ROMAN
TOWNS
IN BRITAIN

ROMAN TOWNS
IN BRITAIN

GUY DE LA BÉDOYÈRE

TEMPUS

Cover picture: *The town centre of Colchester as it may have looked at its height, looking south-east across the theatre and the temple of the deified Claudius*
Painting: Peter Froste, courtesy of the Colchester Archaeological Trust

First published 1992
This edition first published 2003, reprinted 2004

Tempus Publishing Ltd
The Mill, Brimscombe Port
Stroud, Gloucestershire GL5 2QG
www.tempus-publishing.com

British Library Cataloguing in Publication Data.
A catalogue record for this book is available from the British Library.

ISBN 0 7524 2919 1

Typesetting and origination by Tempus Publishing.
Printed and bound in Great Britain.

CONTENTS

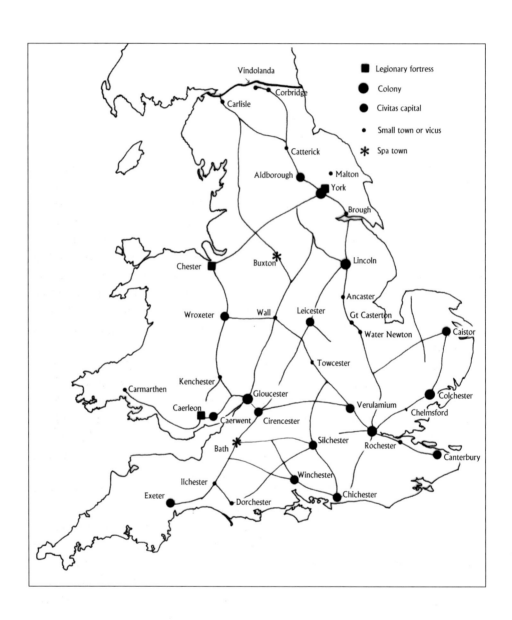

■	Legionary fortress
●	Colony
●	Civitas capital
•	Small town or vicus
✳	Spa town

Vindolanda

Corbridge

Carlisle

Catterick

Aldborough

Malton

York

Brough

Chester

Buxton

Lincoln

Ancaster

Wroxeter

Wall

Leicester

Gt Casterton

Water Newton

Caistor

Towcester

Kenchester

Carmarthen

Gloucester

Verulamium

Colchester

Caerleon

Chelmsford

Caerwent

Cirencester

Bath

Silchester

Rochester

Canterbury

Ilchester

Winchester

Chichester

Exeter

Dorchester

INTRODUCTION

When I prepared this book for the first edition in 1992, it was a privilege to contribute one of the first of the long series of successful titles produced by Batsford in collaboration with English Heritage. It was a considerable challenge to try and provide a summary of a vast subject, trying to take into account the many different views held, while at the same time supplying a general reader with useful information in concise form. The book was well-received and in more recent years I have had many enquiries from new readers who would like to find a copy since it has been unavailable for several years. I am therefore grateful to Peter Kemmis Betty and the team at Tempus (especially Tim Clarke and Emma Parkin) for the chance to produce a brand new edition that could take account of the way the subject has moved on.

I have taken the opportunity to revise the text thoroughly to take into account new discoveries and views, and to update the illustrations, making numerous alterations. A number of key Roman town sites have now been published, making available new information. I have substantially increased the number of examples cited, significantly extended some sections, and modified many parts of the text to take into account how my own views have altered in the last eleven years. The colour section has been completely revised. New discoveries, some made only weeks before this book went to press, have been included as well.

Interest in archaeology has increased enormously over the last decade, led in part by television programmes like *Time Team* and *Meet the Ancestors*. I have been fortunate to take part in some of these, including being able to see the replicated water-lifting device, based on finds made in London, being built for the Museum of London. Visitor numbers to archaeological sites have increased, and so have students taking archaeology courses. Roman Britain, with its unique mix of historical, inscription, architectural and artefact evidence, is one of the most popular subjects. So, the intention is that this edition serves not just as a book to read, but also as a durable work of reference about the towns, which played such a key part in the development of Britain as a Roman province. The appendices have been substantially extended to include ancient references to towns in Roman Britain and what they tell us about civic organization, status and so on. I have also experimented with presenting inscriptions in a new digitally reconstructed format, since the originals are so often difficult to read and are incomplete (see for instance **28** and appendix 2).

Many of Britain's major Roman towns have museums or remains of buildings to visit. The 'Where to visit Roman towns in Britain' section has been substantially enlarged, with telephone numbers and website information. These range from the military town at Corbridge with its street fountain, Lincoln's basilica wall, Caerwent's basilica and defences, to the theatre and the new museum at Verulamium, and the temple precinct at Bath.

Roman towns, like every other part of Britain's past, form a constantly evolving subject and in the last ten years alone a colossal amount of new information has emerged. It should be emphasized that this book is an overview and takes into account excavation work, and publications produced, by many different archaeologists and historians. What emerges into a book like this as an important sentence or paragraph often has its origins in months of their work, sometimes experienced under arduous conditions. It is a credit to Britain's archaeological tradition and her archaeologists that so much evidence is now amassed.

Guy de la Bédoyère, Welby, 2003

1

THE FOUNDATION OF TOWNS

For each of us a town can be one of many things. It may be a place in which to live and work, a place in which to buy and sell, or a centre of government and administration. We take these things for granted, even more so in the twenty-first century when most of the modern British population live in or near a town of some kind. But what makes a town? Is it just a large group of buildings with a high street full of shops, a town hall, a swimming pool, library, police station and a ring road? How do we distinguish a town from a village? Are towns just convenient facilities or are they more important than that? If a place is a town now, how long has it been one, what made it one originally, and how long will it last?

We could ask many more questions than these, but already it seems that something that appeared to be crystal clear is not quite so well-defined. Archaeologists have found that deciding whether an ancient settlement was a 'town' or not is an excellent way of embarking on an inconclusive debate about the meaning of an apparently simple word.

In the Mediterranean world the concept of a town was a more fundamental building-block of society (**colour plate 1**). In a very real sense, the town was synonymous with a community. Greece was divided up amongst city-states in which cities like Athens and Sparta ruled their hinterlands. The city and its territory were effectively a single constitutional unit. Exactly the same was true of Rome, a settlement that had grown to be the dominant city in Italy. Rome became immensely powerful because of its disciplined military force, but also because it developed an intoxicating sense of community summed up in the expression *Senatus Populusque Romanus*, 'The Roman Senate and People', and the way in which Rome herself was often referred to as just *Urbs*, 'The City'.

Rome was far more than just a large accumulation of people on the banks of the Tiber. No other civilisation in the west had ever conceived of the city in quite the same way as the Romans did. The Roman city had become a co-ordinated mechanism of public services, utilities and communications. In this way it exemplified the procession of events leading to our own urban civilisations that have, for better or ill, placed man at an increasing distance from the natural world. The geographer Strabo, who wrote at the time of Augustus, summed this up when he said that 'the Romans have added other blessings to those which Mother Nature endowed their city, thanks to their foresight'. Amongst these he counted roads, aqueducts and sewers, and he praised them for dealing with practicality before attending to beauty.

Roman government did not rule through military power, as is commonly believed. Instead, power was delegated through the government of each province to regional capitals that were organized physically and administratively on Rome herself. Each of these towns was responsible for governing the surrounding area on behalf of the state. Across the Roman world local worthies ran town governments, administered local laws, maintained the imperial cult and generally indulged in the conceit of the reflected glory their civic prominence brought them (**1**).

In return, the town was granted formal status and financial support to give it the infrastructure such as public buildings, to help it fulfil its role in the way

DEAE ·TV ELE ·BOVDIG
M ·AVR LVNARIS SE
VIR ·AVGCOL BOR ·ET
LIND ·ROV · BRIT INF
ARAM ·QVAVOVR
AB BORACI ·EVEC
V · S · L · M ·
PRPRVOF·CORNE

1 *Bordeaux. Altar (cast) erected in 237 by Marcus Aurelius Lunaris, priest of the imperial cult at Lincoln and York, to give thanks for a successful voyage from Britain. The text is transcribed to the right. Note the use of reversed and combined letters, a typical stylistic layout for the period. The names of the towns can be seen in the third, fourth and sixth lines:* LIND *(for Lincoln, Lindum), and* EBOR/EBORACI *(for York, Eboracum). He was almost certainly a merchant,* negotiator, *perhaps in wine. His journey and his position make him an important example of the cosmopolitan trading world Roman Britain's towns were part of. See appendix 2 for a full translation*

2 *City-centre public buildings at Sbeitla (Sufetula) in Tunisia. A remote location in what is now desert has allowed this modest provincial town's public buildings to survive in a remarkable state of preservation. Once Roman Britain's towns could boast buildings like these*

that Rome herself fulfilled her greater role at the hub of the Empire (**2** & **colour plate 1**).

In the Roman world, therefore, the major town had a more sophisticated status and spiritual identity than modern towns. Throughout most of the Empire existing towns were utilized to serve this purpose by being awarded official status, while others were founded where towns had not previously existed. Towns also grew up as a consequence of a thriving network of trade routes, usually at a place where roads met, or beside a bridge.

Britain presents a rather different picture. The existing communities that were conquered by the Romans did not generally have a tradition of living together in permanent concentrated groups (usually referred to by archaeologists as 'nucleated settlements'). In other words towns, or anything resembling them, were not very common. The presence of the Roman army in forts may have encouraged the subsequent emergence of towns but a number of other factors could also lie behind the existence of any one town. Also, for every regional capital there were many smaller towns, few of which were larger than something we would call a village. These small towns are not very well known but unlike the major towns they almost always lack any evidence for having been formally laid-out, or for large buildings. This makes them especially difficult to understand.

Society and settlement in pre-Roman Britain

Legends and distribution of late-first-century BC and early-first-century AD British coins, together with references by Roman historians, show that the tribes were ruled by regional chieftains or kings who tried to assert their power through expanding their territorial control (**3**). Coin evidence is complemented by Caesar's description of what he found in 55 and 54 BC, Strabo's writings, and by the accounts of the invasion campaign in and after AD 43 (Tacitus and Dio Cassius). This sustained confrontation would have provided a dynamic for society but in primitive communities subsistence is the first priority. Only when agricultural production becomes successful enough to produce a sustained surplus (when, for example, a family regularly produces more food than it needs) can the 'luxury' of a chieftain society with an upper tier of non-productive warriors be supported. The medieval kings and their barons are a useful parallel even if their disputes were generally on a larger scale.

Society in pre-Roman Britain was primarily agricultural and sufficiently productive (though probably only just) to support the gradual emergence of an unproductive upper tier in society. Although mixed farming was both widespread and organized it absorbed the efforts of most of the community for most of the time, making significant production of manufactured goods like pottery only possible during slack periods in the agricultural cycle. But by the late first century BC southern Britain had goods to sell and there is an increasing amount of evidence for certain industries becoming sufficiently intensive to imply that specialist activities were involved, good quality pottery and salt production being amongst them. However it was the warrior aristocracy that

3 Oppida *on British coinage. Such pieces are the only non-Roman verification for the names of these settlements.* Left: *silver stater struck at* Calleva *(Silchester), tribal capital of the Atrebates for Eppillus (named on the other side), telling us he is* Rex, *'King of* Calleva'. *Around 30 BC-AD 10.* Right: *gold stater of Cunobelinus of the Catuvellauni struck at the tribal capital of the Trinovantes at* Camulodunum *(Colchester). Around AD 10-40*

appears both to have benefited from the trade in the form of imported manu-factured goods, and probably controlled any domestic production.

In the year 43 there were no settlements in Britain that could properly be described as towns, even if some had similar characteristics. This is part of what made the Roman invasion such a radical event. It was far more than a military conquest. It was also a social revolution. Much of the network of major towns in existence today was created by the Roman state out of the existing pattern of communities in the interests of effectively governing the new province. For sure there were places where large numbers of people had settled in close proximity. For much of the latter part of the first millennium BC the most conspicuous examples are the hillforts of southern Britain. A number of these, for example Danebury (Hants), appear to have grown at the expense of smaller neighbours but it is impossible to tell if this was a response to inter-tribal tension or social changes. In eastern Britain sites like Mucking (Essex) seem to have developed into undefended village-style communities from about 300 BC onwards.

By about 100 BC many hillforts had become disused and it seems that in south-east Britain in particular they were replaced with what classical authors like Caesar called *oppida*, utilizing the Latin word for a town. An *oppidum* was much larger and was located in a more low-lying area than a hillfort. Their most obvious characteristic was the provision of straggling defences (**4**). But if the defences of hillforts and the dykes which marked the limits of the more low-lying and more sprawling *oppida* were fairly durable there is little evidence for any further permanence about them – any kind of buildings, for example, were rare (though this may reflect inadequate excavation), and apart from possibly acting as chieftains' strongholds they were not administrative centres. They may have been little more than elaborate, perhaps seasonal, bivouacs with the lack of defences facilitating the free movement of trade. Indeed, it may have been the very exposure of the south and east to increasing amounts of Roman trade in the century before the invasion of 43 that helped encourage the growth of *oppida*.

Strabo was emphatic in describing *oppida* as only temporary corrals for people and cattle, equipped with timber defences. This description compares well with Caesar's account of his assault on Cassivellaunus' stronghold in 54 BC, in the Verulamium area. Caesar says the stronghold was protected by woods and swamps, though he also adds the general comment that the Britons built ramparts around their defensive settlements. This contrasts with towns in the Mediterranean world. At Pompeii the street grid contains traces of the layout of an earlier Greek settlement dating from at least as early as the fifth century BC. Like many other places in the Mediterranean world, Roman Pompeii was simply a development of a pre-existing town. Amongst the *oppida* that have been discovered in Britain are Camulodunum (Colchester, **4**), Silchester (**17**), Prae Wood (by Verulamium) and Stanwick (North Yorkshire). Extensive areas were defined by lengths of unconnected ramparts that would have been ineffective against a concerted attack by a large body of troops,

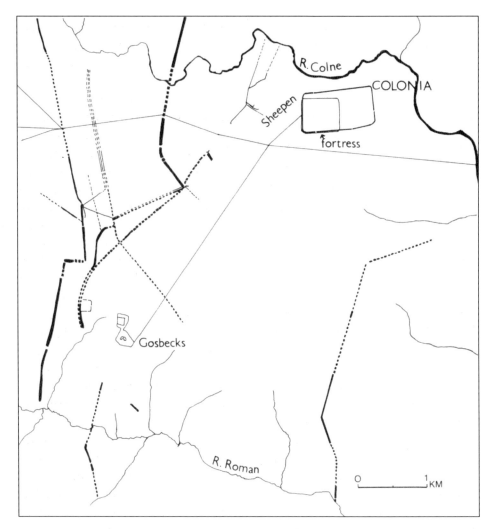

4 *The pre-Roman dyke system around Colchester forming the oppidum of* Camulodunum. *The lines of ditches seem to have acted as a boundary to the movements from the west enclosing a large area between the two principal rivers. Note the fort, of early date, beside the religious complex at Gosbecks, probably a focal point for the pre-Roman community.* After Hull

though they would have been useful in controlling day-to-day movements of people. They represent societies prepared to engage in substantial communal effort and this in itself implies centralization, or at least coercive leadership.

Whether an *oppidum* was the focal point of the community in the sense that this was where the chieftain and his family lived, and from where he controlled his tribe and its territory, is not clear: archaeology does not generally provide evidence for this. It is doubtful whether an *oppidum* actually had much effective control over outlying communities. Caesar only implies that the stronghold that he attacked was that of Cassivellaunus. Even so, it is likely that the community rotated about the person of the chief rather than any particular place. His, or her, prestige would have been the foundation of power and influence. The Trinovantes refused to join the loose confederation that gathered under Cassivellaunus to face Caesar, because Cassivellaunus had recently killed their king.

This was something that the Roman government exploited in the development of towns. This situation played a crucial part in native resistance during the early years of the Roman conquest. Caratacus, son of Cunobelinus of the Catuvellauni, carried the war west with himself as leader of the opposition to the governor Ostorius Scapula (47-51). His prestige was considerable although he was betrayed in 51. Similarly, the Boudican Revolt a decade later appears to have pivoted around the personality of Boudica herself as the foundation of the rebellion rather than a concerted defence of a particular settlement. But we depend totally on Tacitus and Dio Cassius for this version of events, and the possibility remains that Boudica was considerably less important than they imply. She provided an essential literary balance to their agenda, which was to denigrate Nero as an effete, decadent and ineffectual emperor. This does not affect the point that the rebellion was galvanized around a tribal leadership that treated Roman towns as threats, symbolic or actual, to their way of life. With the revolt crushed, the rebels were killed, imprisoned or dispersed. So although this chieftain society was familiar with the concept of large-scale settlements those were not the same as towns because they were not permanent, they were not administrative and, perhaps more importantly, they did not act as symbolic centres for the tribal communities.

Understanding *oppida* has always been complicated by a lack of large-scale excavation. However, Sheepen, part of the Camulodunum *oppidum*, has been partly excavated. By the early first century AD it acted as a centre of industry and trade. Metalworking, sometimes to an extremely high standard, existed as well as the importation of fine pottery from Gaul, and amphorae containing wines, oils and other foods. Despite this the impression is more of an ad hoc settlement rather than a co-ordinated and well-established one with a centralized administration. The buildings found were mostly wattle and daub circular huts and there was no trace of a layout of streets. Only the imported goods and the possible presence of a mint point to the site's importance. However, recent work at Silchester suggests there was in some places a kind of transition period when Roman urban characteristics started to appear, perhaps in a client-kingdom context.

The invasion of 43 and the founding of towns

The traditional view of Romano-British towns is that many developed as a result of civil settlement around an earlier fort. This is a perfectly plausible argument but while in some cases an earlier fort is a virtual certainty it has often been assumed that forts almost invariably preceded a town. This has even extended to 'inventing' forts where none has yet been found, usually on the basis of finds of pieces of early military equipment. These of course prove nothing, soldiers would have been permanently in transit as individuals and in units throughout Britain.

In reality towns might develop for many different reasons. Forts were undoubtedly one of these but others might be the presence of a local native settlement (which may well have been the initial reason for the fort, as at Colchester, **5**) or a place of special ritual significance (Bath), the presence of natural resources such as minerals (Charterhouse) or whether the site was incorporated into the communications system (London). Sometimes there were several reasons. Cirencester and Ilchester were two Roman towns that grew up on the Fosse Way, a major Roman route that ran diagonally across Britain from Lincoln to Exeter and which was established within ten years of the conquest. Both towns were preceded by early Roman forts, which were established because of suitable locations and the proximity of native centres. Only 5km (3 miles) from Cirencester (**6**) was a native settlement at Bagendon. At Ilchester a

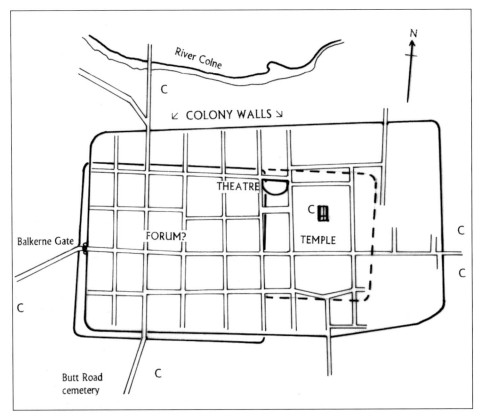

5 *Plan of the developed* colonia *at Colchester. Note the way in which the former fortress and its annexe were submerged by the new street grid.* After Crummy

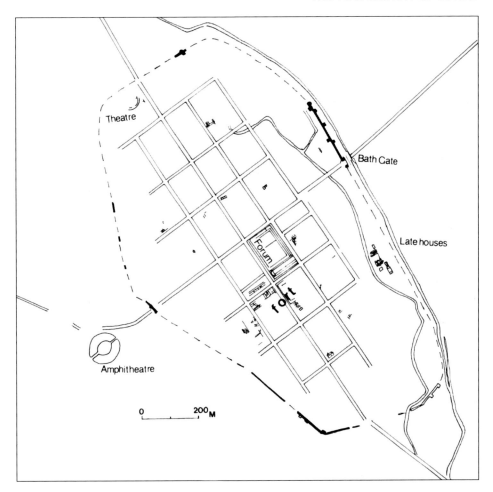

6 *Plan of the town at Cirencester,* Corinium Dobunnorum, *showing the location of the mid-first-century fort in the middle of the later settlement. The Bath Gate cemetery is discussed in chapter 6, and the 'late houses' in chapter 4.* Based on a plan by Cirencester Excavation Committee

16-hectare Iron Age enclosure lay around 300m south of where the fort was established, and 8km (5 miles) to the southwest is the Iron Age hillfort at Ham Hill. The presence of the forts and the road modified local movements by changing the focus and nature of communications, making the old settlements redundant in the new context. Establishing towns at either of these places was probably deliberate, but by the time that happened the new towns probably just confirmed a change that had already happened. It might seem strange that the civilians did not follow the army when it moved on, but if they were mostly local to begin with they will have had little reason to do so. The road itself became a sustaining component of the town's future as a civilian settlement.

The Roman world was held together as much by trade, a natural product of stability, as anything else. The presence of troops introduced people with earnings to spend, though there would have been other groups of people such as government officials and traders. Those who came to supply the military's demands had themselves money to spend, and so it went on. Rome could also be a source of credit, whether it was wanted or not. One of the explanations for the Boudican Revolt was the calling in of loans made to the Trinovantes in and around Colchester. Towns had a crucial role to play in the circulation of goods and money and with the enormous expansion in trade which took place after 43 it is hardly surprising that they should have benefited; in a few cases, London being the best example, a town developed more or less entirely because it lay in a place of outstanding commercial convenience. It would be foolish also to ignore the real needs that people have to come together to collectively express a sense of belonging to a community, or even to be drawn by the attraction of a community over which to exercise power and enjoy status. Equally, 'going to market' or attending ritual and social events would have been an event to look forward to for those who lived outside a town. For those who lived within there would have been the appeal of being involved in all the petty preoccupations of parochial politics and social relations. It is all too easy to forget such aspects of human society and to tend always to want to find obvious rational economic and physical reasons for places being where they were.

These are just general points and of course there are exceptions and many variations to these themes. Roman towns were not founded as fully developed institutions. Their development (or even lack of) was gradual, intermittent, idiosyncratic, and in some cases spontaneous. It would be wrong to imagine armies of surveyors, architects and builders moving into the allocated area overnight and swiftly designing and erecting an instant Roman town complete with forum, basilica and baths while romanized natives loitered in colonnaded avenues discussing Virgil. It was often several generations later before such a town had all the necessary attributes of a miniature Rome, if even then. The main period of public building in Roman Britain lasted sporadically from the 60s and 70s right through to the mid-second century or even later. Throughout the province there were numerous small towns that have attracted limited archaeological attention and about which we know really very little. For the most part their origins and the roles they played in Romano-British society remain a mystery.

Towns in the Roman world

Roman towns fell into several different categories, some of which held a specific legal status and others of which had no significance beyond the fact that they existed. When Rome conquered territory in the eastern Mediterranean area she took control of peoples already accustomed to living in towns. In Asia Minor, for example, the great cities of Ephesus and Miletus had existed for centuries as Greek settlements. In the north-western part of

Europe this was not the case, at least not to anything like the same extent, and consequently there was no existing civilian government infrastructure that could be adapted to Roman rule. It was also the case that the army was perpetually confronted with the problem of having large numbers of soldiers who had come to the end of their twenty-five years' service.

The two problems were dealt with by creating colonies of retired soldiers, called *coloniae*. These colonies were founded in conquered territory by establishing and laying out a town together with a certain amount of land, *territorium*, around it. Britain eventually had at least four: Colchester (**5**), Gloucester, Lincoln (**10**) and York. Each retired soldier was allocated a piece of land within and outside the town. He could therefore enjoy the benefits of Roman urban life and support himself and his family. This was as convenient for the government as it was for the ex-soldier. Not only was a trained reserve available but it also acted as an example of romanization to the conquered rabble. Not all colonies were settlements of ex-soldiers (who were also Roman citizens). Sometimes towns and their inhabitants were elevated to the status as an honour, though instead of becoming full Roman citizens it was possible to grant them only the slightly lesser rank of Latin rights.

The *civitates* were more numerous than the colonies. The Latin word *civitas* means the political community of a body of citizens or 'canton'. Unlike the colonies, which were self-contained legal entities created by the Roman state, the *civitates* were a formalized development of the existing tribal groupings. The *civitas* capitals, like Silchester or Cirencester, were not legally distinct from the tribal region in which they lay. This was reflected in the name. Cirencester's for example was *Corinium Dobunnorum*, '*Corinium* of the Dobunni people'. The meaning of *Corinium* is unknown. In other words the Roman government took an existing tribal area, recognized it and imposed local government from a regional centre.

Roman Britain was not wholly divided into cantonal areas governed from towns. Much of the north and west for example was under military control. Regions existed, but are rarely specified in the record. They were probably components of imperial estates, perhaps ultimately governed from forts or other designated headquarters often by imperial procurators, a word that means literally 'manager' or 'overseer'. One at Castleford (*Lagitium*), which began life as a fort, is testified as *Regione Lagitiense*. Others are testified around Ribchester and Carlisle, as well as Bath (see below).

Occasionally it was necessary to manufacture a tribal area where either a small dispersed population or confusion over tribal boundaries made it impossible to exploit an existing arrangement easily. Winchester is an excellent example – its official name of *Venta Belgarum*, '*Venta* [Market] of the Belgae', merely employs the generic term for the people of south-eastern Britain, rather than an individual tribe. The fact that this was done emphasizes how important it was for Rome to be able to rule through self-governing local communities.

Sometimes settlements within a tribal canton, apart from the *civitas* capital, were granted the formal status of *vicus* that allowed them to be self-governing units within the tribal area, though not separate from it (see appendix 1).

The *civitas* capital was laid out on the model of a Roman town, generally with state assistance, but instead of being populated by Roman citizens it was in theory left to the local inhabitants to run. This meant that pre-existing hierarchies within the social group were allowed to continue in a new, more easily manipulated, structure, though it would be a mistake to think they were left entirely to it. It was commonplace in the Roman world to detach centurions from their units and use them in taxation, police, or other administrative capacities. At Bath a centurion called Gaius Severius Emeritus tells he was 'centurion of the region' on an altar he erected to commemorate the repair work he undertook at a vandalized religious monument, presumably in or near the spa town. We have no idea if Bath fell into a tribal canton, perhaps of the Dobunni or Durotriges. Alternatively, Bath could have been an imperial estate leased or handed over to a local community to manage. Emeritus might have even administered part of an imperial estate nearby rather than anywhere in or around Bath. This just shows how very little we know about the system of management 'on the ground'. In reality there were probably many different ad hoc arrangements, depending on time or place.

On the whole, though, native laws remained effective and the inhabitants were not granted the status of Roman citizens or Latin rights other than in exceptional circumstances. The Roman government also had a vested interest in exploiting existing native social structures and customs in the interests of stable administration. If the existing élite could be allowed to continue to dominate the area in which they lived they would regard a burgeoning town as an advantage, and therefore tolerate their own subjugation. In a town they could retain status and have the opportunity to continue to exploit the local population. While there may have been opportunities for 'ordinary' people to live and work in towns we can be sure that the existing wealthy and powerful tribal aristocracy remained just that.

Occasionally a *civitas* capital was elevated to the rank of *municipium*. This is a word for which we have no convenient equivalent but we might almost consider these towns as honorary colonies. Like a colony a *municipium* would generally have its own allocated territory around it and its population were either made Roman citizens or enjoyed the slightly inferior legal status of Latin citizens. It is not entirely clear what a town had to do to achieve this status. Verulamium (**8**) is the only town in Britain referred to in ancient sources specifically as a *municipium* (by Tacitus) but the reason is not mentioned and no inscription has been found which might be more helpful. Some of the possibilities are discussed in chapter 2.

The various towns discussed above were all official in the sense that they held formal status and were founded by the state and recognized as being run by its delegates. They were all responsible for local government and were equipped with the facilities to do so. They were each governed by the *ordo* (council). The *ordo* was theoretically made up of about 100 local worthies serving as decurions, each with sufficient funds to satisfy the property qualification. The system therefore perpetuated the existing hierarchy and guaranteed that it would effectively be hereditary. However, it would be wrong to believe that local government was dominated entirely by people of local descent. The limited amount of inscriptional evidence we have suggests that some of these people were freedmen, some were descended from retired troops, and some were from other provinces, just to name a few examples. In fact, it has to be pointed out that it is people of demonstrably 'British' origin who are most invisible from our records.

Although thousands of individuals would have sat on a town council during the history of Roman Britain almost none are known by name. This shows just how difficult it is for us to make direct connections between power, wealth and property in the province. Flavius Martius, buried at Old Penrith, was a *senator*, 'councillor', following a term as *quaestor*, in the government of the Carvetii (a tribe in the north-western part of the province), and had a romanized name that tells us nothing about his origins. Even the connection with Mars might mean a military or Celtic origin (many obscure local deities in the north were associated with Mars). At Lincoln the decurion Aurelius Senecio recorded his status on his wife's tombstone, and at York the coffin of Flavius Bellator tells he was a 'decurion of the Colony of *Eboracum*'. We will come across a few of the others later. Caerwent's basilica is extremely well-preserved and remains of the council chamber, *curia*, have been found. It could only be reached through an antechamber, rather than the main hall of the basilica. Those with cases, petitions or pleas, would have had to wait here to be summoned before the council. Councillors here issued their decrees (*ex decreto ordinis*, 'by decree of the council'). These might include aspects of town maintenance, or orders to priests of town cults to make dedications. The councillors faced one another on rows of timber benches, and at one end the magistrates presiding over the hearing sat on a sort of stage.

The members of councils competed for the various magistracies that would further enhance their prestige and influence within the local community. The magistracies were also modelled on those at Rome. The main pair, based on consuls, were known as the *duoviri iuridicundo* and were responsible for justice, supervision of the *ordo* and religious festivals. They were assisted by *aediles*, who dealt with public services like buildings, markets, aqueducts, sewers, the food supply and so on. They were also responsible for arranging public entertainments (**28**). *Quaestores* administered public finance. The *censitor* managed census records, essential for assessing householders for tax liability. Collectively, these men were supposed to keep the town running. Other officials took care of day-to-day problems, for example the *curatores sartorum tectorum*, literally 'managers of wall-surface repairs', who dealt with the patching-up of public works and religious buildings. Evidence for a very few of these posts in Britain is given in appendix 1 (Colchester) and appendix 2 (various). Lesser towns with organized government had similar offices but they only had power within the town, rather than the canton.

Nothing whatsoever survives from Britain to tell us about the process of election, but an inscription from the city of *Malaca* (Malaga) in Spain, dating to the early 80s, does give us an idea. The town was divided into wards (*curiae*) and these wards all went to vote simultaneously. The official overseeing the town's election appointed three men to manage the ballot in each ward. The three had to come from a different ward to the one they were supervising, and they had to take an oath that they would guard and count the votes honestly. They also had to cast their own votes in the ward they were working in. The priority was to elect the *duoviri* first, followed by the *aediles* and then the *quaestores*. Candidates had to be twenty-five or older, and anyone who had been a *duovir* in the last five years was disqualified from re-election to that post. When two men got the same number of votes, precedence went to whichever man was married or who was married with the most children. If the two men were equal in this respect they drew lots. Various other provisions covered the actual process of the election and oaths to be taken by office-holders. Another, similar, inscription naming the nearby town of *Salpensa* adds the interesting information that *duoviri*, *aediles* and *quaestores*, and their families were rewarded with Roman citizenship after their terms of office. There is no reason to believe that this privilege applied to Britain but since both these towns were *municipia*, perhaps Verulamium's magistrates did benefit this way.

So, the town electoral system had order, checks and balances, and incentives. But it is easy to see that in a provincial urban community all those forces of patronage, pressure, moral blackmail and outright intimidation might have played their familiar parts in 'influencing' the outcome of elections. We can also be sure that a small number of local families would have dominated the holding of office for generations, although we have no specific evidence for this in Britain. At Herculaneum in Italy the basilica, buried by mud and lava during the eruption of Vesuvius in 79, was found to contain statues honouring the whole family of one Marcus Nonius Balbus who had paid for the building to be rebuilt at an earlier date. He was of senatorial rank, which meant that he was extremely wealthy and was a member of the Roman Senate. He had served as a consul in Rome, which meant proconsular status, entitling the holder to prestigious posts like provincial governorships. It is clear that this man used his prestige to hold great sway over local politics. By paying for the basilica's repairs he was investing in his family's future.

It is all very well listing off the various legal features of town status in the Roman world but it gives us little idea of what towns were actually like, and the roles which they played in the lives of their inhabitants and those who lived round about. Pompeii, also covered by debris from the eruption of Vesuvius, is of exceptional importance not just because so much is preserved but also because the town was caught at a moment in time. It is easy to forget that archaeology is an imprecise discipline and it is almost impossible to say what the actual state of any building, and even less a town, was at any given moment. Pompeii, however, allows us to glimpse what went to make up a Roman town on one particular day (**9** & **colour plate 28**). Of course it cannot be exactly representative because it lay in a rich part of Italy, close to the sea and was a relatively short distance from Rome. But we have nothing else like it. The better-preserved remains of nearby Herculaneum are confined to a small, predominantly residential, part of the town (**7**). At Pompeii it is still possible to make one's way from the forum to the amphitheatre past dozens of shop fronts, or alternatively explore the back streets of the older part of the town with its brothel and then enter the large houses of the well-to-do.

Everywhere in Pompeii are traces of the bustle of town life and the various comings and goings of people and their goods. At many street corners the paving stones still bear the deep ruts worn by countless wagon wheels, sometimes up to 25cm (10in) deep (**9**). We know from Tacitus that in AD 59 the amphitheatre was the scene of a violent confrontation between locals and visitors from nearby Nuceria. The incident arose from an exchange of insults

7 *A street in Herculaneum buried in AD 79. Roman Britain's town streets in the first and second centuries would have looked similar. Note the upper storey built with a timber frame and supported on columns*

during a gladiatorial bout that degenerated into the drawing of swords. A number of people were killed. Pompeii was forbidden to hold such displays for ten years as its punishment. This gladiatorial display was just the sort of event that would have been promoted and financed by those seeking public office, normally during the course of one of the many annual 'religious' festivals. One of the most interesting features of Pompeii is the lively range of election slogans daubed on walls. Most of them probably relate to the election that would have taken place in March 79 for the magistracies commencing on 1 July. In one instance the goldsmiths collectively recommend one Gaius Cuspius Pansa as *aedile*, though a more practical anonymous pundit prefers Gaius Julius Polybius because he supplies good bread. These are interspersed with advertisements for gladiatorial bouts and references to sexual prowess (or lack of it). One accuses Colepius, keeper of the forum baths, of being excessively familiar with women.

Romano-British town life must have been just as frustrating and as vivid, but unfortunately pages of excavation reports listing broken pottery can sometimes obscure the reality of a human experience. We should always remember that concentrations of human beings invariably produce strains that can sometimes lead to disproportionate consequences, or at least disproportionate emotions. A shortage of bread at Aspendus in southern Turkey caused by speculators stockpiling supplies, led to a riot in which a crowd tried to burn a magistrate. A more innocuous frustration gripped Seneca in Rome and caused him to write his famous tirade against the noise he suffered by living over a public baths, particularly from the shouting of customers having hairs plucked. Roman Britain's towns will have had their good years and their bad years, and shared all the experiences common to towns of occasional bouts of disease, street disorder, pageants and celebrations, rowdy elections, catastrophic fires, crooked builders, well-intentioned benefactors, corrupt officials, well-respected businesses and the polite charms of walking in well-kept town centres late on an English summer evening.

The mechanics of laying out a town

In theory the first stage in founding a town was to lay out roads to create a series of rectangular or square areas known as *insulae*, literally 'islands'. Who did this? The answer is that in Britain we do not know, but the most likely candidates in the first instance were military surveyors detached from their units for the purpose. They had the skills, the experience and the equipment, and they were immediately on hand either from the pool of serving soldiers or the colonies of veterans. Surveying was more than just a technical exercise; it had great symbolic significance and there would have been foundation sacrifices accompanied possibly by the marking out of the boundary with a plough team made up of a cow and a bull to symbolize fertility. Laying out the grid did not mean setting it in stone, and leaving the town stuck with it for evermore. Silchester had at least two, and possibly three, consecutive grids (**17**).

The two main roads that crossed in the centre of town at right angles formed the axes of the grid. They were called the *Cardo Maximus* and the *Decumanus Maximus*. *Cardo* means 'hinge' or 'axis', while *decumanus* is linked to the idea of carving something up into tenths. So *Decumanus Maximus*

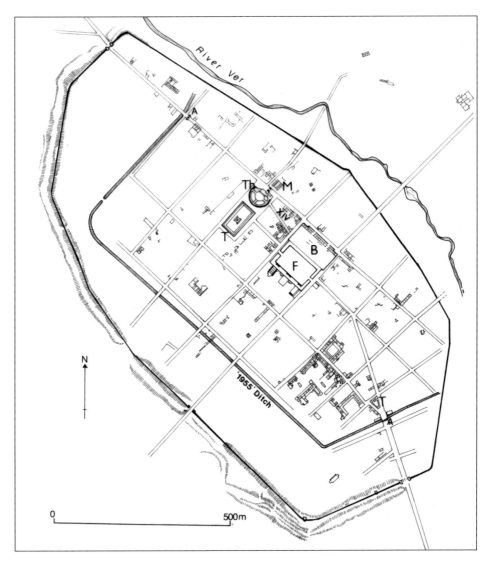

8 *Plan of Verulamium based on excavations and aerial photography. The street grid is fairly regular apart from the entry of Watling Street from the south-east. The basilica (B) and forum (F) dominate the town centre with the theatre (Th) and its attendant temple (T) a little to the north. Close by is* Insula XIV *while in the southern part of the town the Triangular Temple (T) lies at the point where Watling Street met the town grid. Within the third-century town walls is the earlier boundary known as the '1955 Ditch'; two arches (A) marked the former city limits. See also* **30** *for the central zone. After Niblett*

probably means something like 'the biggest of the streets that carves the place up into tenths', except that 'tenths' did not really mean anything precise. This grid formed the skeleton of the new town though there were enormous local variations, taking account of contours, rivers, existing routes, and even earlier efforts at laying out a grid. Verulamium is a prime example. Here the grid was laid out parallel to the banks of the river Ver. The road from London entered from the south at a totally different angle but was accommodated by creating a number of triangular *insulae* (**8**). Similar consequences can be seen at Pompeii, where the town grew. Its original, pre-Roman, layout was fairly irregular but the new developments had grids based on the forum's orientation (**colour plate 28**). However, the new *insulae* surrounded the old roads that led out of the town, created a road fork, like Verulamium's (**9**). At Lincoln the town was divided into an upper and lower town. The lower town was laid out on the steep hillside below the upper town and had special staggered streets to allow wheeled traffic to tackle the slope (**10**). In small towns like Water Newton (**75**) or Kenchester such planning never took place to any significant extent. Instead the main road that runs through both merely formed a spine for the straggling streets leading off it.

9 *Pompeii streets. When the town grew larger a new grid was laid out, based on the orientation of the forum, but this had to accommodate an existing route heading out north-west from the old town centre. The result was this fork. The road to the left is the road out, indicated by the heavy cart-rut wear. The road to the right is part of the new grid and was matched by several parallel streets off to the right. Verulamium had a similar feature (see **8**). Note the street fountain in the centre, and the high kerbs that helped waste water and sewage drain away downhill*

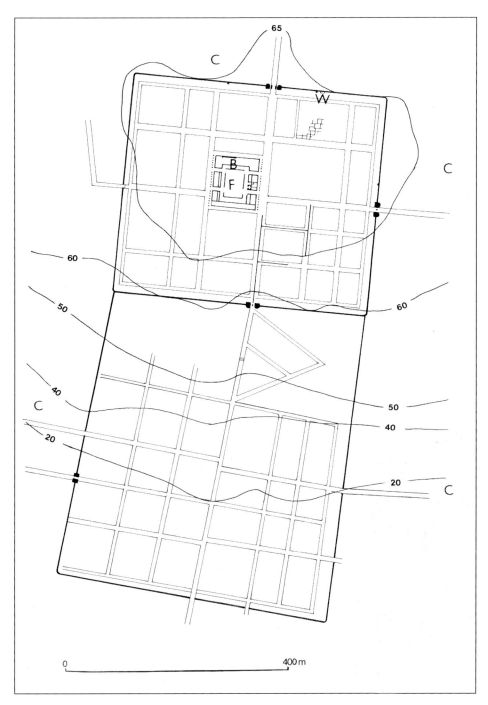

10 *The colonia at Lincoln. There were two quite distinct parts of the settlement with the main centre at the top of the hill over-lying the former legionary fortress. The basilica (B) and forum (F) lie over the fortress headquarters building. W marks the site of the water cistern that supplied public baths. There were a number of burial areas around the settlement (C). Note the diagonal streets to aid wheeled traffic trying to negotiate the steep gradient, the contours (in metres) show the steep slope which the lower town was, built on.*
After Wacher, with additional information

Ideally a town was laid out with fortifications in mind and four gates would have been built, one at each end of the main streets. In Britain town walls were generally not provided before the late second century, perhaps a hundred years or more after the street grid was laid out. Only in the colonies, reusing the site of a legionary fortress, were defences a part of the town from the beginning and even then not necessarily. At Colchester the legionary defences were demolished prior to laying out the new colony (**6**). Part of the consequence of this was that towns developed in a slightly random fashion with the result that the areas eventually walled (not necessarily the entire settled area) were very irregularly shaped. At Silchester the form of the old *oppidum* is thought by some to have helped define the town's later walled shape (**17**). But it is a mark of how opaque the subject is that the early ditch, which lies under the town, could easily have belonged to an early Roman phase of urban development rather than a tribal period. At Caistor-by-Norwich the walled area was considerably less than the town's greatest extent and to this day prominent ridges marking streets still run out to the south beyond the walls.

Laying out the town, and the allocation of plots

The visual impact of Roman public buildings was considerable anywhere and must have been especially so in an island where nothing like them had ever existed before. None survive intact so it is difficult to appreciate the powerful impression they would have created. At Sbeitla in Tunisia the town centre survives in a remarkable state of preservation and although this was a remote provincial town the buildings show that one could be far from Rome and yet still sense her presence (**2** & **colour plate 8**). At Pompeii a modern visitor is drawn to the forum by the way in which the roads appear to lead there. The idea has not been lost on more recent town-planners who have utilized street grids and imposing public architecture to create a sense of power and presence (**12**).

Despite individual variations all the public buildings of Roman towns were similar, something which becomes evident to those fortunate enough to be able to explore several different examples. This was of great importance in the Roman Empire because it promoted the sense of institutional unity, a sense of belonging to a world that was familiar wherever one went. In a world where natural forces were less easily controlled, the underlying feeling of stability which this created should not be underestimated. This was paralleled by the use of common coinage, urban institutions, an Empire-wide army, the same laws, and allegiance to the emperor.

Areas were set aside for the principal public buildings during surveying. The grid itself had been derived from a fixed point in the centre of the future town with a device called a *groma*. This piece of equipment, a kind of primitive theodolite, allowed the sighting of straight lines over distances by suspending weights from the four ends of a cross laid flat on a pivot. The surveyor looked through the *groma* and directed an assistant holding a staff where to place it in the ground. The angles at which the lines intersected could be varied but were usually right angles. The fixed point from which the surveying was done normally marked the site of the future forum and basilica. That the site of this building was earmarked early on has been shown at Silchester where timber structures of early date resembling the later stone basilica have been found underneath (**17**). Silchester was a good choice – although the site of the town is generally flat, the forum and the basilica were placed at the highest point, particularly evident when viewing the town from the lower-lying south-east corner. Verulamium's theatre was not built until the middle of the second century but the plot in which it lies appears to have been vacant until that date, and must have been set aside to help it form part of a town-centre religious complex (**30**).

As far as the rest of a town is concerned we know nothing about how land was allocated for shops, houses or temples in Britain. Some may have remained in the ownership of the town to be rented out, while private landlords bought up others. Plots might have been claimed, much as they were in towns in the Old West. At Pompeii, Gnaeus Allius Nigidius Maius promoted his tenement block in advertisements painted on walls along the town's streets. He had upstairs flats available for rent, and ground-floor shop space. Would-be tenants were referred to his slave Primus to draw up contracts. Papyri from in Roman Egypt also show that it was quite common for families or individuals to buy part-shares in property, or to rent rooms or suites within a house. It is worth noting that the *Malaca* inscription mentioned above, includes regulations that prohibited the demolition of any building within the town without the permission of the town council on pain of a fine equal to its value, unless the structure was to be rebuilt within a year.

Romano-British towns and the Roman world

As an isolated component of the Empire, Britain was regarded with a mixture of fascination and apparent indifference. Very few individuals of Romano-British origin, if any, made any great impact on the history of the Empire and often references to the province are little more than casual asides. Britain, for example, never produced anyone of sufficient wealth, status or prestige to serve as a senator in Rome. Not surprisingly the towns of Roman Britain also feature little in these references though they were occasionally mentioned on inscriptions listing an individual's career that had included a spell in Britain.

In the mid-second century a geographer called Ptolemy drew up a compendium of places in the known world and gave details of location by using a crude form of latitude and longitude. This provides useful information about Britain and which towns were the most important or whether they had some special reputation – Bath, for example, is named as *Aquae Calidae*, which means 'Hot Waters'. However, he rarely gives details of a town's status and even omitted a few, like Gloucester. Many of the otherwise unknown names he listed are probably forts and cannot now be identified. Ptolemy probably drew up his information from a number of sources including old maps and verbal accounts from travellers – both prone to inaccuracy.

Ptolemy was trying to create an equivalent of a world atlas. Travellers would have found it of little value; instead they made use of route maps that listed the places to be found along a given road, a little like a modern schematic map of a motorway and its junctions. Armed with such a map a traveller knew where the next town was and how long it might take him to get there because details of distance were included. The best known is 'The Antonine Itinerary' which lists more than 200 roads and was based on a route map which may have been drawn up for the Emperor Caracalla in about 214. Fifteen Romano-British roads are mentioned and eight start from London. The details of distance, even though sometimes inaccurate, and intended ultimate destination have made it possible to identify many towns on the ground including a number of small ones. In some cases the *civitas* capitals are given their full titles, for example *Venta Silurum* (Caerwent) on Route 14, or *Venta Icenorum* (Caistor-by-Norwich) on Route 9, providing useful confirmation of a town's status and sometimes the only evidence for its existence. Other route maps are known, such as the Peutinger Table and the Ravenna Cosmography, but are either too incomplete or corrupt to provide anything more than supplementary material. Romano-British place names were almost invariably pre-Roman in origin. We know from Celtic coinage that *Camulodunum*, *Verulamium* and *Calleva* were already the names for Colchester, St Albans and Silchester (in fact the Roman site at St Albans is still known as Verulamium today and it will be referred to as such throughout this book, as the site is actually quite distinct from the later settlement).

Where names were purely Latin they were usually new sites, such as forts, with names that were nothing more than descriptive such as *Trimontium* 'three peaks' for Newstead in Scotland. Even the word *Venta*, used for a number of towns, probably meant nothing more than 'market field'. It seems to be a Celtic word, and almost exclusive to Britain in this context. This reflects social continuity from Celtic to Roman Britain, and also the island's isolation from mainstream classical society. This curious mix of adapted native terms, imported words and fabricated labels is found in the western United States where towns grew up with names adapted from native American words like Cheyenne in Wyoming, or were purely descriptive English terms like Twin Falls, Idaho. The difference is that we have all the information at our finger-tips to know how each came about, unlike in Roman Britain.

2

CONQUEST AND COLONIZATION

The development of towns was one of the first effects of the Roman invasion in 43 but the reaction of some of the indigenous population to military defeat and urban administration had been grossly underestimated. As a result the province was very nearly lost during the Boudican Revolt of 60/1. Our understanding of this early period is dominated by what we know about military activities. Dio Cassius, Tacitus and Suetonius provide a limited amount of material that describes the advance of the army both westwards and northwards across Britain. The details are recounted in a number of modern works and need not detain us here. But, in brief, the invading force under Aulus Plautius is believed to have consisted of approximately 20,000 legionaries of *II Augusta*, *IX Hispana*, *XIV Gemina*, *XX*, and a roughly equivalent number of auxiliaries. In fact, only *II Augusta* is known to have formed part of the force. The others are inferred to have participated because they were in Britain in 60. There is other evidence that vexillations of other legions, like *VIII Augusta*, took part but did not stay.

The invasion force landed somewhere on the south coast, probably in Kent, but not necessarily all in the same place or at exactly the same time. After a major river battle, perhaps on the Medway, the main part of the army eventually reached the Thames somewhere in the vicinity of modern central London. Near here the force split up, but if different landing places had been used that might have already happened. The *II Augusta* we know made its way towards the south-west. For the others we have to work back from where they turn up later, and that leads to the conclusion that the *XIV* went across the Midlands towards central and north Wales, and the *IX* advanced north. This sounds very neat but in fact the legions involved were split into vexillations (detachments), and were accompanied by groups of auxiliaries. It is quite impossible to know exactly what each part was up to, other than gaining a very general impression of them fanning out across southern, central and eastern England. Years of seasonal fort and fortress building lay ahead, with units remaining constantly mobile and subject to being split up as required.

For the time being, though, the *XX* and its attendant auxiliaries, however, fell back on Colchester, or *Camulodunum*, now one of the strongholds of the

11 *Colchester, tombstone of the trooper Longinus, an auxiliary in First ala of Thracians. He probably died just before the legionary fortress here was given over to veterans as a colony*

Catuvellauni, which at the time was the dominant tribe in south–eastern Britain (**11**). Since the beginning of the first century, mainly during the reign of Cunobelinus (about AD 10-40), it had been expanding its power from a tribal area centred on Verulamium first at the expense of the Trinovantes to the east at Colchester and later, during the reign of Cunobelinus' sons. By 47 the *XX* legion had been despatched to fight in Wales. Along the way it was based in several places, like Gloucester, that evolved into towns in their own right.

In *XX*'s place a colony of veteran legionaries was established on the site of Camulodunum (**5**). Tacitus' description of this and the impact of the Boudican Revolt both here and at London and Verulamium gives us a vital glimpse of the Roman style of town life which had emerged in the few short years since the conquest. Archaeology has been able to supply us with more detail of how these towns grew up before they were destroyed. Each of the three evolved into a town in completely different ways, as we shall see.

The early province of Roman Britain was relatively small. Although the army advanced swiftly into Wales and south-western England only the south-east experienced civilian development before 60. Even this was very limited. Colchester was the first town but the Thames crossing was a focal point of communications, and the earlier stronghold of the Catuvellauni at Verulamium seems to have been an attractive site for early development. Further west the Atrebatic tribal area was merged with others to the south to create a client kingdom. This area was apparently ruled by a native king called Tiberius Claudius Togidubnus/Cogidubnus (the spelling is uncertain), with nominal independence. He may have been related to Verica, the tribal leader who fled to Rome to ask for help from Claudius, providing the Romans with a pretext to invade. Coins tie Verica to Silchester, and therefore the Atrebates. The arrangement was conditional upon Togidubnus' unconditional loyalty. The major settlements within this area, Silchester, Winchester and Chichester, subsequently emerged as separate *civitas* capitals once the client kingdom was dissolved, probably towards the end of the first century after Togidubnus' death. They too show evidence for early urban development but as they were not destroyed during the Boudican Revolt this gives archaeology less opportunity to distinguish easily features that can be confidently dated precisely to before 60.

The Boudican Revolt

The surviving accounts of the Revolt supply us with valuable detail about some of the towns that were in existence at the time. As we saw in chapter 1, the uprising hung around a mobile tribal leadership rather than attempting to hold or defend any specific native region. The towns of Colchester, London and Verulamium were clearly the primary targets. We are given the impression that once the East Anglian Iceni were mobilized, they did not hesitate in making for the colony at Colchester. The temple of Claudius symbolized their subordination and the colonists are said to have dispossessed many of the Trinovantes of their livelihoods. Thereafter Tacitus says the rebels specifically avoided military installations, instead being attracted to the easy pickings of undefended towns. This led to the massacre of any remaining inhabitants, reputedly totalling between 70,000 and 80,000 though this is probably an exaggeration. While on one hand this gives us the idea that towns were developing swiftly and had attracted a substantial number of people, it also gives us an impression of a section of the wider native population that had been alienated from it. In terms of archaeology, the substantial traces of the sacking and firing of these towns has sealed the earliest layers of urban development.

Colchester before 60

The removal of the *XX* legion from Colchester meant that its earth and timber fortress was left vacant. Recent excavations have thrown light on the extent to which the new colonists utilized the redundant buildings. Instead of the fortress being completely demolished and a neat new Roman town built in its place, the transition was a much more long-term project. Even so there was extensive early investment in public buildings. The whole area of the fortress was surrounded by parts of the former Catuvellaunian stronghold Camulodunum, which before about AD 5-10 had been the Trinovantian tribal centre. Coins were issued in the name of Cunobelinus and bearing the mintmark CAMV (**3**). At Sheepen, 0.8km (½ mile) to the west, lay an important industrial and trading centre. Gosbecks, 5km (3 miles) to the south-west, seems to have been a farming and possible religious zone, later developed in the Roman period with a temple and theatre. An extensive series of dykes defined the whole area that was also enclosed by two rivers, the Colne and the Roman, which run parallel from west to east (**4**). The fortress, which has only been discovered recently, was built on unoccupied high ground in the northern part of the area.

The new colony needed more land than the fortress supplied so the military defences were demolished in order to allow its annexe to be incorporated (**5**). A fort annexe was a kind of subsidiary defended area attached to a fort or fortress, used for storage and perhaps corralling animals. Obliterating the defences was a mistake because it made the town vulnerable to attack: colonies established later in the first century in the former legionary fortresses of Gloucester and Lincoln seem to have retained their defences. The new town was therefore easily attacked by Boudica's supporters in 60. On the other hand, the conversion work seems to have meant that the skulls of the legion's enemies, used to 'decorate' the ramparts, were toppled into the backfilled ditches.

Curiously, the street grid was laid out on a different alignment to that of the fortress despite the fact that a number of the old barrack blocks were adapted into living quarters. In most cases the centurion's house at the end of each block was retained as a house, but the soldiers' accommodation was sometimes demolished to make way for gardens or cultivation. This seems strange considering that colonists were generally awarded additional plots of land outside the town expressly for such a purpose. However, there are unlikely to have been many veterans at this stage. The population was probably much smaller than the 5,000 or so members of the departed legion, unless veterans from other legions abroad were offered land and accommodation here for their retirement. The prospect of ruthless profiteering in 'virgin' territory might have been attractive.

The description by Tacitus of the sack of Colchester in 60 gives us an idea of what work had been done in only thirteen years since 47. Tacitus says that the town had a 'senate house', a 'theatre' and a 'temple'. But Tacitus wrote a generation later. He had never seen any of these places and whether they were actually any more grandiose, and no less pretentious, than a timber town hall in a nineteenth-century frontier town in Montana is a moot point (**105**). Obviously the destruction of the town means that we have no idea of the extent to which these buildings had been completed but it is clear that Colchester was already emerging as a 'typical Roman town' in a province that had seen nothing like it less than a generation before. This reflects the colony's purpose as an example of civil and civic government based on law. These public buildings were sited in the former fortress annexe though strangely the theatre, if the known remains of the later theatre lie over the theatre of 60, was built directly over the filled-in ditches of the fortress. Much the most imposing would have been the classical temple dedicated to Claudius (**12**) that, along with its precinct, was large and secure enough to have served as the last stand during the sack. Of course, it might have been far from complete at this date. In effect this created a kind of public building zone, isolated from the rest of the town rather than being in its centre. Perhaps it was felt that placing imposing new buildings in amongst the old barracks would have diminished their impact.

12 *The Temple of Claudius at Colchester. The façade of the Supreme Court in Washington DC is similar in scale and proportion, as well as the number of columns, to the probable appearance of the Colchester temple and provides an excellent impression of how remarkable this building must have appeared to mid-first-century Britain. It also reflects how visionaries of later ages modelled their cities on classical archetypes to create a sense of grandeur and power*

The new town was more than just a showcase of Roman public life. Its Roman inhabitants would have become swiftly discontented in their remote provincial exile if they had been prevented from living in the style to which they were accustomed. There would have been an influx of merchants and craftsmen eager to supply goods and services. Archaeology has provided evidence for their presence, often in burnt layers that can be associated with the destruction during the Revolt. Not only was there the well-known 'samian shop' which contained the burnt and fused remains of hundreds of fine red-slip wheel-thrown bowls, dishes and cups from southern Gaul, but also remains of a clay oil-lamp factory. Large quantities of perishables, such as wine and foodstuffs, would have been imported, as well as grown and traded locally.

Colchester at this time has been described as a 'boom town' and also as a 'converted army camp'. Both are true but the town was designed to be more than either. By being sited so close to the principal Iron Age settlement of pre-Roman Britain it may have been planned as the provincial capital with its official title of *Colonia Claudia Victriciensis*, following Claudius' triumphal entry to the town in 43 (**13**).

However, Tacitus' description of the Boudican Revolt clearly implies that the procurator of the province, Catus Decianus (the financial administrator, acting as deputy to the governor Suetonius Paullinus), was based elsewhere. Unfortunately he doesn't say where. London ought to be the most likely but a fort is a possibility too. Whatever the situation, it may have been decided that the town was too closely associated with the unacceptable sides of Roman rule to function as an effective capital after 60. The temple was regarded as the prime symbol of Roman power and Colchester's colonists had been unduly harsh to the Trinovantians who lived around the town by summarily seizing

13 *Claudius (41-54), on a brass* sestertius *struck at Rome around 41-2 and found in Britain. Actual diameter 36mm*

their property. That insult was made worse when some Trinovantians were obliged to serve as priests in the temple, though it is possible that some of them complied in order to enhance their status in the new arrangements. But they were forced to hand over even more goods as 'offerings'. This was correctly interpreted by the Trinovantians as a racket that apparently left them nothing to lose by participating in an armed rebellion.

Verulamium before 60

Tacitus naturally concentrated on the dramatic and symbolic details of Colchester's destruction in the Boudican Revolt. We therefore know less about the other two principal towns involved: Verulamium and London. Tacitus said that the *municipium* of Verulamium suffered the same disaster as London and Colchester, though far less archaeological evidence has been found here for widespread burning and destruction. What this also appears to tell us is that Verulamium had achieved the status of *municipium* by the year 60. As we saw in chapter 1 this was normally only conferred on an already existing *civitas* capital. It seems unlikely that such an elevation could have taken place so swiftly. Tacitus may have been unintentionally using the town's title at the time when he was writing (around the beginning of the second century). But in the absence of a confirmatory inscription we have to take his reference on trust and assume that this was a possibility.

Unfortunately this brief reference is all we have. But if the town was important enough to attract the attention of the rebels, and also the provincial governor Suetonius Paullinus as he withdrew, it must have become a place of some significance. The area was already a centre for the Catuvellauni who issued coins in the name of the king, Tasciovanus, in about 20-15 BC. The coins were struck with the name of the settlement in various forms, for example VER or VERLAMIO. The exact location of the settlement is uncertain – it may have been on the higher ground to the west of the east-facing slope on which the Roman town was built, overlooking the river Ver. Subsequently Tasciovanus' son Cunobelinus extended the tribe's power eastwards to Camulodunum. The situation became more confused during the reign of Caligula (37-41) when Cunobelinus' son, Adminius, was banished. He surrendered himself to Caligula, an act which was conveniently interpreted for political purposes by the emperor as a gift of Britain to himself and therefore an invitation to invade.

Caligula's failure to fulfil this intention may be linked to the subsequent early development of the settlement as a Roman town as a way of making up and, more importantly, because Adminius would probably have been perceived as a useful ally amongst the British nobility. This is pure speculation and any connection is rather tenuous but there must have been a reason for the town's favoured status – it is after all the only Romano-British town we know was a *municipium* at some point in its history, and one of the earliest to have been equipped with masonry public administrative buildings. It may simply have been a reward for exceptionally successful urban development or playing a significant role in a provincial crisis, perhaps the Boudican Revolt. Another possibility is that the Catuvellauni became a client kingdom and Verulamium's early development as a Roman city benefited from the arrangement. A wealthy tribal burial was found at Folly Lane to the east of the later Roman city in 1992. Dated to the mid-50s by the Roman pottery found within, the burial later had a Romano-Celtic temple built over it. It has been suggested this was where Verulamium's last tribal leader was buried, with his memory later forming the centre of a cult, and that this might even have been Adminius himself. It is impossible to verify this attractive, but possibly fanciful, theory.

If there was ever a fort established at Verulamium, no firm physical evidence has ever been found for it. Fragments of military equipment prove nothing. They can turn up almost anywhere and reflect a world in which soldiers were a part of everyday life. Their equipment needed repair, and could be manufactured or recycled almost anywhere. None of the Verulamium pieces, like a section of armour nearly cut-up and buried, have been found in definitively military contexts. A stretch of turf bank and a passageway through it under the centre of the later town were once thought to be evidence for an early fort, supported by the way in which Watling Street ignored the street grid, presumably heading for an earlier fort. But Rosalind Niblett has now shown that the bank has been totally reinterpreted as remains of a brushwood causeway. She also points out that no military buildings have been found and very few of the 'copies' of Claudian bronze coins have been found on the site. These are normally associated with forts of this date. Not only that, but Watling Street apparently did not cut across the grid until the 70s.

All this need not preclude the possibility that a short-lived fort did indeed exist at Verulamium. But if a fort ever was built here it was probably only used briefly unless it was on a different site and has yet to be found. The fact that Verulamium lay on a major route and was already a prominent native centre was undoubtedly of greater importance and it is likely that the town benefited from the involvement of the local tribal nobility. Either way, it is clear that Verulamium started life in a very different way from Colchester.

The fort/no-fort debate introduces us conveniently to the rather simplistic tradition that pervaded studies of Roman Britain in the nineteenth and much of the twentieth centuries. Places tended to be regarded as military or civilian. If military evidence was found then that meant the place had to be military, and had therefore to have been a fort. In fact, and this is plain from Roman literature and inscriptions, as well as from studies of other parts of the Empire, individual soldiers, or small detachments, served as escorts to government administrators (particularly the governor), as customs officials, as policemen, and in a host of other mundane duties. They also contributed to city surveying and even architecture, especially in more remote provinces where professional technical skills were not so readily available. So soldiers were everywhere and that was especially true in Britain, where inscriptions recording them dominate the record in towns where there was a military period, however brief. Cirencester is a particularly good example. Ironically, Verulamium is the one major Romano-British city where there are no inscriptions of soldiers (or indeed anyone else) and this fact alone suggests that Verulamium's military population was both small and transient, especially in the first century. We will return to the implications of Britain's lack of urban inscriptions later (in chapter 3, and also under 'Death and burial' in chapter 6).

The main source of evidence for the early development of Verulamium is the row of buildings in *Insula* XIV that fronted the main through-route from London (Watling Street). This elementary timber-framed construction, which resembles a barrack block, might have been built by soldiers using existing military timber components for the benefit of settlers. But almost all residential or small-scale industrial and retail units in the Roman world consist of variations of this style, at least as they appear in plan. Moreover, some of the techniques seem to have been in use at some native sites before the Roman conquest so it is just as likely that the buildings were a private venture (**14**). The idea that a street grid had already been formally laid out by this date has now been abandoned, so this cannot be used to support the idea of organized Roman urban development. It was based on an incorrect survey of the forum-basilica, which appeared to show that the complex had been built to fit into an earlier, different, road layout.

More important than the origin of the *Insula* XIV row is that it existed at all. It appears to have contained a number of separate establishments whose occupants were engaged in various manufacturing concerns. Most of these involved metalworking including bronze, iron and gold. There may also have been an eating house or small inn. This is significant because it shows that at an exceptionally early date there was already business to be had in the manufacture and repair of goods that were not functional, for example bronze statuettes and gold items. That the buildings fronted Watling Street suggests that some of this trade was passing trade; after all there would have been a considerable amount of traffic connected with the advancing army. Far to the northwest along Watling Street at Wroxeter, probably the legionary fortress of the *XIV Gemina* by the late 50s, there is evidence for metalworking in Celtic styles and techniques (such as enamelled bronze) by this date. Perhaps local smiths were supplying the local community, or army, or artisans from other parts of Britain had followed the legion and its auxiliaries into the Welsh Marches. Clearly the traders at Verulamium, whoever they were, were making a living and we can assume that they represented not just a source of supply but also demand. There were similarities with the pre-Roman industrial and trading settlement at Sheepen (Camulodunum) but the *Insula* XIV shops differed in being buildings of a Roman type, and being sited beside a major road.

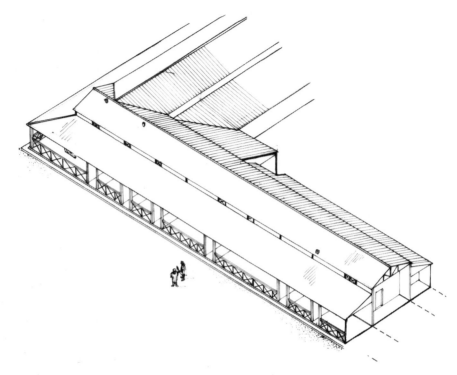

14 *Isometric reconstruction of the timber shops at Verulamium in* Insula *XIV as they may have appeared around the year AD 60 before being burnt down, probably in the Boudican Revolt. The site remained in almost continuous occupation throughout the Roman period but went through many stages of reconstruction. It was typical of urban industrial and retail buildings in Roman Britain during the first and second centuries*

So at Verulamium we can tentatively identify the early stages of an urban economy based on the concentration in a small area of a group of people who were not primarily engaged in providing food for themselves, but had the income to allow them to buy it from elsewhere. This is the basis of all towns and depends on an agricultural economy with surplus. So long as this group continues to make a living from its trades then the town has life. At Verulamium this is reflected in the finds of imported goods, especially pre-60 samian, found in *Insula* XIV and other deposits across an area that would later become the middle of the town that developed over the next century.

There is nothing particularly profound about this but it is important to recognize that the group of shops in early Verulamium existed for some of the same reasons that lie behind our own urban society. It would be interesting to know whether the individuals concerned were operating independently or whether they were in some way tied to a master, Roman or native, who had financed their premises and exacted a tithe from their income. On the evidence of places on the continent, we might imagine a single landlord who had erected the building in order to rent out street-frontage space to businesses, while individuals and families rented upstairs apartments.

London before 60

While Colchester was certainly a town with official status, and Verulamium probably so, London was a town with no formal standing at all. Dio's description of the Revolt only says that two cities were destroyed. These must be Colchester and Verulamium. Tacitus specifically says that while London was not a colony it was already a very well-known and prosperous trading and business centre. This implies that it was effectively functioning with all the prestige and activity of a colony. It was even important enough for Suetonius Paullinus to consider making a stand against Boudica there. After the Revolt the new procurator of the province, Gaius Julius Alpinus Classicianus, seems to have been based there instead of Colchester. His tombstone survives, found reused in the late defences of Roman *Londinium* (**15**).

The striking feature about this is that London had apparently developed without any deliberate intent to found it. While the Roman government was considering the political expediency of instituting client kingdoms, *civitas* capitals and colonies, the underlying factors of trade and communications led to the spontaneous growth of a town where conditions were right. Until the conquest in 43 the River Thames had served as a tribal boundary and apart from isolated traces of native settlement in the area (for example the hillfort at Wimbledon and a concentration of Iron Age coin finds to the west of Roman London) no evidence has been found for a late Iron Age *oppidum*. The river will have already served as a communications route of course but the combi-

15 *London. Computer reconstruction of the text from the tombstone of the procurator of the province of Britannia Gaius Julius Alpinus Classicianus, c.65. This remarkable survival of a historically testified major provincial official is a key piece of evidence for London's early status as capital of Britannia. See appendix 2 for a translation.* Based on work by R.S.O. Tomlin

nation of the vast increase in continental and inland traffic under the Roman occupation and a politically neutral location close to a convergence of a number of roads at a river crossing made it almost inevitable that it would attract settlement.

Excavations in London have also yielded evidence for an early town with a thriving commercial base that was destroyed in 60. There is no more evidence here for a military presence before the town developed than at Verulamium. Traces of military-style ditches have been identified to the west of the town, by modern Fleet Street and also at Aldgate, but these cannot yet be attributed to a fort, and there is no concentration of early military artefacts. Another possibility is that there was a fort south of the river in Southwark where a number of military artefacts and coins dating to *c*.40-65 have been found. So while there may have been a military base in the vicinity at some point, it is unlikely to have been connected with the subsequent or contemporary growth of London around an early bridgehead across the Thames.

The road network suggests that the traditional crossing of the Thames was about a mile to the west of the Roman town, close to where Westminster is now. Later the roads were diverted to converge at the Roman bridgehead. The trading settlement grew up on a site which was more suitable for development as a port, making a new crossing and later a bridge essential. The northern slope of the riverbank drops relatively steeply here and this would have made it easier either to avoid or limit the inconvenient beaching effect of low tides once a quayside had been built. Caesar might have been taken by surprise when his ships were damaged by high tides a century before but the founders of early London had a very much better idea of how to cope. To the south, Southwark consisted of a number of islands at this date. The most northerly was exploited to build the bridge at the point where the river was at its narrowest (**16**). With the communications network adapted, London's development was assured. Although settlement has moved around, especially after the Roman occupation, the situation has remained more or less unchanged ever since.

Despite London's unofficial status the settlement was still laid out around a grid. This could simply reflect the practical habits of early Roman Londoners who reproduced what they were used to elsewhere, or perhaps the occasional presence of military or other official personnel passing through what was obviously developing into a key communications hub. At least two roads were laid out running parallel to the north bank of the Thames, connected by a road that ran down to a possible bridge. The northerly road remained the principal east-west axis of the town. At the centre of this grid was an open gravelled space on what eventually became the site of the forum. It may be that here we have some of the earliest circumstantial evidence for public administrative buildings. Of course it may have been nothing more than a market place, or possibly part of an otherwise unidentifiable military compound, but its location and the later use of the site suggests something more significant.

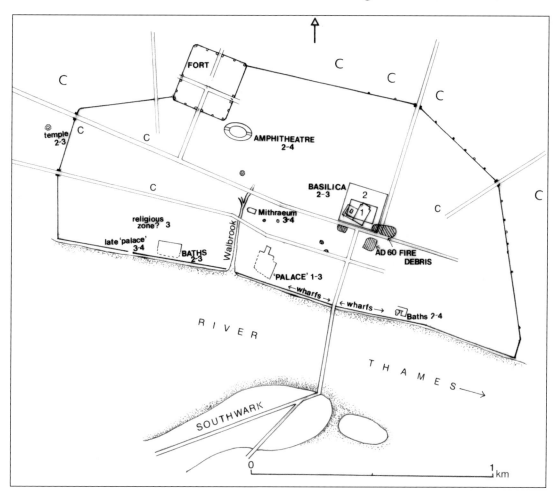

16 *Plan of London. Although a number of much later features are shown here various excavations have revealed traces of extensive burning dating to the mid-first century. These are often attributed to the Boudican Revolt. Traces of settlement of this date have been found all the way along the two main east-west roads. Subsequently the town was rebuilt with two successive basilica and forum complexes and is now known to have had an amphitheatre, almost certainly associated with the second-century fort later incorporated into the third-century defences. 'C' marks the site of a cemetery, the smaller 'c' within the third-century walls denoting cemeteries associated with the first-century town. Approximate date ranges for buildings are indicated, e.g. 2-4 = second to fourth centuries*

By about the year 55 a number of rectangular timber-framed buildings were put up on the eastern side of the gravelled area. These extended to having some sort of frontage, resembling the 'shops' of *Insula* XIV at Verulamium (**14**). However, no evidence was recovered to indicate what they were used for. There is plenty of other evidence for structural remains in London at this time, including stone foundations and traces of water-pipes and drains. Excavations on the Roman riverfront have shown that by about the year 50 efforts were already being made to develop the north bank around the bridgehead, with timber being used to create revetments to serve as quays. Destruction debris from possible Boudican levels also indicates that trade was indeed thriving here with numerous remains of imported luxury goods. Evidence for metalworking has been found and even for the manufacture of engraved gemstones (intaglios) – a group of four from a pit included one that was discarded before being finished, implying it was made locally. At Colchester such comprehensive urban activity can be attributed to the presence of military veterans. In London it is less obvious who could have been responsible for what seems to have been an organized programme of land allocations and harbour development. It has been suggested that a body of Roman citizens, intent on making the most of the commercial possibilities in London, settled themselves there and set about the task of creating a trading centre. This is reflected in the distribution of settlement along the roads whose intersection at this place had created the catalyst for a town. However, it is equally possible that London was already being used by the Roman government as an administrative centre. This was certainly so later, but the town's convenience as well as the advantages of a politically neutral location can hardly have gone unnoticed.

Chelmsford

Chelmsford lay in the heart of Trinovantian territory (roughly equal to present-day Essex). Little is known about its origin though it has been attributed to the presence of a fort and, perhaps, an attempt to create a tribal capital for the Trinovantes to foster an impression of Rome acting as a liberator from Catuvellaunian oppression. The presence of early buildings destroyed in a fire associated possibly with the Boudican Revolt was thought to give this some credence, but the burnt samian supposedly found there has now been shown actually to be materially originally recovered in London. Chelmsford's important-sounding Latin name, *Caesaromagus* ('Caesar's market place') is unparalleled in Britain and gives no indication that there was any earlier place-name available for adaptation: quite the contrary, in fact. The name bears all the hallmarks of an artificial and official foundation, though we do not know when the town was awarded the name. It may have been granted during later reorganization of tribal government. Whatever the situation, however, Chelmsford did not develop into anything particularly significant, or perhaps even anything at all. Tacitus and Suetonius do not mention it even by implication, and lying so close to Colchester may have deprived it of economic stimuli. Chelmsford is therefore an instance of a 'town' of sorts which did not develop swiftly in the years between 43 and 60 because it was neither originally an important native settlement nor did it have the advantage of lying at both a major road junction and river crossing.

The other towns of early Roman Britain

The other principal settlements that have shown traces of early urban development are Canterbury, Silchester, Winchester and Chichester, but these are of a completely different character. Canterbury lay close to the place the Roman forces may have landed in 43 and was already a large native settlement with its own mint, probably clustering around a pre-Roman shrine centre for which some archaeological evidence has been found. Canterbury's name, *Durovernum*, means 'town by the alder swamp', perhaps itself once the focus of cult activity. It seems that some sort of street grid was laid out here shortly after the invasion though on closer examination this has turned out to be less regimented than originally thought, perhaps taking account of the Iron Age shrine area. There are also fragmentary traces of early timber-framed buildings. To some extent it all depends on whether eastern Kent was a major military landing area during the aftermath of the Conquest. If it was, tolerating a native settlement so close was unlikely and this could have provoked swift supervised development of Canterbury as a Roman town. Even so, some round huts of pre-Roman type appear to have remained in use for some time after 43 and there is as yet no evidence to suggest that any of the public buildings were begun at this time.

At Silchester the *oppidum* of *Calleva* remained in occupation after the invasion. The possibility of a fort exists but since this remains limited to military equipment rather than anything structural that is definitively military, any army presence was probably brief. Silchester was something of an ordered community because during the early first century AD metalled streets were laid out and rectangular buildings erected, though evidence for this 'grid' is limited to two roads appearing to converge at right angles. But other evidence, like palisades and ordered rubbish pits, has led the excavators to call this period one of 'proto-urbanism'; in other words, a kind of halfway house between an *oppidum* and a Roman town. The so-called 'inner earthwork', which resembles in form the later shape of the third-century walled town, could belong to this very early stage of urban development though it clearly preceded the baths (**17**). Re-excavation of *Insula* IX in the town has produced traces of rectangular timber buildings in existence as early as AD 50. Finds generally of imported luxury goods also create an impression of a tribal chief trying to present himself as a sophisticated Roman-style ruler or a Roman town being create in and out of the old *oppidum*. Verica's mission to Claudius for help in the face of Catuvellaunian expansion reinforces the image, and it is even possible the client king Togidubnus ruled the canton from Silchester rather than Chichester, or even both, especially as Silchester later emerged as the *civitas* capital for the Atrebates. But another, *Calleva*-based, client king is just as plausible.

The archaeological evidence suggests that the *oppidum* was reorganized as a more romanized town in the 50s or 60s. No evidence for a fort has been found. A new street grid was laid out and we know that tiles were being manu-

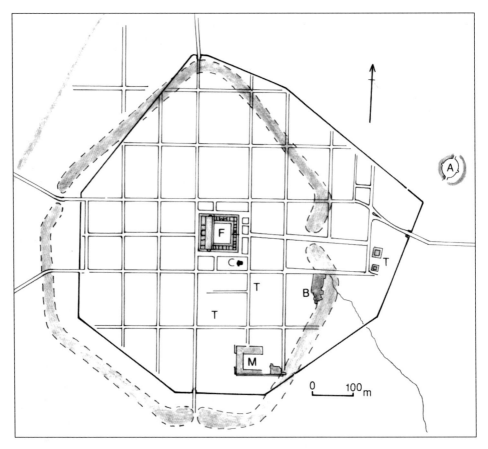

17 *Silchester. This simplified plan shows the third-century town walls that crossed the earlier main street grid. This grid itself superseded an earlier grid, evident from the angle the forum-basilica (F) and baths (B) were built on. Traces of an even earlier grid, on a totally different orientation, have been found in the forum area. The first grid might have been contemporary with the 'inner earthwork', which might have defended the mid-first-century Roman town. Temple sites are marked T; note the* insula *with temples close to the east gate and the amphitheatre (A). The late Christian (?) church is marked C.* Based on work by Hope, Boon and Fulford

factured in the vicinity during the reign of Nero (54-68) because they bear his name (**18**). This is an exceptional instance for Britain of a tile bearing an emperor's name in a civilian context and it is reasonable to assume that official resources were being supplied to the community in the interests of urban development. It may even have had a timber administrative structure in the centre (perhaps the one for which the Neronian tiles were produced), a site that was subsequently used for a Flavian timber basilica and later stone basilica. Modern clearance and excavation of the amphitheatre has shown that the earliest phase, of earth and timber, may have belonged to this period. London's amphitheatre is now known also to have had an early phase. The old name was retained with the addition of the tribal name, making it *Calleva Atrebatum*, 'the woodland town of the Atrebates'. Perhaps it was one of the principal centres of the client kingdom of Togidubnus, which would explain the apparently special treatment the town received. But there is absolutely no evidence to verify that, even indirectly.

Chichester is particularly interesting because an inscription found in the town names Togidubnus as approving the dedication of a temple to Neptune and Minerva. If the currently accepted restoration of the inscription is correct, he did so in his capacity as *Rex Magnus*, 'Great King' (**108** & appendix 2). The inscription is undated but must belong to somewhere between *c.*50 and *c.*80 and at least associates him with a specific location, something which Tacitus never does. As the town is now completely built over, excavation has been limited, but there was certainly settlement of a romanized nature at a very early date evidenced by the presence of metalworkers and potters, following the demolition of military-style structures *c.*50. A military presence is not certain but we do know that the army had a compound of sorts at nearby Fishbourne and the area may have formed part of a supply base for the *II* legion's advance to the south-west. A series of dykes to the north of the town may indicate the presence of an *oppidum* but no obvious centre has yet been identified.

As Nero received a dedication from Chichester's senate in 59 we can assume that the settlement had received an official charter (appendices 1 & 2). It was probably not yet a *civitas* capital or else the inscription would have mentioned it. The town subsequently emerged as the *civitas* capital for the Regini, a tribe artificially created in the absence of any convenient grouping, but this probably belongs to the period after Cogidubnus' death. The same applies to Winchester, which was made into the capital for the vaguely-titled Belgae of the area (*Belgae*

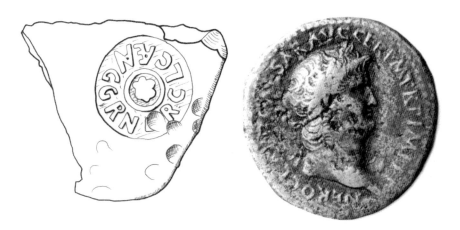

18 *Silchester.* Left: *tile stamp from the public baths' latrine bearing the titles of Nero,* NER(O) CL(AVDIVS) CAE(SAR) AVG(VSTVS) G(E)R(MANICVS). *Three other examples were found on the basilica site and together suggest an imperial tilery was set up between 54-68 to initiate public building projects.* Right: *brass sestertius of Nero, struck at Rome between 64-8. The manufacturer of the wooden (the grain can be seen on the tile) stamp die may have used a similar coin as a source of Nero's titles*

was just a general name for the peoples of south-east Britain, and originating in *Belgica* on the continent). Like Chichester, ambiguous evidence for some sort of early Roman presence has been found but nothing has been discovered to confirm if this was a fort, and whether it was associated with an as yet unlocated pre-Roman settlement still in occupation in 43.

Collectively Canterbury, Silchester, Chichester and Winchester make an interesting group of settlements. While they all emerged as conventional *civitas* capitals that never became especially prominent, all of them seem to have been influenced by Roman town-planning. However, nothing has been located to indicate any of the thriving commercial activity so evident in Colchester, London and Verulamium. This may be a false impression because the latter three have benefited from enormous amounts of excavation in modern times, much of which has been fully published. Nevertheless, the date 60 is useful because it seems to have been a point up to which urban development was piecemeal yet surprisingly intense in concentrations. London is the key because its spontaneous development reflected the arrival of a completely new social, economic, legal and logistical order. But it would be wrong to overrate the kind of towns that these settlements were. Rivet for example once described Verulamium and London respectively at this time as being 'a straggle of shops and shacks' and the equivalent of a 'corrugated iron-roofed trading centre'. These were, after all, in every sense frontier towns on the fringe of the known world. On the other hand to those who had never seen a town before they may have seemed exceptionally interesting and exciting or perhaps even intimidating places.

We cannot attribute the various stages of later development in the towns to such a short period because we have neither the literary nor epigraphic evidence to pin things down so clearly. Even so, a picture has emerged of extensive and more consistent urban development in the rest of the province in the aftermath of the Revolt, lasting from the Flavian period right through until the middle of the second century and later (**colour plates 2**, **3**, **4** & **25**). The days of piecemeal street grids and shadowy traces of timber buildings give way to the arrival of monumental urban architecture, whose function and importance are not in doubt, and unprecedented economic activity. The rest of the book explores this development through the various different aspects of the history, and commercial and religious life of the towns.

3

RECONSTRUCTION AND GROWTH OF TOWNS

Although the northern part of Britain remained distinctly unsettled until the early part of the third century, by the late first century the south had entered a period when urban and rural life could develop reasonably peacefully. This was not an overnight activity. In the towns destroyed during the Boudican Revolt there is evidence to suggest that some sites may have remained vacant for ten or more years. By 75 the rot was over, and there is far more evidence for sustained urban development. Apart from the growth of the *civitas* capitals, two more colonies were created by the end of the first century at Lincoln and Gloucester. London also emerged as the provincial capital, if it was not already, though to this day we have no idea if it was ever formally classified in any way. The tombstone of Classicianus (**15**) and the appearance of procuratorial tiles is the only evidence that we have (**69** & **colour plate 24**).

This stability and its effects should not be underestimated. During the pre-Roman period most of the population would have been accustomed to almost perpetual insecurity. Tribal boundaries and fortunes fluctuated along with the rise and fall of the respective individuals who ruled them. This does not mean that the ordinary people lived in permanent fear of plunder and rape, huddled in corners of wattle-and-daub shacks. But it does mean that a great deal of economic and nervous energy was expended in the exercise of tribal rivalries and the pursuit of individual status. Tribal warfare was dependent on an economic surplus because the surplus fed the leaders and warriors. If inter-tribal warfare was terminated and armed resistance quashed the surplus could then be redirected into supporting towns. Similarly the members of the tribal elites would seek to assert their influence and power within the structure and offices of local government, and were being educated to do so by the Roman authorities as a matter of policy.

In almost all the major towns a long period of construction work began in the two decades after 60 and continued well into the second century. This picture has been largely created by the extensive excavations that have taken place in a number of the larger towns during the last hundred years or so. The traditional reliance on Tacitus' description of Agricola's promotion of urban development between 78 and 84, and the chance survival of Verulamium's forum inscription from the same date, originally created the impression that intensive urban development was concentrated in the Flavian period (**110, colour plates 2 & 4**).

It now seems clear that while several towns like Silchester and Lincoln may have had early timber administrative buildings many of the more elaborate masonry forums and basilicas belonged to a much longer-term programme of building. The structures were the equivalent of medieval cathedrals in scale so they may also have taken generations to plan, finance and build. The difference of course is that, apart from the fact that the island was being ruled from Rome, we have no idea of where the money came from. We have very little epigraphic evidence in Britain for what has been described as the 'competitive munificence' seen elsewhere in the Empire. This was the way wealthy members of communities vied with one another to build the most lavish and generously endowed public buildings, usually embellished with inscriptions that recorded their status as priests of the imperial cult, or listed the public offices they held. The lack of this sort of evidence is a particularly interesting aspect of Romano-British towns that we shall examine in closer detail later.

The development of public buildings was followed by a marked general improvement in urban housing with a distinct move away from the congested commercial quarters of the first century. By the end of the second century widely-spaced stone housing was becoming normal. These houses contain evidence for an urban population that had surplus wealth to spend on decorations like mosaics and wall-paintings. The enormous quantities of archaeological material excavated from the late first- and second-century levels in towns show that the building programmes were matched with a thriving urban economy (see chapter 5). By the third century, though, the energetic development of towns seems to have slowed. Whether this represents the onset of decline or simply a period of stabilization is a problem explored in later chapters.

The forum and basilica

A forum was an open square or rectangle, which in Roman Britain was surrounded by covered colonnades on three sides, with the basilica forming the fourth. Access was through a small number of entrances that would normally have excluded wheeled traffic (**19, 20 & 23**). Very few Romano-British forums had temples incorporated into the structure, even though this was common practice on the continent. Only Verulamium seems to have been built like this (**30 & colour plate 4**) while at Caerwent a temple was added later. London's modest first forum and basilica, built in the Flavian period, had a free-standing temple built in a precinct annexed to the forum. Perhaps the ill-feeling created by the Temple of Claudius in Colchester during the

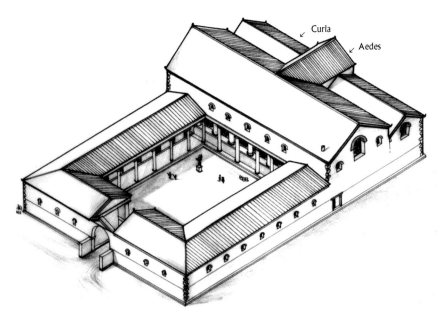

19 *Reconstructed isometric view of the basilica and forum at Caerwent, built in the early second century. This new drawing takes into account recent excavation work on the basilica that showed the side facing the forum was an open colonnade, and the roofing has been revised. Although one of the smallest in Britain it is plain that this was still a substantial and imposing complex (about 80 by 58m), and was originally around 20m high. The building survives in an exceptional state for Britain, with walls up to 2m high (see 25)*

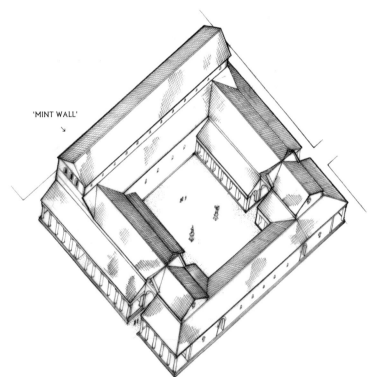

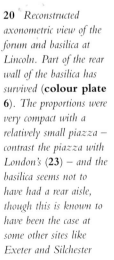

20 *Reconstructed axonometric view of the forum and basilica at Lincoln. Part of the rear wall of the basilica has survived (**colour plate 6**). The proportions were very compact with a relatively small piazza – contrast the piazza with London's (23) – and the basilica seems not to have had a rear aisle, though this is known to have been the case at some other sites like Exeter and Silchester*

Boudican Revolt (it was perceived as a particularly potent symbol of Rome's domination) encouraged a low-key approach to enforcing official religion during the period in which the *civitas* capitals were being instituted.

The forum served as an open meeting place for the whole town. It was used as a market and as a gathering place for public pronouncements. It was an essential means of promoting a political and social sense of civic unity within the context of Roman town life. Consequently it was also a place where honorific statues of emperors or local worthies were erected, and also a place where religious dedications were made to the Capitoline Triad of Jupiter, Juno and Minerva, and the Spirits of the Emperors, sometimes in a dedicated temple (**colour plate 8**). This is what we would expect on the evidence of other parts of the Empire. In Britain so little survives that we face a choice of either assuming that things would have been much the same, or suggesting that perhaps the lack of evidence implies that things were different. Suetonius commented in his *Life of Titus* (79-81) on how the emperor was so popular in Britain and Germany that statues and busts of him were plentiful in both provinces. Many of these would have been on public display in forums and basilicas. None survive but substantial fragments of monumental figures have been found, the most famous being the bronze bust of Hadrian (**21**) found in the Thames in London that would almost certainly have come from the forum, and the bronze eagle from the basilica in Silchester (**22**). Other smaller pieces have been found in other towns, for example a piece of a bronze horse's mane from the Gloucester forum; this would probably have once been part of a statue of an emperor seated on horseback waving to the population, a stock posture.

21 *Life-size bronze bust of Hadrian dredged from the Thames. Height 41cm. It probably formed part of a major statue displayed in the forum or basilica*

22 *Bronze eagle found in the basilica at Silchester during the Victorian excavations. Height 15cm*

The basilica was a long covered rectangular hall with nave and aisle(s), and with an apse at one or both ends (**23** & **colour plate 16**). A number of Romano-British examples were built in a slightly curious form and had only a single aisle, for example at Silchester and Lincoln (**20** & **25**). The height of the roof was roughly equivalent to the width of the nave and one aisle added together (early churches of basilican type in Italy provide parallels). Vaults or timber beams supported the roof. It was in rooms here that the council of the *civitas* met, where justice was dispensed and where civic records and funds were stored.

The basilica would have towered over surrounding houses, just as medieval cathedrals still do. The site chosen in London was especially prominent. A road led up the hill from the north bank of the Thames to the forum, and the basilica would probably have been visible behind the forum's entrance all the way. Inside the basilica there would have been some elaborately painted wall-plaster and a large amount of ornamental stucco and stonework. London was a special case, though. Excavations beside Cannon Street station have revealed traces of a monumental terraced complex that included an ornamental garden with a pool and a substantial hall. It has been tentatively identified as the palace of the provincial governor, built in the late first century. However, there are doubts about both whether the complex was all built around the same time, and also its function. It may have been the headquarters of the imperial cult in Britain or even a leisure complex with baths.

The forum and basilica site seems to have been set aside as an open area from an early date in many towns. Both London and Silchester, for example, seem to have had gravelled areas laid out before the Boudican Revolt. In both cases the sites were subsequently used for the forum proper so it seems likely

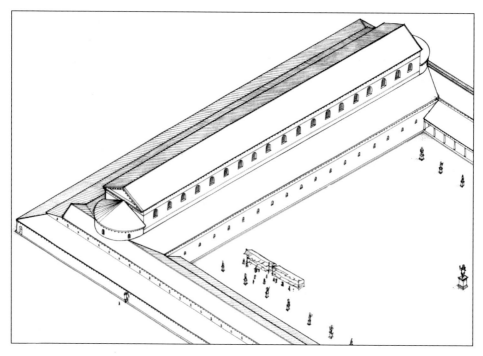

23 *Reconstructed isometric view of the monumental Hadrianic basilica in London. The building may never have been fully completed and is now known to have had at least two separate periods of construction, as well as superseding an earlier and smaller predecessor. The apse in the foreground is hypothetical*

that they were fulfilling some of the forum functions already. We know that Verulamium's forum had been officially dedicated by the year 79 or 81 (though this does not necessarily mean that it was finished). London's modest first stone forum and basilica appears to have been erected at a similar time. Silchester and Exeter appear to have had timber forums and basilicas built around 80-90 (with an even earlier phase at Silchester dating to about 60).

IMP·CAES·DIVI·TRAIANI·PARH
CI·FIL·DIVI·NERVAE·NEPOTI·TRA
IANO·HADRIANO·AVG·PONIFI
CI·MAXIMO·TRIB·POT·XIIII·COS·III·P·P·
CIVITAS·CORNOVIORVM

24 *Wroxeter, computer-generated restoration of the forum inscription, based on the surviving fragments (the lighter areas) recording a dedication made in 129-30 during the reign of Hadrian. Note that the building is not specified. See appendix 2 for a translation*

This is interesting because the remains belonging to Silchester's timber period have only recently been identified even though the site was cleared during the late-nineteenth-century excavations. Elsewhere most evidence points to masonry structures being erected in the early second century, as at both Leicester and Caerwent. An inscription from Wroxeter records that here a formal dedication did not take place until Hadrian's reign in the year 130 or 131 (**24**), just a few years after Caerwent's basilica was built. In the construction levels of the Caerwent basilica a virtually uncirculated *sestertius* of Trajan struck 112-14 was found. It is unlikely to have been available in this condition for many years after those dates, but it depicts the port of Ostia and is a very rare type so could have been preserved by an owner for a while. Nevertheless, it provides a good case for pinning the building's erection to within the reign of Trajan's successor Hadrian (117-38) (**25 & colour plate 3**).

It may be that some of these towns also had post-Boudican (or even pre-?) timber administrative buildings that have not yet been identified. Or, on the other hand, perhaps this essential component of Roman civic and provincial government was not automatically constructed in towns once the *civitates* were instituted. Silchester's later street grid (**17**) shows that some of the principal buildings, especially the forum-basilica and baths, correspond to a slightly different grid than that which subsequently defined the town. Evidently, urban development was prone to quite significant change. What we can be certain of is that from around the year 65 a long period of public administration building works was undertaken in Roman Britain with many not being constructed in

25 *The second-century basilica at Caerwent during excavation in the 1990s. The view is east (see also **19**)*

stone until well into the second century. Caerwent is an interesting case because the evidence for the first-century town is limited to fairly scrappy timber buildings scattered along a roadside. It makes the forum-basilica look like a very deliberate official effort to create a *civitas* community with its own small, but perfectly-formed, cantonal capital.

The excavations on the site of London's second basilica in the mid-1980s showed that construction had involved at least two separate phases with the nave erected first, following the demolition of housing. The reason for the break, and its duration, are unknown but may have been connected with money and man-power. Whatever the circumstances it would obviously be wrong always to assume that these buildings were planned and built in an orderly and sustained fashion. It is also possible that some were never finished either inside or out and together with some evidence for these buildings becoming redundant in the third century makes it possible buildings were being provided for functions that in some cases were never really instituted. London's Hadrianic basilica was as large as a cathedral (**23**). The basilica's nave was about 150m (492ft) in length, 14m (46ft) wide and would have been about 25m (82ft) in height. Although the basic fabric of the building was made up of fired bricks cemented together (common practice in the Roman world) it would have been extensively decorated inside with carved stonework such as columns, capitals and architraves, and veneers made up from cut pieces of exotic stone like porphyry and marble, much of which would have been imported. All this assumes the building was completed and that was not necessarily the case. Medieval cathedrals sometimes took centuries to build, and in Roman Britain the circumstances of the third century in some towns suggest that basilicas were becoming redundant in terms of their original function.

Walls not decorated with stone veneers would have been plastered and painted – fragments of this have been found. London was not unusual in these respects even though as the premier town in the province it was probably intended to be the most lavish. The modest basilica at Caerwent had decorated stone capitals, and others have been found at Silchester and Cirencester. As an early showpiece, Verulamium's basilica would have been particularly interesting but the structure is almost completely inaccessible beneath a later church; and in any case we can be almost certain that any significant stonework would have been removed for use in constructing the nearby medieval abbey of St Alban. The only significant pieces of any Romano-British basilica surviving are part of the rear wall at Lincoln (**colour plate 6**) and at Caerwent (**19 & 25**).

The *macellum*

The forum was not always sufficiently large to accommodate all the market activities that went on in a town. Sometimes it was supplemented with a *macellum*, a building that was really just a small version of a forum. The word means literally a 'meat market', but was used in the more general sense of a food market. Likewise the term *forum boarium* meant 'cattle market', but this was more likely to be at the town's edge so that slaughtering could take place where the mess would be less intrusive. The butchered meat could then be carted into town for immediate sale.

In the year 59 construction of Nero's *Macellum Magnum* ('Great Macellum') was completed in Rome. Not very many have been identified in Britain but Verulamium, Leicester (**colour plate 11**) and Wroxeter (**26**) appear to have been equipped with one, though in no case is identification certain. Evidence from Pompeii suggests that while most of the booths were shops of various kinds there may have been a religious presence, perhaps in the form of a meeting place for priests involved in the imperial cult, or the cult of a *Genius* (literally the spirit, or something akin to a patron saint) of a trade.

Verulamium's *macellum* had a long history. It enjoyed a central location, just across Watling Street from the theatre and close to the forum. It was originally built in the first century and consisted of two rows of nine 'shops' facing one another across an enclosed courtyard. It seems not to have been particularly well-used for it was subsequently reduced in size, though by the fourth century it had been completely rebuilt with a monumental façade. Conversely, at Leicester the building interpreted as the *macellum* seems to have been modelled on the basilica and forum in size and form. Erected by the early third century it could represent an attempt to cope with a lack of facilities to accommodate demand.

26 *Wroxeter. The* macellum, *built into the* insula *that contained the main public baths. A number of small chambers, probably shops, were arranged around a small covered portico with an open central space. It was just across the main road from the forum* (**56**)

Arches

Monumental arches were common throughout the Empire forming a kind of architectural statement representing power as well as acting as a symbolic entrance from one zone to another. Totally functionless apart from acting as advertisement boards to brag about the emperor's achievements, and as plinths for statuary, in general they commemorated imperial military victories. The only instance of a 'triumphal' arch known in Britain is the Richborough arch that probably marked the formal entrance to Britain. The others were built as gates into towns, or as entrances into religious precincts.

Only four certain urban examples are known from actual remains: three in Verulamium and one in Colchester. The latter, now known as the Balkerne Gate (**27**), was incorporated into the city wall at a later date and became the west gate. The Verulamium examples seem to have remained as markers of the town's early boundaries and were erected in the later second century, at about the same time as earthworks were being constructed to enclose a much larger area (**30**). Similar examples are still visible at Pompeii, and they provide a good impression of how arches were used to define zones within towns (**colour plate 28**). Inscriptions record a small number of other instances. The little town at Ancaster had an arch, dedicated to the local god Viridios, and probably served as the entrance to the god's precinct, and another was erected in York in the year 221 (**44**).

27 *Colchester. The Balkerne Gate from within the town walls looking west. The visible stonework formed part of the southern tower and pedestrian passageway added to the original monumental arch*

Civic amenities

Of course there was more to public town life than purely administrative and honorific buildings and activities. Anyone who has visited the remains of better preserved Roman towns around the Mediterranean will have seen how the almost regimented format of town life was extended to all civic facilities and amenities. Almost every town had at least one theatre, a major bath house and some sort of centralized water supply. In Britain we cannot say with confidence that this was the case in every town but the combination of literary, epigraphic and archaeological material gives us the impression that many would at least have aspired to emulating longer established continental towns.

Theatres and amphitheatres

Although religion is dealt with in more detail in chapter 6, Roman theatres cannot be considered without it. Theatres and amphitheatres were an integral component of religion in the Roman world and cannot be separated from it. Urban theatres and amphitheatres were nearly always next to temples or were linked by a roadway. In Britain this was the case at Colchester, Canterbury, Verulamium and Silchester. Silchester's amphitheatre actually lies outside the town walls but a road led from it straight into the city and an *insula* with temples in it. Outside Colchester another theatre was located in a religious precinct with pre-Roman origins at Gosbecks. Processions and celebrations starting in the theatre could progress to the temple as a full part of the ceremonial. Games and entertainments played a vital role in the activities, especially those linked directly to religious festivals (see chapter 6), but these also included enactment of myth.

We have already seen that Colchester had a theatre by 60. It may have lain beneath the later theatre known to have existed beside the precinct of the Temple of Claudius. No other literary references for theatres exist, but at Brough-on-Humber some time between 140 and 144 an *aedile* called Marcus Ulpius Januarius recorded his gift of a new stage to the town's theatre on an inscription that, in part, survives (**28**). This is interesting not just because as an inscription recording a personal gift of a civic amenity it is extremely rare for Britain, but also because Brough was a remote town which was not a *civitas* capital. If Brough had a theatre then we might reasonably suppose that all the major towns would have had one.

Curiously, however, this does not always seem to have been the case. Silchester and Caistor-by-Norwich are all *civitas* capitals that can be examined relatively easily. Silchester has been explored in great detail. It has an amphitheatre, and a very early one at that, but apparently no theatre. Caistor has not been extensively excavated but aerial photography would probably have

OB · HONOREM
DOMVS·DIVINAE
IMP·CAES·T·AEL·HADRI
ANI·ANTONINI·AVG·PII
P · P · COS · III
ET·NVMINIB · AVGG
M·VLP·IANVARIVS
AEDILIS·VICI·PETVAR
PROSCAEN·ET·COL
DE · SVO · DEDIT

28 *Brough-on-Humber. Inscription recording the gift of a theatre stage* (proscaenium) *by the aedile Marcus Ulpius Januarius, c.140-61. The use of decorative crescents* (peltae) *at the side resembles military inscriptions of the period, and the donor's name and location suggests he was probably the son or freedman of a soldier who received his citizenship under Trajan (98-117).* Top: *the surviving part of the inscription.* Bottom: *computer-generated restoration of the complete text. See appendix 2, part 2 for a translation*

revealed theatres by now. Only a depression outside the south-east corner of the town walls at Caistor suggests that it may have had an amphitheatre of sorts. The town that grew up at Richborough, one of the ports-of-entry to Roman Britain, had an amphitheatre on high ground to the south of the late-Roman shore fort there. Even Verulamium's well-known theatre is not a conventional Roman type. Instead, it appears to have been based on a modified amphitheatre design, being not only more than semi-circular but also built out of raised earth banks (**29** & **colour plate 17**). Only Colchester and Canterbury certainly had theatres in the classical form, while traces of possible others have also been identified in Cirencester (**6**) and London (both the latter also had amphitheatres). Canterbury's theatre was not built in more conventional stone classical form until the third century – before that earth and gravel banks built in the late first century had been considered adequate.

This apparently sporadic pattern is almost certainly misleading. At Wroxeter a rectangular enclosure beside a classical temple precinct has been tentatively

identified as the possible setting for religious theatricals and associated entertainments that better-appointed towns had amphitheatres for. A pair of concentric walls surrounded the arena on three sides, and it has been suggested these
supported wooden seats. So elliptical arenas and semi-circular theatres might be
a reflection of our rigid expectations of what a Roman town had to be. A
variety of literary references from the period mention the use of temporary turf
and timber theatres and amphitheatres. Nero had a wooden amphitheatre built
near Mars Field in Rome. In older times, gladiatorial bouts were even held in
the forum, and it is not impossible Britain's public piazzas were also occasionally used this way. Even in Rome the Colosseum was the city's first permanent
amphitheatre, and was not dedicated until the reign of Titus (79-81).

If a Romano-British town had a timber amphitheatre erected as required
on an open field nearby it is highly unlikely that we would chance upon
evidence for it. But in some cases, plans were rather more definitive.
Verulamium's theatre site seems to have been reserved at an early date next to
a large town-centre temple precinct but it was not until well into the second
century that it was actually built (**30**). Clearly the theatre had been planned
from early on, and even in its first form was made of earth and timber. At
Rome an inscription recording the events of the Secular Games for the year

29 *The theatre at Verulamium looking north-east, built originally c.140 in earth and timber. It was later
reconstructed in stone, and subsequently enlarged and modified. The remains of the stage are visible in the
centre left. Four columns supported a cover for the stage and one survives. The seats were supported on earth
banks, revetted in stone. By the fourth century it was disused and had become a rubbish dump, perhaps as a
result of legal restrictions on pagan worship and festivals. See also* **colour plate 17**

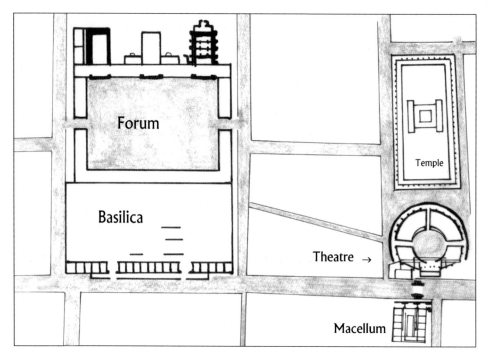

30 *Verulamium town centre. To the left (south) the forum-basilica complex dominated the town centre. A short distance away, and connected by road, was the theatre with its adjacent temple precinct. The arch marked the site of earlier defences but may also have symbolized entry to a religious zone*

17 BC mentions that Latin plays were to be performed in the 'wooden theatre close to the river Tiber'. But Verulamium's theatre fell out of use long before the other civic buildings, despite extensive alterations. Does this mean that the Romano-British never really took to theatre-going? No, because the religious usage of an urban theatre was far more important. By 313 universal religious toleration was imperial law, but in the decades that followed more and more legal restrictions were imposed on paganism until it was banned altogether. In fact, this was extremely difficult to enforce but not in towns where, with some exceptions, paganism was more successfully suppressed.

There is certainly evidence that some of the Romano-British had some acquaintance with classical literature of the kind that could form part of more conventional theatre entertainments. Wall-plaster from the villa at Farningham in Kent bears a couple of words from Virgil's *Aeneid* and the mosaic floor at nearby Lullingstone bears an inscription also alluding to a passage in the *Aeneid*. The small town at Baldock (Herts) has yielded a fragmentary life-sized theatre tragic mask and pieces of others are known from London. While London would almost certainly have had a classical-style theatre, possibly even two (one being an 'odeon', used for literary readings and the like), Baldock probably did not. It may be much more likely that theatres were erected as temporary, maybe seasonal, structures of timber. The Baldock masks could be the surviving traces of a strolling band of players who visited various settlements throughout the year.

Unlike their counterparts in the Mediterranean world, which consisted of a network of interlocking vaults surrounding an elliptical arena, Romano-British amphitheatres were not elaborate structures. Instead they were almost invariably built out of raised earth mounds around a sunken arena. Natural depressions were ideal, and so were redundant Neolithic henge monuments. The earth banks were revetted with timber or stone. Of course this style of construction and the minimal use of masonry gives Romano-British amphitheatres a good chance of recognizable survival. They are often the only buildings surviving above ground level, for example at Chichester, Carmarthen, Silchester and Cirencester, and even at the mining settlement at Charterhouse in the Mendips. At Dorchester (**31**), a Neolithic henge monument was adapted into an amphitheatre by lowering the central ellipse to create a sunken arena. This thoroughly practical solution was not always adopted. At Catterick, a denuded henge monument was ignored by the Roman road builders who simply laid Dere Street, the highway to the north, right across it.

Silchester's amphitheatre (**32 & 33**) has now been comprehensively excavated and has been shown to date from as early as the middle of the first century. London's amphitheatre is thought to have been built around the beginning of the second century but it also overlay a timber predecessor. London's does fall into a very different category. Exceptionally, London had a

31 *Maumbury Rings amphitheatre at Dorchester, Dorset, built out of a Neolithic henge monument (a round or oval bank enclosing a ditch and central area) by lowering the central area to create an arena*

32 *Silchester, the amphitheatre looking through one of the entrances. A stone revetment wall contained the seating banks which were probably once fitted with wooden seats. The visible remains belong to the early third century, but at least two predecessors lie underneath. The first may have been built as early as the reign of Nero (see **18**)*

33 *Silchester, amphitheatre niche. A niche was located in the middle of the long sides of the arena wall. From examples elsewhere, we know that these contained shrines to Nemesis (Fate). It supported a kiosk for civic or visiting dignitaries*

small fort that almost certainly housed a garrison of troops detached from around the province to serve on the governor's staff. The amphitheatre lies so close to the fort it was almost certainly built as a military facility in the first instance, where displays of fighting and parades could take place. However, no artefactual traces of the kind of entertainments that went on have ever turned up in urban amphitheatres or theatres in Britain (nor have they been found at any other Romano-British amphitheatres). We can be sure that these would have included cock-fighting and bear-baiting, and probably extended to matched pairs of gladiators. A gladiator's helmet from Hawkedon in Suffolk may have come from a town originally but how it came to end up in the countryside is a mystery. Gladiators were certainly known about in Britain. One of the mosaics at Bignor depicts several pairs of cupids, dressed as fighting pairs. Wild animals were also depicted: the Rudston (E. Yorks) villa illustrates several in a hunting context (**colour plate 9**).

The third form of public entertainment building, the stadium or circus, was apparently absent from Roman Britain at least as a permanent feature of town life. None are known at all though this does not mean that chariot races did not take place. Chariots feature prominently in Roman descriptions of British tribal warfare, so it is unlikely enthusiasm for expertise had diminished. Across the Humber from Rudston in Lincolnshire the Horkstow villa had a floor that included a panel depicting four chariots, each pulled by a pair of horses racing around the *spina* (central axis) of a circus (**34**). The comparatively remote situation of both houses suggests chariot racing must have been well known elsewhere in Roman Britain unless the owner had a specialist interest. The designs are believed to have North African connections but that could simply be the source of a pattern book used by a local mosaicist rather than implying anything about the house's owner. If the towns had circuses these were probably laid out as temporary structures outside the confines of the settled area. Even on the continent circuses, unlike theatres, were rare additions to towns so the situation in Britain is hardly surprising.

Bath houses

The town of Pompeii in Italy had at least three large public bath houses. This was common for any Roman town. The pastime would have been entirely new to most of the British population and although it undoubtedly became widespread it does not seem to have been a major priority. Bathing was of course regarded by the army and other members of the Roman establishment as a vital and necessary activity so it is not surprising that fortresses and forts are the places in which we find some of the earliest and most elaborate bathing structures.

At Silchester the public baths were erected early in the town's history because they appear to be aligned on a street layout that had already been

34 *Horkstow (Lincs) villa. Mosaic depicting, amongst other subjects, a chariot race (see also* **colour plate 9***). Although the design was possibly influenced by North African styles and topics, the design might have reflected a familiarity with the sport in Britain. Chariots were a traditional part of late prehistoric British tribal warfare. Fourth century*

superseded by the end of the first century (**17** & **35**). Indeed its portico had to be demolished to make way for one of the streets of the new grid. That this represents an intermediate phase in the town's evolution is plain from the fact that the baths overlay the 'inner earthwork' that either fortified the pre-Roman *oppidum* or defended the earliest phase of the Roman town. But as we have already seen, there is a good case to be made for Silchester being developed early as a Roman town with imperial help, perhaps for the benefit of a client kingship. Elsewhere, the Romano-British were more equivocal in their approach. Exeter, almost certainly the fortress of *II Augusta*, was given over to the canton of the Dumnonii in the last quarter of the first century. The fortress seems to have contained only one major stone building. This was a substantial vaulted bath house with the full range of rooms: *frigidarium* (cold bath), *tepidarium* (warm bath), *caldarium* (hot bath) and *palaestra* (exercise hall). Built as early as the 50s it is the first monumental piece of Roman architecture yet known in Britain, but it was partly demolished after only about thirty years and converted into the civic basilica (**colour plate 13**).

On the face of it, this is difficult to explain. Why demolish a perfectly good, prestigious building that could have been adapted for use by the town residents? Perhaps a basilica was considered, at that stage, far more important. Similarly, public bathing might not yet have become (if it ever did) a pastime that appealed to indigenous peoples rather than immigrants, soldiers or veterans. In London around the same time the massive Huggin Hills baths were being built, and went through later periods of rebuilding and design. Bath, that most celebrated of all Roman Britain's bathing facilities, was particularly popular amongst soldiers. Developed from the late first century on, it may even have been built in the first instance by the army as a spa and leisure facility for troops. This is known to have happened on the continent. London also had a large military population, demonstrated by the military tombstones and the fort.

Conversely, at Wroxeter the first attempt at erecting town-centre public baths begun in the late first century was knocked down before completion, in order to make way for the new forum and basilica. Only subsequently were public baths provided in an adjacent *insula* during the second half of the second century, only a little after the baths at Leicester (**colour plate 18**). Verulamium's public baths have only recently been identified in an *insula* a couple of blocks south of the forum towards the south gate, and were probably started around the end of the first century. A possible earlier, but short-lived, baths might have been sited close to the east gate. But it was destroyed in a massive mid-second-century fire that ravaged Verulamium and it was left in ruins until the beginning of the third century. Evidently it was a facility the locals felt could take second place to other priorities. Certainly few of the houses here, and in other towns, had their own baths.

This all suggests very variable civilian enthusiasm for public baths that contrasts with Tacitus' description of the Romano-British being skilfully tempted into Roman ways with such amenities. In some towns they were

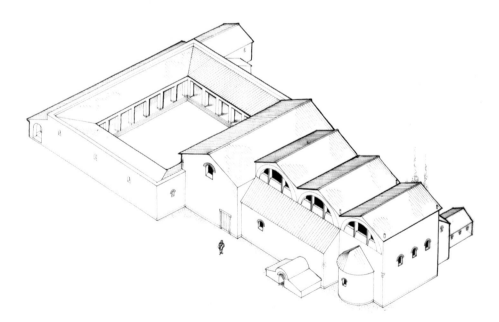

35 *Reconstructed isometric view of the baths at Silchester in their first-century phase. The open* palaestra *was a Mediterranean feature not often used in Roman Britain and resembles better preserved examples still visible in Pompeii. The three vaulted chambers acted as the cold* (frigidarium), *warm* (tepidarium), *and hot* (caldarium) *rooms respectively while the larger roofed hall* (apodyterium) *was used for changing and preparation*

provided early, in others they were not. The only conclusion can be that demand (and resources) varied from place to place. Even so, while most of the towns have been found to have had public baths eventually, very few seem to have had more than one main set and no inscriptions at all have been found which refer to them. Inscriptions referring to public buildings at all are very rare anyway but considering that almost every town had baths we might expect to have at least a semi-restorable example from somewhere.

This is even more curious when one considers that bath houses had to have vaulted roofs if they were to last, because of the effects of heat and damp. This made them relatively massive and it was therefore inappropriate to build them out of timber, hence the Exeter legionary baths being the only stone building in the fortress (**colour plate 13**), and similarly the Silchester baths at a time when the basilica and forum were still built of timber. At Bath, a timber roof supported on stone piers had to be replaced with a stone vault, work that required massive strengthening of the supports (**36**). In addition, unlike the Mediterranean version where the *palaestra* was an open space, Romano-British baths often had covered exercise halls modelled on basilicas. The result is that where bath houses survive their remains are usually quite substantial. At Leicester and Wroxeter sections of walls survive to a considerable height known as the 'Jewry Wall' and 'The Old Work' respectively (**116** & **colour plate 18**).

Despite their scale and essential role in Roman life the urban bath houses of Roman Britain have supplied little evidence either for internal decorations or for the kind of activities that went on inside. We know from better-preserved examples elsewhere that there would have been a complicated plumbing system using brass and copper boilers and taps, and lead piping, to carry water to the different chambers. In some, water would have been pumped into stone basins for washing, or into plunge baths. It is likely that the walls and vaults would have been decorated with stucco and painted wall-plaster. Furniture would have included benches and shelving for clothes and there would probably have been a number of statues and busts of deities (**colour plate 15**).

Water supply and drainage

In Britain water supply is not generally a problem but coordinating provision of fresh water into towns, and disposing of waste is. Managing water supplies as an administrative and architectural problem was a major issue at Rome and it had provided plenty of experience in hydraulic engineering. That meant bringing water in without any disruption, and servicing a constant flow to public baths, public fountains and the private houses of the wealthy, as well as dealing with people who illegally tapped into pipes for a free private supply. Sextus Julius Frontinus, governor of Britain in the mid-70s, later rose to be Commissioner of Aqueducts in Rome in 97 and wrote a treatise on the issues involved in

36 *Bath, the Great Bath vault.*
Above: *pier in the Great Bath. Note how the piers have been substantially strengthened with extra masonry. This was to support a masonry vault, which by the late second century had replaced an earlier timber roof.* Below: *roof section from the Great Bath at Bath. The massive potential weight of the new vaulted roof was reduced by cementing hollow box tiles together. In spite of this, the old piers still had to be massively reinforced, a mark of the engineering skills and scale of public architecture in Roman Britain*

sustaining urban water supplies. He might even have done some footwork when in Britain, since development of the facilities at Bath began around the time of his governorship. Many Romano-British towns had public baths, and as urban populations grew so provision had to be made but as we shall see many people in Britain probably continued to depend on private arrangements.

Roman public water supplies through aqueducts into towns were continuous. In other words, water was always flowing. This is called 'constant offtake', and it required special arrangements. Water reached the town at its highest point and poured into the *castellum divisiorum*, 'dividing reservoir'. Sediment sank to the bottom, and the water then carried on into the town through various pipes for different destinations. Sluices allowed the different supplies to be stopped or limited, or opened up for special jobs. Getting the water reliably to the town at all required a lot of pressure, and if the town was built on a slope (however slight), that pressure would only get worse as the water flowed down through the town. Since this might be far too much for pipes and taps in fountains and houses, the pressure had to be reduced. This was done by running the water into tanks on columns at street corners, as are found at Pompeii. The elevated tanks were not as high as the *castellum divisiorum* or the original source of the water, so they reduced the pressure but still provided a head. They did not overflow, because water was constantly running off into fountains and baths. Drainage involved piping or channelling water away from houses into sewers that then ran into a river.

There is very little evidence for such elaborate systems in Romano-British towns though at Wroxeter a system of wooden pipes brought water to a roadside wooden tank that served as a water fountain. At Carlisle, 'junction boxes' have been found. Large blocks of wood were drilled through to join lengths of wooden pipe inserted into the holes. The little town at Catterick, *Cataractonium* (N. Yorks), had an unusually elaborate stone fountain in the courtyard of the *mansio* and at Lincoln a large octagonal fountain (6m wide) was found close to the south gate of the upper town. At Pompeii street fountains were distributed so that most of the population had no further than 50m to walk to get water (**9**). A similar example is still visible at Corbridge (**115**).

Providing water in substantial quantities means coping with local topography. Britain is not particularly mountainous, but even the lowland zone can be fairly described as undulating. This presents problems with locating a water supply at a point higher than the town and bringing it in. The solution was an aqueduct but these were only rarely built in the form of a channel or duct suspended on a row of arches. Raised aqueducts tend only to appear in areas where water had to be brought from so far away that it was necessary to cross plains or deep valleys. Even so aqueducts seem to reflect not just circumstances but also the preparedness of any settlement or individual to finance one.

Most Romano-British aqueducts were conduits laid in the ground along natural contours. An exceptionally fine example is known as the Eifel aqueduct near Cologne in Germany. Here a trench was dug and a brick conduit constructed with access manholes for maintenance placed at intervals. The trench was then back-filled. In Britain, Dorchester was served by a leat fed from a reservoir seven miles away at Frampton. A dam created the reservoir, and water flowed to the town along a timber-lined channel running along a terrace, and was installed by the late first century. Later, the timber was replaced with ceramic piping laid on concrete but this scheme was apparently never completed. Wroxeter's arrangements were similar but made do with a clay-lined channel. These systems sound effective but it is obvious that round-the-clock maintenance to clear out blockages, dead animals and rubbish will have been essential.

Lincoln is an interesting example where local difficulties were met with different solutions. Most of the main part of the Roman town lay some 50m (165ft) above the surrounding landscape making the water available from the rivers Till and Witham at the bottom of the steep slope to the south as good as useless (**10**). The east range of the forum contained a well with a well-head which was such a serviceable public utility that it was still in use during the Middle Ages. There would have been many other wells but these were not enough. Water was also taken from somewhere to the north-east and carried into the town through an earthenware pipe supported on arches. This was not as simple as it sounds – one of the possible water sources is only about 1.8km (just over 1 mile) away but is actually 21m (70ft) below the height of the town. So water would have had to be tapped from much further away, up to 32km (20 miles). Whatever they were, the arrangements at Lincoln clearly worked because a *castellum divisiorum* was built beside the town's north wall to store the supply. Probably dating to the first half of the second century, it corresponds well with the evidence for provision of other civic amenities in the town. From here gravity would have supplied the needs of the baths built in an adjacent *insula* in the north-east corner of the town, though these are currently still only known from limited records of excavation in difficult circumstances nearly fifty years ago. Water-pipes running under the road at Cirencester's north-east gate might have carried supplies from a similar, but undiscovered, cistern fed by an aqueduct.

In theory providing running water as a civic amenity symbolized organized Roman town life, however limited in scope. Nothing like this had ever existed before. Erecting public buildings was one thing, but with the provision of a civic water supply and drainage system we can see the Roman town government at work in a practical day-to-day sense. At Verulamium at least one water-pipe across an *insula* was still functioning right on until the end of the period, and possibly beyond. In Exeter the pipes once used for the military bath house (now adapted into the basilica) were reused, perhaps to supply private houses or street fountains. But in practice there is very little evidence for water being made available for use or collection by individuals in Britain. Most ordinary people would have been accustomed to taking water from wells and rivers, or from a street fountain fed by a conduit like those found at

Verulamium, York, Catterick and Corbridge, the latter still being visible at the site today. Evidently at Dorchester the townsfolk had to resort to traditional methods when the reconstructed leat was left unfinished.

In London excavations in 2001 close to the fort in the north-western part of the city in Gresham Street revealed the substantial remains of two similar mechanisms designed to lift water from timber-lined wells around 4.5-5m deep. The systems both worked with a chain made of wooden buckets connected by iron links, similar to a modern bicycle chain (**37**). Power was provided by animals or men who turned a wheel that was connected by gears to the shaft around which the chain rotated. Although it has proved possible to manufacture a replica (now on display at the Museum of London) it is very far from clear how the water was transferred from the buckets into a conduit, without large amounts spilling back down over the mechanism, as they rose up and over the driveshaft. The device seems to be similar to one described by the Roman architect and engineer Vitruvius but he says that the buckets 'as they pass above the axle must tip over and deliver into the reservoir what they have brought up' (X.4), which does not explain exactly how.

The first of the two Gresham Street systems was in operation in the late 60s, and was abandoned when some of the well lining collapsed. The second well was installed by *c*.110 and lasted until the well-house was destroyed by fire before *c*.150. Damaged components were dumped in the well where excavators found them. Presumably, serviceable parts were removed for reuse elsewhere. In fact, components of a third example, from London's Cheapside

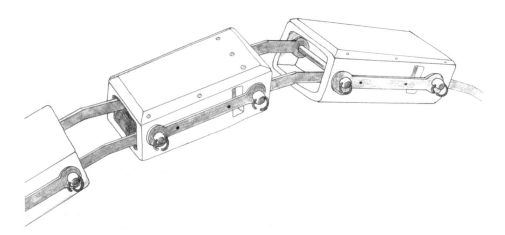

37 *Gresham Street, London. Drawing based on finds of wooden water buckets and iron linkages, found in the remains of a 5m-deep timber-lined well built from timber felled c.108-9. Twenty oak buckets were driven on a continuous loop chain made from the links, gathering water from the well. As the filled buckets rose up and over the drive shaft at the top, water was tipped out into a channel, though how this was achieved without losing an unacceptably large amount into the drive wheel is unclear. It may be that spouts, now lost, were fitted to the buckets. The most likely function was servicing the demands of a single establishment, perhaps a baths, either because aqueduct supplies were insufficient or not yet available*

baths, were subsequently identified in museum stores but since far less had survived they had not been understood before. The fact that the mechanisms were very similar shows that they were built according to a standard technique so it is unlikely anyone at the time would have regarded them as unusual.

However, it is obvious that the bucket-and-chain device involved a phenomenal amount of continual effort to produce (compared to an aqueduct) a very small amount of water. At Pompeii and Ostia, bucket-and-chain systems were used to raise the water for bath house roof-tanks to provide a local head of water. This suggests they were considered useful for special applications and may even have become redundant when aqueduct supplies were introduced. If that was what happened in London, it might help explain why the Gresham Street systems were not replaced.

Unfortunately, with so little evidence to hand it is very difficult for us to have any idea how much continuous aqueduct supplies were ever available in Roman Britain's towns, and how much ad hoc arrangements had to be made. At Silchester George Boon said 'the supply of running water was very limited' but it is unlikely he was ever in a position really to make this judgement. At London the Thames was not the solution a huge river might seem. In 1326 low rainfall revealed just how salty the tidal Thames could be and led to complaints. In any case moving water from the river up to the highest points of the town on a large scale in an age without motor-driven pumps was a very different matter from bringing up bucket-loads for individual needs. Private wells were the only easy solution for the most part until the seventeenth and eighteenth centuries, starting with the New River Company in 1613 when its first reservoir at Clerkenwell was made operational. Even so, it was not until the early twentieth century that London's water supply came under the control of a single authority.

Natural drainage would have taken care of much waste water and not all towns appear to have had some kind of proper sewer system, despite the fact that Britain's towns were laid out as new facilities and it would have been relatively easy to install underground stone drains before streets were metalled. But even Pompeii had limited drainage facilities, despite the opportunities afforded when the town's grid was extended, and largely made use of open drainage (**9**). It is clear from the crossing blocks for pedestrians that water ran away in the gutters. Silchester, for example, virtually did without drains at all and what it had consisted of open channels running beside the street – a feature common enough elsewhere in the Empire. While that sounds unpleasant, the 'constant offtake' system of aqueduct supply would (if it was provided) keep up a continual flow of fresh water through drains. Nevertheless, it is plain enough that the modern popular belief that Roman settlements were invariably characterized by hygienic, maintained and reliable sewerage systems, is exposed for partial fiction it is. However, there were exceptions. York's sewers are the best known. Like the Cologne aqueduct they were built as vaulted masonry conduits under the streets and were fed by subsidiary drains that ran down from adjacent buildings. The whole system was built with a slight gradient to ensure the waste flowed away. At Verulamium drains that kept the streets clear around the basilica were regularly maintained and do not seem to have fallen out of use until the fifth century. Ultimately of course sewage and waste was not treated. It flowed into rivers, or out into fields where it was supposed to soak away.

Inns and staging posts

The Roman government could not possibly have ruled its provinces through towns without an effective means of communication. Roads are all very well but it was also necessary to make provision for food and shelter for those travelling on official business. This system was called the *cursus publicus*, literally 'public passage'. Along all major routes inns (*mansiones*) were established providing baths, food, a bed for the night and probably fresh horses. In his *Life of Augustus* the historian Suetonius said that the Emperor instituted the system so that a piece of official post or a message could be carried by a single individual all the way in order that he could be quizzed by the recipient for further details. Most known examples are found within towns, rather than as isolated facilities, but unlike other public buildings they appear to have been as much a feature of small towns and villages as they were of major towns. Their function is plain enough from the word *mansio*, which means 'a stay' in the sense of remaining in one place for a while.

However, not a single example of a *mansio* in Britain has been recognized for certain. They have been identified purely on the grounds of their size compared to other houses in the towns, and take the form of a substantial courtyard house. There is, for instance, no inscription or graffiti that labels one of these buildings. The principal differences lie in the fact that the individual room sizes tend to be small compared to the size of the building. They usually have a bath-suite (sometimes a pair, perhaps to allow segregated bathing), and occasionally have granaries.

The examples believed to have existed at Silchester (**38**) and Caerwent lie in peripheral parts of the enclosed area. On one hand this might reflect their relatively unimportant role in *civitas* capitals. On the other, as is plain from Silchester's plan, the *mansio* lay close to an entrance through the city walls and one internal road off the grid ran right into it. Proximity to the town's periphery was probably just convenience, just as motels are located on town limits and ring roads today. Similarly a recently discovered possible candidate for a *mansio* in London of Flavian date lies in what was the straggling suburb of Southwark, on the south bank of the Thames (**16**).

The *mansio* is more easily picked out from plans of small towns, discussed in more detail in chapter 5. The settlements at Wall (**45**) and Catterick, for

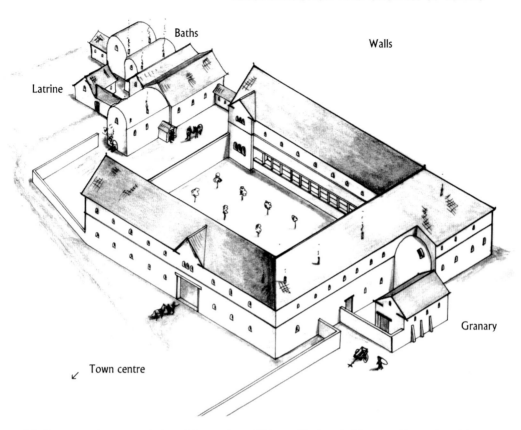

38 *Reconstructed axonometric view of the* mansio *at Silchester. The large building resembles a substantial private house but had the added features of a bath-suite (unusual for houses in towns) and a granary*

example, might have begun as forts but in the longer run the most prominent structure at both places was the *mansio*, as it was in numerous other small towns, and in many senses the official legacy of the army period. The *mansio* demanded support services, attracted traffic, and provided a focal point for a small town's economy. Evidence of a granary beside the Catterick *mansio* has been used to suggest that this was where locals were obliged to pay taxes 'in kind', with the goods being stored in the *mansio* granary for distribution to official users like the army. Even in a comparatively large 'small town' like Water Newton the only prominent structures are two central courtyard buildings, one of which may very well have been an inn (**75**).

At Godmanchester a small basilica-like structure in the centre was built around the early third century. It may have been used for local government but it was both dwarfed and preceded by a probable inn and baths constructed a hundred years earlier. This *mansio* lay right next door to a temple precinct, possibly dedicated to a local god called Abandinus. The concept of the religious pilgrimage was well-known in antiquity, just as it was in the Middle Ages. Travellers made use of shrines en route to thank the gods for safe passage, even if they had more mundane business to attend to. Pilgrims might target shrines on their way to visit a more important temple. Shrine and *mansio* could therefore be economically dependent on one another. Ancaster is another instance of a small town with a lot of evidence for religious activity, though no *mansio* has been found yet. But given that it lay on a major road it is inconceivable there was no provision for travellers (**45** & **79**).

At Wanborough near Cirencester a settlement grew up around a road junction during the late first and early second centuries. There is no evidence for the site having a pre-Roman origin and no structural evidence for a fort either. Even if there was a fort it has been suggested that the site owed its principal influence to the construction of an inn that has been identified from aerial photography. Excavation that has taken place in the town has shown that the roadside structures were small, simple and mostly made of timber. The substantial courtyard building is therefore quite conspicuously out of proportion to the rest of the settlement, though it has yet to be excavated. The problem with arguing that an inn could help stimulate a settlement's development is that it is clear from the letters of Pliny the Younger that the costs of providing them fell on to the local communities and that he regarded them as onerous impositions. So possibly the presence of an inn in some minor towns may actually have ensured that they stayed as just that.

Who paid for public buildings?

Who paid for Roman Britain's public buildings? Tacitus says that Agricola provided official assistance for the building of forums, temples and houses. The Verulamium basilica inscription implies that this was not empty praise (**110** & appendix 2), though the Neronian tiles from Silchester show he was not the first (**18**). In London tiles stamped P.P.BR.LON (*Procurator Provinciae Britanniae Londinii*, 'the Procurator of the Province of Britain at London') often turn up on the sites of public buildings suggesting that they were built with official funds (**colour plate 24**). Town authorities could also instigate and finance projects in the name of the canton (**69**). The money came from official grants donated by Rome, local taxation, interest on loans, renting out public property or charging admission to public facilities. At Wroxeter the civic authority of the Cornovii seems to have been responsible for the forum (**24** & appendix 2).

The picture in Roman Britain is very incomplete. The forums and basilicas for almost all the major towns in Britain have been located (twelve or more), and the theatres (five or more), amphitheatres (six or more) and baths at several have also been found. Just two have produced legible inscriptions. A third, from Brough, refers to an as-yet unlocated theatre (**28**). Elsewhere in the Empire inscriptions are often found which record the munificence of communities or individual citizens who had contributed money (sometimes the actual sum is specified) towards the building of a particular public amenity. The money could either be given during the benefactor's lifetime, or as part of his will. This is sometimes described as competitive munificence. Wealthy men repaid the community for their status as magistrates, or bought that status, by providing facilities and advertising the fact.

Since remains of the buildings exist either this means Romano-British towns and their prominent citizens did not produce inscriptions, or that they have not survived late- or post-Roman demolition and stone-robbing. In the south there was a shortage of stone suitable for dressing, and anything needed had to be shipped in to places like London and Silchester. A particularly fine marble Trajanic inscription from the legionary fortress at Caerleon had been shipped over from Italy, for example. Not only might this shortage have diminished the number of urban inscriptions made in stone rather than wood, but also any wooden ones would have rotted away, and surviving dressed stone would be very attractive to stone-robbers.

Moreover, any Romano-British public building inscription erected during the reign of Domitian (81-96) was liable to be destroyed after 96 because after his murder his memory was officially damned (see **110**). Since the late first century was one of the peak public-building periods in Britain, it is obvious that this could have affected quite a few. If they were never replaced in the name of one of his successors, we would have little or nothing to find. Relatively unscathed towns like Caerwent, Silchester, Wroxeter and Verulamium have been extensively examined with limited results. It is a curiosity of Roman Britain's inscriptions that temples and shrines are much the most frequently mentioned amongst buildings, usually of late-second or early-third-century dates, that at all times and most places soldiers are disproportionately responsible for general inscriptions like altars and tombstones, and that civic magistrates are relatively absent from the record.

So, London for instance, despite all its public buildings, has produced two inscriptions only referring to temples of Isis (**86**), and of course Chichester's one and only building inscription records a temple to Neptune and Minerva (**108**). Similarly, two inscriptions from York refer to temples and a third to an arch and shrine (**44 & 87**), but nothing referring to secular buildings. Cirencester has just the text from the base of a Jupiter column (**100**). There are still unexpected surprises though. Little is known about Winchester's Roman buildings, but a fragment of a colossal imperial inscription with foot-high letters must have come from a town-centre public building or a temple (**39**). Fragments of another, very nearly as large, were found in Silchester's basilica in the 19th century but are totally beyond restoration of any sort. Otherwise, Silchester has several semi-restorable slabs from a temple referring to donations by a local guild. Caerwent's well-preserved basilica has produced nothing at all. The existence of the two massive Winchester and Silchester inscriptions obviously begs the question of whether there were once many more on display.

IMP·CAES·T·AEL·HADRIANO·ANTONINO·AVG·PIO·P·P

39 Winchester. Monumental imperial inscription from Middle Brook Street. Despite being brief, the lettering is easily restorable as [A]NTO[NINO]. Although this name was used by several emperors, the style makes Antoninus Pius (138-61) or Marcus Aurelius (161-80) the most likely candidates. The restoration at the bottom shows the titles for Antoninus Pius. At 29.2cm (11.5in) these are the biggest letters from any inscription found in Roman Britain. Together with the fact that it was found in the town centre the original text must once have adorned the basilica-forum or a major temple

Just Wroxeter and Brough alone have produced two tolerably complete inscriptions referring to secular buildings, except of course that Brough's theatre was very probably linked to a temple, while Verulamium's is so badly broken and incomplete we only know the date and location. A crucial point of course is that all these buildings were demolished at some point. Any inscriptions displayed on them had to be pulled down, if they hadn't already fallen off. Tombstones and altars were generally inserted in the ground to begin with. So, it is fairly obvious that public building inscriptions were unlikely to escape being severely damaged to the point of destruction. Both Wroxeter's and Verulamium's were found shattered.

When we know who was responsible for a public building, they turn out mainly to be the *civitas* government, the governor, or a *collegium* (**108**). What we scarcely have at all is individual civic worthies doing what normally came relatively naturally to them in most other provinces: financing public works and bragging about it. This makes the Brough theatre inscription all the more incongruous, since here we have an exceptional instance of a civic magistrate recording his personal donation of a theatre stage. Brough was an obscure minor town. Surely it must be a freak survival of inscriptions that were once far more widespread, or is it just a freak? We do not know where Marcus Ulpius Januarius, the *aedile* who provided Brough's new theatre stage in the 140s, came from but his name means he or (more probably) his father or was awarded his citizenship under Marcus Ulpius Trajanus (98-117), perhaps in January one year (**28**). Such an adoptive name is frustrating for us because it totally obscures his, or his father's, original family name, which might have told us what his ethnic origin was.

What Januarius did, and how he recorded it, would have been a common-place in most other provinces, but for Britain it is so unusual that it makes the absence of almost anything comparable all the more conspicuous. The most likely explanation is that he was from the family of an auxiliary soldier who completed his twenty-five years' service, or perhaps was the freedman of a citizen soldier or administrator. The decorative devices on the slab closely resemble those produced by the army on the Antonine Wall at the same time. Brough was of course in northern Britain and was close to the fortress at York, and the ferry crossing for the road south to the veteran colony at Lincoln. Moreover, soldiers as a group are responsible for more inscriptions recording buildings than any other in Britain.

The only 'town' where we have several examples of urban men of status is York, and even then some of the evidence connected with the veteran colony there actually comes from abroad. The Marcus Aurelius Lunaris altar (**1**) of 237 was found in Bordeaux, and also serves as the most important instance of a man of this status from Lincoln. Like Januarius, his full name suggests an award of citizenship to a military predecessor or to a freedman – as a *sevir Augustalis* he was most likely to have been a freedman. He was a trader but his Bordeaux connection means he might actually have come from Gaul. Lucius Viducius Placidus was a trader who came from Rouen (**44** & appendix 2). We only know his full details because he left another dedication in Holland.

So, in fact it starts to look rather as if indigenous British urban officials rarely adopted the inscription habit if they ever really did at all. When it comes to inscriptions by individuals most of what we have comes from the military zone, colonies, abroad or from individuals likely to have had military origins. Something like three-quarters of all the inscriptions surviving from Roman Britain come from the military zone, and a fair number of those from the 'civilian south' are by soldiers too. Even at Winchester the only building implicit on an inscription is a temple or shrine to the Mother Goddesses dedicated by a soldier on the governor's personal staff, who had restored it. Foreigners make up a large proportion of the rest (**55**), as we will also see from tombstones in chapter 6.

On balance it's likely that in Roman Britain inscriptions recording individuals, their works or achievements, in southern towns were very rare as a matter of culture, though destruction and rebuilding since then has probably made things worse. The explanation need not only be inclination. Given that not a single Briton is ever recorded as rising to the status of a senator in Rome, something that many Gauls managed, the possibility is that Romano-British *per capita* wealth meant that very few members of the decurial class had the individual means to finance such projects between *c*.70-200 when public building was at its peak. We cannot know who paid for Romano-British public buildings with so little to go on. The only conclusion can be that since imperial grants, *civitas* initiatives, *collegia* initiatives, and occasionally individual gifts, are all testified, each remains a possibility in places where we have no clues. As so often with Roman archaeology in Britain we are confronted with possibilities rather than facts.

It is, incidentally, worth bearing in mind how haphazard and incompetent management of public building works could be, even in richer parts of the Empire where major architectural works had a much longer established tradition. Pliny the Younger's letters to Trajan in the early second century are particularly interesting because, as governor of Bithynia and Pontus, Pliny was plagued by the problems that resulted from civic building projects. The town of Prusa needed new baths that were to be financed by diverting funds and also calling in debts to the town government. Trajan approved this but only on condition that no new taxes were imposed and that no more money was re-allocated. This sort of rational arrangement was not always employed: at Nicomedia enormous sums were spent on two separate aqueduct projects, both of which were abandoned before ever being used. At Nicaea poor planning left a theatre subsiding and created a disorganized and potentially dangerous gymnasium, while at Claudiopolis baths were being built on an unsuitable site. In Mauretania in North Africa in the mid-second century, the city of Saldae got itself into a mess with an aqueduct being bored through a mountain. Starting from opposite sides, the tunnels missed due to faulty surveying. The city had to called in a retired legionary called Nonius Datus to sort the mess out. He recorded the work on an inscription. These tales paint a picture of disorganization, petty rivalries and hasty decisions and no doubt these were problems in Roman Britain too.

Who built the public buildings in Britain?

Inscriptions tell us nothing about who actually designed and executed the work. There is no evidence for an architect in Roman Britain, so we have no way of knowing to what extent urban public building projects were designed and managed by civilian professionals or detached military architects. In fact, there is very limited evidence for architects in the Roman world at all, most of whom were of relatively lowly status. Two examples are: from Lambaesis in North Africa the tombstone of Marcus Cornelius Festus, an ordinary soldier and *architectus*, of *III Augusta*; and from the theatre at Pompeii, a slab that states 'Architect: Marcus Artorius Primus, freedman of Marcus'. We only know the latter built the theatre because the stone was found there.

The basic form of the Romano-British basilica and forum resembles closely the military headquarters building, but there was nothing exclusively military about the basilican form, or the piazza with a colonnade. All we can say is that it is likely military architects and surveyors played a role, but it is possible that civilians (mainly slaves and freedmen) on the governor's or the emperor's staff, were also used. Equally, many 'civilian' architects will have learned their trade during a term of military service. As far as labouring is concerned, there is no avoiding the fact that key skills and trades were disproportionately represented amongst soldiers and veterans. They also had, when they were not fighting or building their own forts, the time. Thus a writing tablet from the fort at Vindolanda at the end of the first century records that thirty men were working on building a residence block under the direction of a *medicus* (doctor), while others were busy quarrying the stone.

To begin with there was, by definition, no such pool of skilled and experienced civilian labour in Britain. This would have changed radically over succeeding generations as soldiers retired into the broader community and handed down their skills, as immigrant craftsmen moved in, and as the Britons became integrated into the economic demands of Roman Britain. Wroxeter's basilica-forum was dedicated in 129-30, a period when extensive legionary building work was being undertaken on the northern frontier to build Hadrian's Wall, and thus hardly likely to make military labour available for civilian projects. A plausible scenario is that it was designed and laid out by imperial staff accompanying Hadrian when he visited Britain in *c.*119, but that the work was executed by civilian contractors engaged by the *civitas* government. Amongst them might have been a man like Sulinus the sculptor recorded on religious dedications he made at Bath and Cirencester (**93**).

Housing

Marcus Ulpius Januarius, the *aedile* in Antonine Brough, is a rare British example of a man who had status in his local community and had enough money, inherited or earned, to sustain that status by contributing something to his town (**28**). He was a member of the upper tier of Romano-British urban society that the Roman government depended on for maintaining order in the province. Ulpius Januarius was representative of individuals who manned the town councils and we can be sure that they exercised lucrative controls over local land and trade.

If the emergence of public buildings can in part be attributed to men such as these, then the appearance of more solidly built and better-appointed houses in the second century can be attributed to a natural desire to enjoy their wealth privately as well. Towns in Roman Britain were more than administrative or economic centres and as examples of romanization they would have had no purpose if none of the Romano-British had become accustomed to living in, and identifying themselves with, them. Once more we have to turn to Tacitus for the only instance where official policy is mentioned. Agricola, he says, encouraged the Romano-British to build houses and the word he uses, *domos*, refers particularly to town houses and in the sense of them being homes.

Excavations in towns have shown how buildings, apart from public works, seem to have been commercially orientated in the first century. Usually built out of timber and wattle-and-daub, with a street frontage, they often contain some sort of evidence for a trade or light industry like metalworking (**14**). As we saw earlier, Silchester's *Insula* IX had rectangular timber buildings by the mid-first century. Within a generation the walls of these structures had been rebuilt with flint and mortar, which is exceptionally early for this kind of 'improvement'. Only in the second century did significant numbers of stone buildings begin to appear in Romano-British towns but it would be quite wrong to assume that timber construction had been abandoned. The Silchester buildings of *Insula* IX went through another timber phase, but this was unusual. Townhouse ground plans were more developed and although solid floors and plastered walls were a common feature of earlier houses the new ones were much more likely to contain a mosaic floor or two and plastered walls painted with a colourful decorative scheme. This preceded similar developments in the countryside by up to a century. Whether these houses directly represented family wealth accrued from earlier commercial activities we cannot say because the evidence does not exist for us to draw this kind of connection.

In their most elaborate forms town houses might have several mosaic floors, out-buildings and an integral bath-suite though the latter was much rarer than in the affluent country villas (they were fire risks and usually public facilities were available). Much has been made of their ground-plans but these are for the most part no more than simple variations on rows of rooms and arguing for patterns of influence and development based on such elementary forms seems very suspect. Equally the idea that one can analyse social structures on the basis of room size and numbers seems hopelessly optimistic as we rarely have the slightest idea of what a single room was used for. Likewise, we have almost no knowledge at all of the nature or names of any house-owners in Roman Britain at any time. We need only consider the various different residents in a row of modern identical semi-detached houses to realize that we cannot make assumptions about who lived where.

No town houses seem to have reached the extravagant heights of the great villas like Chedworth or Bignor. But then few town houses in the last three centuries equal the extent and luxury found in the greatest English country houses. The wealthy have always tended to leave towns and invest their capital in rural seats. A removal to the countryside may have happened in Roman Britain too. The perceived reduction in the urban population may have been paralleled by a decline in investment in public buildings (see also chapter 5), perhaps further evidence of a withdrawal of the curial class from towns. There are problems with this theory (see chapter 4) and the picture is a very difficult one to analyse. Excavations in towns tend to be piecemeal, compromised by limited opportunities and the effects of later occupation like eighteenth-century rubbish pits and Victorian foundations. The few towns that have been extensively excavated, such as Silchester (**40**) and Caerwent (**41**), were dug at a time when techniques were unlikely to help locate structures made of wood. The recent work at Silchester and Wroxeter has shown how *insulae* featuring widely-spaced town houses might be a totally misleading picture.

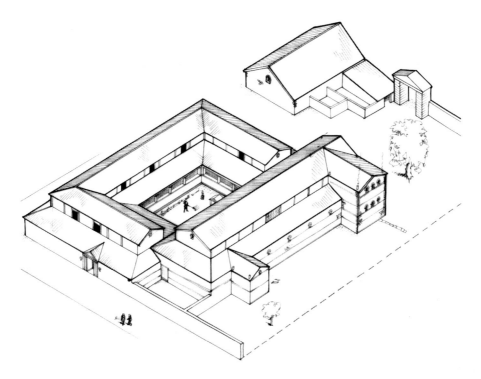

40 *Reconstructed isometric view of a substantial courtyard town house at Silchester (Insula XIV.1). Note the out-building, perhaps for livestock, and the gateway. The house may therefore have been involved with farming land outside the town limits*

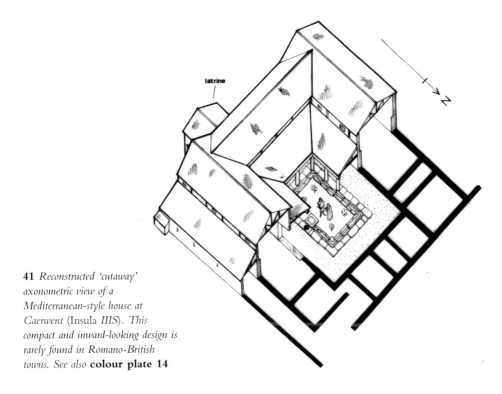

latrine

41 *Reconstructed 'cutaway' axonometric view of a Mediterranean-style house at Caerwent (Insula IIIS). This compact and inward-looking design is rarely found in Romano-British towns. See also* **colour plate 14**

House-types

Not surprisingly town houses resemble rural villas as structures. We do not have to assume that one derives from the other, or that both were derived from somewhere else. The idea of using rectangular or square rooms arranged in sequences was a relatively new one, but not unknown in pre-Roman Britain. Beyond that it is difficult to see what the alternative was to building in what were usually no more than two parallel rows. Anything wider would have required complicated roofing and made internal lighting a problem. Equally it is hardly surprising that larger houses made use of rows at right angles to one another. This minimized the distance a resident would have to walk to get from one room to another. The only alternative to a 'courtyard house' (**40**) was building an extremely long row of rooms that would have been enormously inconvenient. This elementary observation makes the time-honoured series of classifications of house types a tool of dubious merit, apart from being conveniently descriptive.

In general, town houses consist of nothing more sophisticated than one, two, three or four rows of rooms arranged approximately at right angles to one another. The observed series, though this need not necessarily be chronological, begins with the 'strip-house'. This type of building seems to have been typical of most towns that were thriving during the first two centuries. Verulamium and London have the best examples but other towns like Cirencester had similar buildings at about the same time. They were usually small rectangular structures built of clay and wood (a perfectly effective and quick way of producing a place to live), divided into several rooms and erected at right angles to a street. This maximized the number of establishments that had a street frontage and makes it likely that there was some sort of commercial activity going on.

Obviously we know nothing about land ownership, since no documents have survived in any one case, but we might speculate that an entrepreneur could buy a plot of land and put up several of these buildings to increase his rent yield. This has been plausibly suggested as being the case at Verulamium's *Insula* XIV where a row of separate businesses seem to have been housed in a single, purpose-built, structure (**14**). Despite the simplicity of the design the method was fairly durable apart from the need to replace ground timbers every fifteen to twenty years or so and there is evidence from many sites, for example at Gutter Lane in London, that the owners were prepared to invest in painted wall-plaster and plain tessellated flooring or even mosaics.

The main problem was the risk of fire but it seems that at London and Verulamium it took serious conflagrations before more substantial house building in stone (or at least in part) took place. Both towns experienced fires that appear to have damaged extensive areas, in *c*.125 and *c*.155 respectively. The inflammable nature of the houses and the congested layout with narrow alleys must have made it easy for fire to spread swiftly (just as it did amongst the medieval houses in the London fire of 1666). Thereafter London and Verulamium appear to have joined a trend for better built and more widely-spaced housing which had already begun elsewhere, for example in Cirencester and Canterbury, unless timber structures in between have escaped notice.

The largest town houses were little more than elaborations of the strip-house that was easily expanded into a simple 'corridor house'. Here, slightly more rooms were accessed by a corridor that allowed both privacy and more insulation from the elements. The corridor types are all fairly simple and apart from a row of perhaps six to ten rooms, usually vary only to the extent of having one or two flanking corridors, occasionally with an extra room, perhaps an outhouse, tacked on. If a larger house was needed then it made sense to build on wings. Very few examples of winged corridor houses have matching symmetrical wings. Instead they were built according to requirements and convenience. They would have limited wing length and if additional rooms were needed then a fourth wing was also added to create an enclosed courtyard.

The principal exception to this rule is the Mediterranean type of house, found in very limited numbers in Britain apart from the legionary fortresses where they were used to house senior officers. The best-known urban examples have been found in Gloucester and Caerwent (**41** & **colour plate 14**) where the proximity of the fortress at Caerleon, the colony status of Gloucester and an earlier date for the buildings concerned makes such a house style less surprising. The Mediterranean type of house is distinguished by being much more inward-looking. Almost invariably they consist of four compact wings packed tightly around a very small internal courtyard. Surviving examples in Italy show that the roofs were pitched inwards so that water drained off into gullies around the courtyard. They were much more suited to a hot sunny climate so they were probably considered unsuitable for Britain and never became a popular alternative.

Many Romano-British houses were built with at least stone footings from the second century onwards. It is normally impossible to be sure whether the whole wall was made of stone or not unless a collapsed wall is found where it fell, for example at the Meonstoke villa. The thickness of the stone footings proves nothing either way; we cannot assume that all foundations were built exactly according to the precise structural requirements of the building and that the buildings were maintained properly either by their owners or landlords. There is plenty of evidence to show that this was far from the case. The poet Juvenal cursed the way lives were placed at risk by appallingly botched repairs in Rome and the dangers to passers-by from falling tiles. All we can say is that houses would have been built either entirely in stone, entirely of wood, or a combination of both. All would have been completely serviceable on a day-to-day basis if constructed properly. The choice of building materials and whether to maintain them must have reflected costs and tastes, and greed, which must have been as prevalent then as it has ever been.

The relatively poor dating evidence from extensively excavated towns makes it difficult to be sure which houses existed at the same times as others. From the town plans it is possible to see that the *insulae* generally have from one to five significantly-sized masonry houses so that the spacing between houses had apparently become much greater by the third to fourth centuries than in the 'boom' of the late first century, with interesting relevance to the discussion of population figures. There is a great contrast with most continental towns of the period that tend to be much more congested than the 'garden cities' of Roman Britain. Only Colchester remained relatively tightly-packed though some of the small structures within the same *insula* may be outhouses belonging to a larger house or an independent residence.

One thing that is generally beyond us to work out is how many people might have occupied a single building. The buildings tightly hugging the eastern sides of *Insula* XXVIII at Verulamium (**42**) would, for example, have been able to offer prime sites near the forum, perhaps leading to expensive small apartments. A single house might be the home of a wealthy family that owned other properties within and without the town. But quite apart from the possibility of undetected timber buildings, one house need not mean one family. As we know from places like Pompeii (see chapter 1), a large building owned by one man could easily consist of several upstairs apartments let to tenants, while traders rented the ground-floor premises below. In addition of course, the arrangements could change in the course of time. In the so-called *Insula* of the Menander (*Regio* I, *insula* 10), by the year 79 a number of traders were running businesses from shops that had once been internal rooms of the houses. The individuals probably lived in rooms above their shops. Perhaps a modern equivalent is the way in which large Victorian and Edwardian town houses have so frequently been divided up internally into flats to reflect a very different housing market in twenty-first-century Britain. As we will see in chapter 4 Roman Britain presents evidence for a very varied picture as towns moved into the third and fourth centuries.

Restrictions on space naturally make upper storeys desirable in towns, but since no Roman town house survives even remotely complete in Britain it is impossible to say what the situation was. The number of houses which had upper storeys has probably been underestimated, though for the structural reasons outlined above it is not usually possible to demonstrate exactly which ones did. The more solidly-built stone town houses are more likely to have had an upstairs, which would thereby have increased the amount of urban accommodation available than is apparent from the ground-plan. This is certainly often found in houses at Pompeii, and more particularly at Herculaneum where the town was buried beneath scalding mud and lava. The conditions at the latter carbonised and preserved wooden structural components showing that many buildings had stone lower storeys but timber-framed upper storeys, which were sometimes self-contained (**7**).

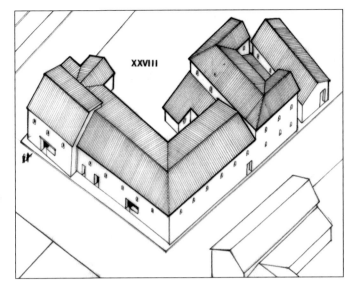

42 *Late second-, early third-century town house at Verulamium in* Insula *XXVIII (axonometric reconstruction). Although a single structure the house appears to have had several components including various establishments on the street front including a latrine and a small eating house. These may have been individually owned or rented*

Decorations

Above all other things the internal decorations of Roman houses, mainly wall-paintings and mosaics (which are normally all that survive), are regarded as amongst the most distinctive features of the whole period. The evidence for them in Britain parallels chronologically the structural evidence for houses. But even in the most well-appointed houses mosaic floors were rarely installed in more than a small number of rooms and wall-paintings usually survive in much too fragmentary a form for us to have a detailed knowledge of them (**colour plates 10 & 11**). There was more to house embellishment than just mosaics and painted walls. It is worth noting that while window glass only occasionally turns up on first-century sites in London, the quantities found from the second and third centuries is much greater and says a lot about the improvement in domestic standard-of-living as Romanization proceeded apace.

Amongst the earliest mosaic floors known in Roman Britain were those of Flavian date found at Fishbourne 'palace'. Some houses in London, destroyed in the fire of *c*.125, had mosaic floors even though they had timber walls. These may have been laid in the late first century and demonstrate an unsurprising trend in what must have been the most cosmopolitan town in the island. However, it is only at Verulamium that there is fairly general evidence for the laying of mosaics during the second century associated with the new houses put up after the fire of *c*.155. Like examples of similar date from Colchester, Silchester, Cirencester, Leicester and Aldborough, they tend to be geometric with very little figure content (**43**). The mosaics were generally colourful and accomplished but reflect quite conservative and unadventurous tastes.

If many of the better-off households were finding they could afford mosaics at this time we can assume that they would also have been commissioning wall

43 *Aldborough (N. Yorks). Late second-century geometric mosaic from a town house in the northernmost* civitas *capital of Roman Britain,* Isurium Brigantium. *Urban mosaics are generally earlier than rural mosaics, and most are purely geometric*

paintings. Panels have been found in many Romano-British town houses, especially at Verulamium and Leicester (**colour plate 10**). The painters largely confined themselves to very conventional formats based on the standardized tradition of a dado a little under a metre in height (3ft), a main area around 2.5m in height (7-9ft) and a narrow upper band. The main zone was usually divided into vertical panels that featured the main themes employed in any one room. These could be quite simple, for example imitation panels of polished exotic stonework, divided by imitation columns; or they could be more sophisticated attempts to exploit the medium's potential for depicting fantastic architecture and figures as in examples from Leicester. Ceiling paintings were more usually straightforward patterns based on hexagons, diamonds, circles and squares containing various motifs (**colour plate 11**).

The mosaics and wall paintings tell us more about Romano-British society than they do about themselves. Arguments about schools of mosaicists and artists are rather academic because we have no satisfactory evidence that reliably distinguishes the work of one craftsman from another, though there is no doubt that some styles or motifs are peculiar to regions around a specific town (**colour plate 12**). But what is clear is that by the second century polite Romano-British society was now prepared to spend significant sums of money on completely non-essential items. A decorative mosaic is no more functional than a simple tessellated floor and painted wall-plaster no more so than plain. The improvements in house structures which had taken place were much more functional in terms of simple comforts. What this means is that a portion of urban society had surplus wealth by the second century, a wealth that supported luxury industries. Wall-paintings and mosaics were ways of displaying and enjoying that wealth and were an alternative to spending large amounts of money on public works.

4

INSECURITY
AND URBAN DECLINE?

The third century in Roman Britain was a time when fewer public buildings appear to have been put up, apart from urban defences, and when cramped commercial quarters in towns had partly given way to more widely-spaced large houses. These apparent facts and the known history of disorder in Rome and wars on the continental frontiers have all contributed to a belief that this was a time of economic decline, or at best stagnation, and insecurity in Roman Britain, affecting public and private projects especially in the towns. However, interpreting archaeological evidence from this period has always been complicated by a marked reduction in the supply of bronze coinage between *c*.180-260 and the difficulty of dating pottery from the third and fourth centuries to within twenty or thirty years. Both these limitations in the evidence are now recognized as such, rather than necessarily meaning that there was an absolute decline in the amount of activity. Even so, while changes in the character of Romano-British towns were undoubtedly taking place it is less easy to generalize about what was going on. Instead local factors seem to have played an increasingly important part in the development of individual towns and ironically this is a period from which we have some of our most specific evidence for thriving commercial urban communities (**1** & **44**).

Britain ceased to be a single province and instead was divided into two. These were called *Britannia Superior* (the south) and *Britannia Inferior* (the north). This occurred around the beginning of the third century and was almost certainly a consequence of the civil war of 193-7 during which the governor of Britain, Clodius Albinus, the governor of Syria, Pescennius Niger, and the governor of Upper Pannonia, Septimius Severus, fought it out to become emperor. Clodius Albinus and Niger were the losers and the episode showed how powerful the governor of Britain could be, given the disproportionately large garrison of three legions and various auxiliary forces. Septimius Severus (193-211), the victor of that civil war, had good reason to divide up Britain.

Whatever the reason, the two *Britanniae* now each had a governor and a capital. London presumably remained capital of *Superior* while *Inferior* was ruled from the legionary fortress of York, where the attendant civilian settlement was

NEPTVNO·Ŧ·GƎNO¹LOCͭ
Ŧ·NM·AⱯGG·LVⅮVCᵢVS
L·F·PLACIDVS·DOMO
CIVIT·VELIOCⱯSSIᵛM
SEVIR·NEGOTIⱯTOR
CRET·ARCW·Ŧ·IANVM
D·D·L·D·D·D·GRATO·Ŧ·
SƎLEVCO·COS

44 *Lucius Viducius Placidus, a trader from Rouen, at York. Computer-generated reconstruction of his dedication of an arch, probably to a religious precinct, in the year 221. This is important, and rare, evidence for a civilian individual's gift to an urban community but in this case, as so often, there is a foreign connection (see also* **55** *for example). See appendix 2 for a translation and explanation of the text*

elevated to colony status around this time. A further division took place a century later (by 312) reflecting a contemporary policy of reducing the size of provincial administrative units across the Empire. *Superior* was divided into *Britannia Prima* and *Maxima Caesariensis* whilst *Inferior* was divided into *Britannia Secunda* and *Flavia Caesariensis*. The boundaries are unknown but it is generally accepted that *Maxima* and *Prima* were ruled from London and Cirencester respectively, and *Secunda* and *Flavia* were ruled from York and Lincoln respectively. These reorganizations will almost certainly have had implications for the status of the *civitas* capitals and lesser towns, but we do not know precisely what.

Literary sources more or less ignore Britain for the period 212-86 leaving us with little idea of what happened in Britain. This is in contrast to the first and second centuries where historical records and imperial inscriptions have made it possible to link sites and features with key events. The building of Hadrian's Wall, which we know began in or around 122, is one of the most significant. Samian ware, found along the Wall, can be classified according to styles and potters. The products of those who were working then can help date levels in towns when their wares are found elsewhere (see chapter 5). By the third century the situation was totally different. After the end of the Severan campaign into Scotland in 212, there were no other great events that involved major building work that are also testified by historians of the time. The great samian industries of Gaul were in terminal decline, and British industries that stepped into the market did not produce pottery in a way that allows us to distinguish different workshops. A reduction in coin supply to Britain during the early third century meant relying for longer on worn coins that were a century or more old.

Britain was probably experiencing a protracted period of internal stability – the northern frontier seems to have been peaceful from 212 until some time close to the end of the century. This explains the lack of literary references, which traditionally usually only referred to Britain when wars or unrest had occurred. There are several inscriptions from the third century, including one as late as 297-305, that tell us some forts and their buildings on the northern frontier had been allowed to decay into ruin, rather than having been destroyed. However, during the third century towns started being equipped with more elaborate defences, while a series of fortifications were erected at coastal sites. These include the forts subsequently described as the Saxon Shore command in the fourth-century compilation of army units called the *Notitia Dignitatum*.

Britain formed part of the breakaway Gallic Empire from 259 to 273 (**68**) and acted as an independent province during the revolt of Carausius and Allectus from 286 to 296 (**67**). Carausius was the successful commander of the Roman fleet stationed in Britain and the north coast of Gaul. He had been ordered to patrol the sea in search of pirates from northern Europe. He decided to capitalize on his popularity by setting himself up as another emperor, until his associate Allectus murdered him in 293 and seized power himself. Both episodes indicate the province's maturity and self-sufficiency, but they were also a product of an age when the legitimate empire's prestige had been dented by military defeat, civil war and barbarian incursions. Ordinary people had little reason to trust the Empire, and so more easily turned to regional military commanders who were popular and successful generals. The success of Carausius' enterprise gives no hint of domestic dissent at his seizure of power and he had fought off at least one earlier attempt to dislodge him. A panegyric to Constantius Chlorus, who recovered Britain in 296, praised Britain's resources and wealth. Obviously the war of repossession had to be presented as having been worthwhile but there is likely to have been some truth or else Britain would indeed have been abandoned. Sidelined from the worst effects of imperial civil war and barbarian invasions, in some respects Britain was more settled and productive than she had ever been.

Public buildings and temples

By the early third century the major towns of Roman Britain seem to have been equipped with the necessary public buildings to act as centres of local government, recreation and religious ceremony. Urban public building inscriptions, rare at any time, are almost entirely unknown from this period and this has sometimes been taken as a mark of decline in the sense that no one was prepared, or able, to fund civic projects. The truth is much more complicated. In some places, and London is the prime example, there is evidence for major building activity in the third century.

A number of milestones are known from the third century, for example one from Kenchester, a minor town in the canton of the Dobunni ruled from Cirencester. The milestone is dated to *c.*283-4 in the name of the canton and shows that the authorities had the funds to maintain roads in a remote part of their sprawling canton. Even in the north at Brougham, in the canton of the Carvetii, a milestone shows that in c.259-68 under the Gallic Empire this local authority was maintaining roads. Ten milestones alone belong to the reign of Gordian III (238-44) and another nine to that of Trajan Decius (249-51). However, the penal system provided for prisoners to be obliged to repair roads as part of their punishment, so this may not have been a particularly expensive activity.

Now, of course roads are essentials and one might argue that these would be kept up come what may. But would it really have been necessary to embark on large numbers of extravagant urban public building projects at this time? The existing buildings would have served well enough unless they had been damaged by fire or structural collapse, or unless circumstances at any one town had changed. The public buildings may have required maintenance and alterations, but as this would have affected the now almost universally absent superstructures it is hardly surprising that we have little evidence for this kind of work. Had it not been for the Second World War, and opportunistic post-war developers, southern and central England's towns and cities would today be making do with many more Victorian public buildings than they already are. This brings us back to the problem of the lack of inscriptions. The first half of the third century in Britain is a key part of the problem. In the north many inscriptions have been found from this period that refer to restoration or repair work at forts. For example, at Lanchester the fort baths and exercise hall were restored between 238 and 244. The building itself has never been found but the inscription is complete and explicit. There are many other examples across the military zone with the building, or repair of, baths and temples being particularly frequent. The inscriptional evidence from towns for the same period is almost non-existent and there is nothing like this for any of Britain's basilicas, forums or theatres.

So if repair work was being undertaken at, say, Silchester's basilica we might be lucky to find out because we have no superstructure and no inscription. The impression that could give to an archaeologist is one of stagnation, but it could be totally misleading. At Leicester the new market hall (?) seems to belong to the early third century, but we would never have guessed the existing facilities were inadequate just from their evidence alone. At Caerwent, the basilica was totally refurbished in the late third century to the extent that the hall was taken to pieces, repaired, and re-erected. Evidence has been found for this in the form of post-holes for scaffolding, and strengthening of components. But this has only been found in extensive modern excavation work, and the structure is the best-preserved in Britain.

It is even possible that some of Roman Britain's public buildings were still being finished off. The very limited evidence that we do have, like the Wroxeter and Verulamium inscriptions, tells us nothing about what stage the work had progressed to. We only need to consider the medieval cathedrals to realize that the public buildings of Roman Britain could have been under intermittent construction for a very long time, like London's basilica (see chapter 3). There is some evidence for public projects going on very late in the second century and into the third century. The forum fires at Verulamium and Wroxeter, in about 155 and 165 respectively, were followed by repairs and reconstruction. The date ranges involved are not very precise but it does seem that there was no sign of gradual decline and work may have been in progress over many years. A further fire at Wroxeter in the late third century destroyed the forum but this time it was not followed by reconstruction (the public baths appear to have become derelict at this time too). Canterbury was able to afford to rebuild its earth and timber theatre in about 220. It was replaced with a monumental free-standing theatre of classical design associated with a temple precinct.

Recent excavations in London and York have yielded traces of monumental buildings belonging to the third century. They are mostly of a 'religious' nature, such as an arch in London thought to be an entrance to a temple precinct, a temple in York, and another arch (**44**). Verulamium built two monumental arches on Watling Street to mark its earlier boundaries (**8 & 30**). A governor in mid-third-century London was able to finance the rebuilding of a temple to Isis that had collapsed. The legate of the *VI Victrix* legion built the York Serapis temple, a project perhaps associated with the presence there in the early third century of the Emperor Septimius Severus and his family, between 208 and 211, during his campaigns in Scotland (**87**). Other work is more explicitly private in nature.

Severus has also been tentatively linked with the London arch which may have acted as the entrance to a large complex of religious buildings in the south-west part of the town. The arch had been subsequently demolished and its blocks used in the town walls by the early fourth century, hence the lack of certainty about its function. Also, substantial alterations seem to have taken place on the 'palace' site to the east around the same time. London's riverside wharfs were extended by building new quays further out from the banks. Timber frames were erected on piles driven into the riverbed and the voids filled in with rubbish and rubble. This may have taken place as late as the mid-third century and suggests that commercial activity was far from dead, even if it was not as vibrant as it had once been.

Close to the probable site of the London arch the foundations of a major building have been identified on Peter's Hill. It has been attributed to the reign of the rebel emperor Allectus (293-6) on the grounds of tree-ring evidence from its timber piles. The site may have been intended as a prestigious palace for the short-lived regime. However, it is unwise to form such a precise historical association in the absence of a confirmatory inscription. Instead the timbers may have come from stocks of felled wood and the building could easily belong to the period following the rebellion. Even so it is an interesting incidence of major construction work going on at a time when the basilica and forum of London seem to have been demolished. These two cases show that it is sometimes rash to make deductions about a town's fate based on the fate of individual structures.

The basilica at Silchester has produced some very interesting evidence for the building being given over to metalworkers in the mid-third century (**68**). Partitions were erected in what had once been an open hall with nave and an aisle to divide it up into separate metalworking workshops. Oddly, the basilica was ideal. It provided shelter but the huge volume and high roof meant that noise, heat and fumes could disperse. On the face of it, this hardly seems evidence for an economic crisis provoking an urban decline. Instead it almost looks like an economic revival. But since this was Silchester's principal public building, the idea that this was done under civic or state control is a good one. That raises all sorts of questions. Does it, for instance, mean that the basilica had always been overkill, an unnecessarily elaborate facility that could easily be dispensed with when there were more pressing needs? It was built under Hadrian or Antoninus Pius (**colour plate 3**) but little evidence has been found for flooring, raising the possibility that like London's monumental Hadrianic basilica, it had never been finished. If so, does this mean administration of the canton was relocated elsewhere in Silchester? Or was control so sewn up by the local magnates, the idea of accountable government had become a nonsense? Alternatively, was there a crisis that meant urgent state supplies of coinage and arms became a necessity?

The Silchester basilica raises the interesting question of whether the whole nature of local administration had changed in later Roman Britain, perhaps diminishing the requirements for government buildings, or even that they were never really needed in the first place. This would help explain the abandonment of the forum at Wroxeter in the late third century, and the demolition of London's basilica and clearing of its forum somewhere around the same time. The so-called church that lies beside the forum at Silchester was probably built during the third century (**17** & **90**). It seems that although towns were origi-nally equipped with similar buildings, local arrangements and circumstances from the mid-third century could lead to completely different fates. At the small town of Wall the *mansio* baths were reconstructed during this time (**45**). Ironically Caerwent's basilica fell into the hands of metalworkers, but not until *c.*350. In other words, the picture facing us seems to change from place to place.

Defences

The question of economic decline and urban stagnation becomes even more complicated when we consider the appearance of circuits of earth and stone around the towns. The problem is to decide whether they were built out of necessity or choice, when they were built, and whether they were the result of

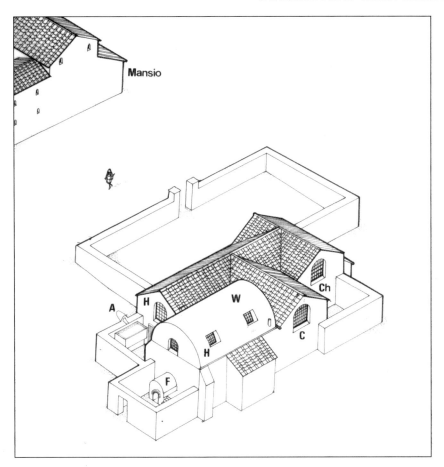

45 *Isometric reconstruction of the* mansio *baths at Wall in their final phase. The main rooms are indicated:* H *(hot rooms,* caldaria*);* W *(warm room,* tepidarium*);* C *(cold room,* frigidarium*);* Ch *(changing room,* apodyterium*). Note also the furnace (F) and the aqueduct outflow (A)*

independent urban initiatives or were ordered by the provincial government; and there is no easy answer. The urban defences of Roman Britain form the most conspicuous visible remains today of the province's towns — at Aldborough, Canterbury, Caistor-by-Norwich and Silchester, for example, almost nothing else can now be seen above ground. Even at Caerwent where a remarkable amount is visible, the defences are substantially more impressive than anything else (**49** & **103**).

The history of urban defences is a long one and goes back well into the first century but the most intensive phase of their development was during the third century. A small number of towns like Colchester built defensive works in the first and second centuries. As a colony it was entitled to do so and so a free-standing masonry wall was erected in the early second century, incorporating the exceptional monumental west gate built around 100 (**27**). Verulamium as a *municipium* was a special case. It was surrounded with a bank and ditch on three sides in the late first century, with the river forming the fourth side. Since it was later demolished to allow the town to expand, dating this has proved rather difficult. The local best estimate is *c*.75–80 but that depends on the rather tenuous evidence of pottery, rarely good enough to pin anything to closer than ten years either way and even that is rather optimistic (**8**).

Apart from the other colonies of Gloucester and Lincoln (which utilized and added to elements of the legionary fortress defences, see **10**) the only other towns known to have had early defences were Silchester, Winchester and Chichester, where banks and ditches were put up in the first century (**17**). All three are thought to have been part of the client kingdom of the pro-Roman chief of the Regini, Togidubnus/Cogidubnus. If that was true (and it is far from certain) this could have exempted them from the legal restriction on defences for provincial towns that required the emperor's permission.

So, to begin with most towns were not legally able to install urban defences. The last thing the Roman government wanted to allow was the creation of possible enemy strongholds. By the second century, circumstances were very different and many towns started to erect earthwork defences. In general, stone facing walls came later. Verulamium for example now enclosed a larger area than before (**colour plate 20**), and a large number of the minor towns scattered about the province such as Ancaster and Great Casterton installed defences (**46**).

46 *All that remains of the late-Roman defences of the small town at Ancaster (Lincs) looking west along the south rampart. The fortifications had stone revetments and bastions (not now visible) and enclosed a much smaller area than the original settlement, as was typical for these late examples of Romano-British urban defences. The church stands on the western defences, and probably partly overlies a temple precinct – a number of religious sculptures have been found around it*

1 *A* Tyche, *or patron goddess of a town, indicated by her mural crown. The Tyche symbolised the Mediterranean concept of the town as an entity, and was frequently depicted on local coinages struck in towns in the Eastern Empire. From a villa at Brantingham, just outside the town of Brough and close to the main road to York. The floor is believed to have been influenced by mosaicists who worked in the Cirencester area, but the design probably originated in a pattern book*

2 *Flavian emperors. The Flavians:* top, *Vespasian (69-79) and his sons,* below left, *Titus (79-81) and* right, *Domitian (81-96). During their reigns Romano-British urban and economic development in the south proceeded at a pace never to be matched again*

3 *Hadrian (117-38) and Antoninus Pius (138-61). During their reigns Britain's urban public building passed its peak*

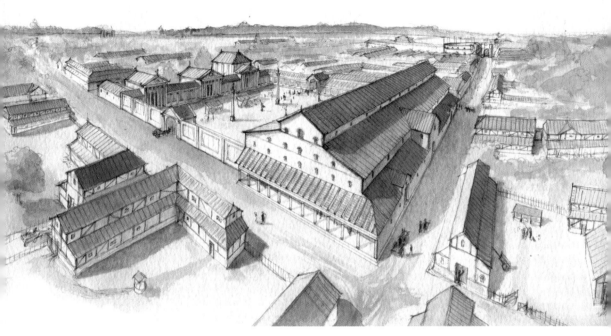

4 *Verulamium's forum and basilica as they might have appeared in the late second century. Dedicated around 79-81, the complex is the earliest testified in Britain*

5 *Constantine II on a bronze coin,* nummus, *from the Langtoft (E. Yorks) no. 2 hoard, found in September 2000. Struck at the short-lived London mint between 320 and 324, just before its closure in 325. The type was matched by similar examples struck at other mints in the West. The reverse reads* Beata Tranquillitas, *'prosperous peace', and carries the mintmark PLON for* Pecunia LONdinii, *'Money of London'. See also* **67**. *Actual diameter 20mm*

6 *The 'Mint Wall' at Lincoln, now known to have almost certainly formed part of the basilica's north wall, survives with a height of over 5m (16ft) and length of 21m (69ft)*

7 *The north gate of the colony at Lincoln as it survives today, the only Roman gate in Britain through which traffic still passes*

8 *The capitol at Dougga,* Thuggensis, *in Tunisia. This spectacular building preserves the impact of Roman public buildings, even in a remote provincial town*

9 *Rudchester. Rudston villa (E. Yorks). A panel from the 'Venus' mosaic, depicting* Taurus Omicida, *'The man-killing bull'. The crescent on a stick was a symbol of a North African circus team of animal-killers. Despite its remote location, Rudston lay close to a road leading west to York, and a junction that connected it to smaller towns at Brough and Malton, linking it commercially and socially to the greater Roman world. The crude execution of the floor shows how diluted the influence had become by the time it reached Rudston. Fourth century*

10 *Leicester. Wall-painting from a second-century house close to the basilica, depicting fantasy architecture with decorative motifs and trims. Finds like this are exceptional in Britain but were probably typical of well-appointed town houses in major settlements by this date*

11 *Leicester. Painted ceiling from a room in the additional market hall, built in the late second or early third century. The building was modelled on the forum-and-basilica complex, and lay just across the road from the main facility, but seems to have been designated as an overflow for the town's commercial activity as it lacked facilities for administration*

12 *Dinnington (Somerset). This newly-discovered villa mosaic is a typical fourth-century geometric floor for the period and region. Most of the mosaics associated with the style are clustered around Ilchester and Dorchester, leading to the belief that the mosaicist and his assistants worked from one of the towns. Dinnington villa lies a few metres from the Fosse Way, 10 miles (16km) south-west of Ilchester*

13 *Exeter. Reconstruction model of the mid-first-century legionary baths (the* caldarium*). This provides an excellent idea of the complex structural engineering applied here, and at later town baths like Wroxeter (**116**) and Leicester (**colour plate 18**). Exeter's military baths were converted into the town's basilica by c.80. The external wall at the left became the rear long wall, with the* curia *located immediately above the left-hand apse*

14 *South Shields house. South Shields, fourth-century commandant's house (replica). Although this courtyard house was built originally in a late military context it preserved a Mediterranean type of town house found at various places in Britain, for example Caerwent. The enclosed courtyard distributed light into the house but provided privacy, of equal validity in a fort or town*

15 *London Lower Thames Street baths. London, model of the Lower Thames Street bath-house (see* **50** *for a view of the outstanding remains). It is not clear if this was private, public or both. It sat in a courtyard, surrounded by three wings of a building that might have been an inn, or a private house*

16 *Ravenna, Italy. The fifth-century nave of St John the Evangelist (restored after the Second World War). Although this is a Christian church it perfectly preserves the government basilican form and provides us with an excellent idea of the interior of a Romano-British town hall*

17 *Verulamium, the theatre looking north-west. Built c.140 in earth and timber, it was later rebuilt and enlarged with stone. By the fourth century it was derelict. See 29*

18 *Leicester Jewry Wall. This monumental piece of masonry formed part of the town baths. The bottom of the doors marks the Roman ground level, beneath which was the substructure of the bathing establishment including drains. Incorporation into a medieval church (the visible church is later) accounts for its survival*

19 *Vindolanda* vicus. *A long series of forts was built here from the late first century on. Eventually a straggling settlement grew up outside the fort to the west. Most of the other forts of the northern frontier had similar settlements, which provided services typical of towns and villages in the more settled south*

20 *Verulamium. This section of the north-east walls stretch now stands in isolation. Built around the middle of the third century, it was systematically robbed out for building stone in the medieval period. This created the level surface as the stone-robbers worked their way down the wall*

21 *Roman town rubbish. A collection of typical material mostly gathered from London's Roman wharves and the Thames foreshore: samian, black-burnished wares, flagons, mortaria, glass bottles, beakers, bone and coins. From the 70s until the third century vast quantities of this material poured into Roman London from abroad and from production sites in Britain*

22 *Samian ware. Fragments from two Form 37 (hemispherical) mould-decorated bowls from rubbish below the wharfs of Roman London at Billingsgate. Both are 'mint' because the original bowls were probably broken during the sea trip from Gaul, or were shattered in a dockside warehouse, and were promptly dumped in the river. Left: South Gaul, c.70-85. Right: Central Gaul, c.100-125*

23 *Nene Valley potter's signature. Painted inscription on a mortarium from Water Newton. This exceptional example records that Sennianus the potter fired (VRIT) the piece at DUROBRIVIS (Water Newton). Probably third century and a very useful reference for other sherds*

24 *Greenwich, London. Stamp bearing the abbreviation P P BR [LON] for 'Procurator of the Province of Britannia at Londinium'. The type is well-known in London and indicates official sponsorship of public buildings*

25 *The north-east corner of London's Hadrianic basilica under excavation. This one tiny corner of the immense building gives a small idea of its scale. The remains are now buried under a modern building*

26 *Canterbury defences. The church of St Mary Northgate preserves part of the town wall in its north wall, showing that it stood almost 9m (29ft) in height*

27 *Lincoln's south-west gate. Built in the fourth century as a simple archway it was subsequently remodelled with two projecting towers. The towers were built partly out of reused stonework and a large carved piece can be seen in the plinth. It may have come from a demolished temple or other public building*

28 *Pompeii. View north from the forum past the temple of Jupiter (left) through a pair of brick arches (their stone facing is lost). Niches once held statues. Urban arches are testified from physical remains in London and Verulamium (30), and on inscriptions from other towns (44). Like Verulamium's, the Pompeii arches helped define passage into different zones, and mark the former boundaries of the older, smaller, town*

29 *St Albans abbey church. Most of building was constructed in later centuries from the ruins of the Roman town. The tower is built almost entirely from Roman tile*

30 *Towcester, Lactodurum (Northants). Limestone slab carved into a face, probably from a tomb. It has similarities to theatrical masks. Height 53cm*

During most of the third century many towns proceeded to consolidate their defences by cutting into the outer face of the earth banks and building stone facing walls (**47**). Few fragments stand to their original height, unless they have been incorporated into later buildings as at Canterbury (**colour plate 26**). In some cases, including Verulamium's London gate and very probably the western gate of London (Newgate), these new walls incorporated stone gateways that had previously been free-standing parts of the earth defences. London's new walls also incorporated a small fort that had been built during the second century (**48**). Much later, around the latter part of the fourth century, some of these stone walls were augmented with external stone towers (**49**). The town gates formed impressive entrances to the towns though few survive in recognizable form today (**27**, **103** & **colour plate 7**). These are the 'facts', or what passes for them, derived exclusively from archaeological evidence.

Evidence that earth defences started going up in the late second century depends on the dating of features buried by the banks and waste material contained within them. Obviously the latest date of the latest object is the earliest date for the work, a rather vague and unreliable method as the 'latest' object could be a residual piece of late first-century pottery. Apart from the fact that building these defences would have technically required the emperor's approval we know absolutely nothing else about them. No inscriptions have been found and no literary sources refer to them but we can assume that the towns (or exceptionally wealthy individuals) financed their own projects or were provided with resources from the government.

So defences are not a fruitful source of firm evidence and only at London and Verulamium have the recovery of coin hoards in a gate-tower and an interval tower provide a little more evidence for the stone curtain. The London hoard ends with a coin of 235, so it is obvious the tower was still standing at some point in the years after that date, and the same applies to the Verulamium hoard where the tower had to have been standing at a time when a coin of 273 was circulating and could be hoarded. In fact, a coin of 273 will not have been any use after the end of the century when the coinage was reformed so that gives us a time zone of about 25 years for the hoard to have been placed in the tower. It does not tell us when the towers were built, or when they were destroyed. Even so that corresponds with the evidence of pottery and stray lost coins located in recent excavations on the defences at Silchester.

Debate about Romano-British urban defences has concentrated on trying to decide if the late-second-century earthworks and the third-century stone walls form part of concerted programmes in response to centrally planned initiatives. The truth is that while this is likely we do not know what the reason was, though it is clear that the work was monumental in scale. It may simply have been part of general policy linked to imperial initiatives. Between 193-7 Britain's governor, Clodius Albinus, took the province's garrison into a catastrophic civil war. But he is unlikely to have expended resources on a

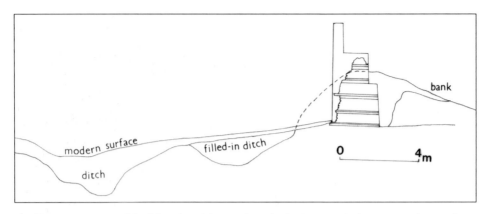

47 Above: *cross-section of the defences at Silchester. The earlier bank was cut back to receive a facing wall of stone. The associated ditch behind was filled in, and a new one dug further back. After Fulford* Below: *view of the defences at Silchester today in the south-east sector. The facing stones have been robbed out but the levelling courses of tile can be seen. The church (left of centre) lies within the town walls on the site of three temples*

48 *The south-west corner of the second-century fort in London. The fort was incorporated into the third-century defences and the junction can be seen in the upper left part of the picture where the much thicker town wall abuts the fort's curved corner (arrowed). Compare with the London plan (see 16)*

49 *The south wall of the third-century defences at Caerwent, the best-preserved urban defences of any Roman town in Britain. The projecting bastions were built at a later date, probably during the fourth century*

protracted project which would have only had any value had he been forced to fall back on Britain.

Perhaps defences were a retrospective precaution following disturbances on the northern frontier around 184. In most cases the new defences were erected over long periods of time and enclosed a space that contained the most concentrated area of settlement (there were exceptions like Caistor-by-Norwich but the contraction here is merely further evidence for the town's generally retarded development). At Verulamium the new earthworks at this time almost doubled the size of the town and were eventually abandoned, the third-century stone walls only following their alignment in part and enclosing a smaller area. The fact that here there was money and time for monumental stone gateways, and triumphal arches to mark the town's earlier limits, hardly smacks of a crisis, military or economic.

The possibilities are almost endless. The legitimate Roman emperor between 270 and 275 was Aurelian, an emperor who ordered the wholesale construction of a monumental circuit of walls, gates and towers around Rome herself to protect the city from barbarian invasions, completed under his successor Probus (276-82). Significantly, Aurelian used civilian labour. Soldiers were too badly needed elsewhere. Perhaps Britain's cities, and those of other provinces, were inclined to emulate Rome's example, and if they used civilians too then given the pattern in Britain the last thing we would expect would be a useful inscription to date any of the work.

Britain was part of breakaway regimes in 259-73 and 286-96. Building stone curtains might have been a response to the instability, or was directed by the rebel regimes to help defend their urban strongholds against an invasion from the legitimate Empire. Indeed this was exactly what terminated the rule of Allectus in 296. On the other hand, town walls might have been linked to the supposed maritime threat posed by pirates in the North Sea and the English Channel, a threat thought to have helped provoke the building of the forts of the Saxon Shore. It does not matter what that threat amounted to in practical terms; what does matter is whether there was a *belief* that it was significant. The promotion of Carausius shows that it was bad enough for the government to mobilise a naval force against coastal raiders.

However, the only new forts that appear to belong to the first half of the third century were at Reculver in Kent and Brancaster in Norfolk. Since anyone manning them could have done little more than watch raiders sailing past, it is difficult to see what use they might have been. But during the rest of the century more were built, characterized by massive freestanding walls with projecting bastions like Portchester (**104**), Richborough, Dover and Bradwell-on-Sea. Other compounds continued the system on the other side of Britain at, for example, Cardiff and Anglesey. They were likely to have served as supply bases for mounted troops dealing with sporadic coastal raids, corrals for horses and supplies, and even as fortified refuges for civilians. Another use could have been that they provided traders with safe locations to store imported supplies or goods for export, and to conduct their business. One literary reference from the late third century even raises the possibility that they were used as well for accommodating prisoners of war. If these were not really forts at all, but fortified corrals for accommodating civilians, stores, soldiers, or prisoners as required, it is much easier to see those forts and urban stone defences, as really all part of the same phenomenon. It may not have been until much later that the shore forts were drawn together in the *Notitia Dignitatum*, creating the impression they were always part of a system when in fact that had not necessarily been the case to begin with.

London's early-third-century landward walls are particularly difficult to reconcile with an emergency. Here the riverfront formed something like a third of the town limits, yet remained unprotected for the meantime (**16**). The landward wall had neat rows of squared facing stones broken by carefully laid levelling courses of tiles, surely not the product of a hasty attempt to protect the town. It enclosed virtually all the area known to have been settled and incorporated the second-century fort. The public building works now known to have been going on in London around this time reinforce the idea that carefully considered projects were under way.

Yet towards the end of the third century a massive wall was erected on London's riverfront, possibly augmented by watchtowers downriver looking out over the Thames (one has been located at Shadwell 6km (4 miles) east of the town defences). There are at least two possible reasons: if the Saxon Shore system was designed to help defend the south-eastern coasts from raiders,

London would have been susceptible with its exceptional frontage on a major tidal river. Secondly, London fell to Constantius Chlorus in 296 during the recovery of the province after the rule of Carausius and Allectus. Either of the latter could have seen fit to provide London swiftly with more defences in an effort to create a stronghold.

There were two distinct styles of construction used in the new London riverside wall. The eastern part, attributed on tree-ring evidence from the foundation piles to the late third century, seems to have been built in a competent manner but only a small part has been located. The western part, of which much more is known, was constructed quite differently to the older landward wall. It had elementary foundations of blocks and used a lot of stone taken from demolished buildings of second- and third-century date. We do not know whether they were demolished expressly for this purpose or were already in ruins. It is noticeable that towns in Gaul seem to have remained unwalled until after a massive raid across the Rhine by the Alamanni (a German tribe) in 276. Subsequently walls were built but this usually involved significant contraction of the settled area, and the extensive reuse of masonry from demolished buildings. What all this means is that in London there is an instance of a late riverside wall which bears the hallmarks of being a response to some critical situation, whereas the main sequence of earlier town walls, including London's landward wall, seem to be the product of a careful and leisurely programme.

Whatever happened in London, it still does not explain the main programme of urban defences. The truth is we will never know for certain. Various military contexts are possibilities, but so are others. Possible reasons may have been a desire to impress, to tax the coming and going of goods more easily and control land rents more effectively, or even to restrict access to towns in order to keep undesirable elements out. In the early 280s in Gaul a landless class called the Bagaudae caused a great deal of trouble, and led to an imperial army being sent against them. A combination of circumstances, including barbarian incursions, had caused social and economic disruption. This result was a variety of communities being evicted as their incomes collapsed, and eventually they coagulated into a dangerous band of outlaws that presented a major threat to towns in northern Gaul. It might not be coincidence that in the war against them, Carausius earned his reputation, leading to his appointment as commander of the fleet in the English Channel. There is no evidence that the Bagaudae, or an equivalent, existed in Britain but that it not a relevant objection if the fear of armed bands of disaffected people existed in Britain. Carausius seems to have been a popular usurper in Britain, and unease about civil unrest might have helped. Were some townsfolk determined to protect themselves in fortified communities like the wealthy in today's Rio de Janeiro? We know so little about what went on in Roman Britain at the time in terms of how the curial classes controlled their position and the politics of town management that we do need to consider all of these as plausible reasons for choosing to concentrate on walls rather than buildings. It may have simply been a regional custom, in the sense that building impressive defences was perhaps the Romano-British way, and needs no more profound explanation. There is also the possibility that it was considered necessary for town governments to be seen to be spending accumulated reserves on projects intended for the public good. In the absence of any confirmatory evidence we will have to content ourselves with recognizing a range of possibilities.

Houses

The stone houses built in the second century in many of the towns would have had long lives, even if they were substantially altered. So it is hardly surprising that there is less evidence for house building in the third and fourth centuries for the simple reason that demand would have diminished closer to replacement levels once the housing stock had been built up. The house known as Building XXVIII.1 at Verulamium seems to have been built around the beginning of the third century on a site abandoned after the fire of c.155. Occupation layers from the basement contained coins running right up to around the mid-fourth century, suggesting that the house was in use until at least then and very probably beyond (**42**). A house in Lower Thames Street in London with its own substantial bath house (possibly run as a business) seems to have been built in the late second century and was still in use up to two hundred years later (**50** & **colour plate 15**).

There appears to have been quite a dramatic decline in the number of sites in London that were occupied as dwellings from the later second century onwards, but this may be partly an illusion. New houses were larger but fewer and many sites seem to have fallen vacant with a layer of dark earth, possibly agricultural, burying them. This picture could be partly due to a reduction in the supply of coinage, a decline in imported datable pottery, and destruction of upper Roman layers during the medieval period. It is also partly a product of archaeology, and the sites that happen to get excavated. The site at No. 1 Poultry, London, showed a series of tightly packed wooden buildings clustered along the roadside. This basic arrangement continued, and was rebuilt after the massive fire of c.125-30. In the third century, stone extensions were built onto the rear of some of the timber buildings and even once the timber structures fell out of use in the fourth century the stone extensions continued to flourish. It was not until the later part of the century that significant decay set in.

Excavations at Milk Street were initially thought to have shown dark earth arriving on sites as early as the late second century. But in Southwark, London's extensive suburb that grew up around the southern end of London Bridge and the roads from Kent and the south-west, dark earth was found in

50 *London, Lower Thames Street baths. Although the site was built around the beginning of the third century, it seems to have remained in use for the rest of the period. The baths were entirely of the 'Turkish' variety – there is no plunge pool, and sat between the wings of what was either a private house or an inn. See* also **colour plate 15**

contexts that suggested other factors had been at play. Amongst these are maggots that would have lived in the dark earth and consumed any late timber buildings that the dark earth had originally covered. This would create the impression the dark earth had sealed earlier layers. If this sounds confusing in a sense it is, because it shows how evidence can be interpreted in totally different ways. This makes it really very difficult for archaeologists to understand how a town was functioning, when evidence from sites near to one another can seem quite contradictory. For example, there is no doubt that the volume of material from London's later wharves is down on the amounts dating from the late first century.

There are all sorts of possible explanations for a change in the character of towns. The configuration of an economy can change. At a time when exports and imports are at their height, a port town can thrive. If the economy changes to one of more regional self-sufficiency the wharves might decline, but not the rest of the town. There is also just fashion. In Rome all the complaints familiar to us today were regularly trotted out. Rome's property was expensive and the annual rent for a small apartment reputedly cost more than buying a small country estate outright. The city was intolerably noisy and congested, and there were all the inconveniences of unpleasant smells, industry, and the risks of poor and dangerous building practices indulged in by cowboy developers.

Not only that, but towns were liable to go up in smoke with catastrophic losses of money and property.

Rome of course was an extreme, but some of this was bound to be reflected even in far-off Britain. Removing to a back-garden stone extension away from the street might have been a solution for residents of No. 1 Poultry, whereas in other *insulae* the residents might have moved away. Conversely, perhaps some zones in London had become a kind of garden city lived in by the well-to-do (especially during the winter months) who liked the peace and quiet but also the prestige of being in the capital, instead of other busier commercial centres. Certainly there is evidence that the provincial economy was becoming more self-contained during the third century, and one in which a major port would have had less of a role to play. In Lincoln, examination of the dark earth layers have produced no evidence for agriculture or plant growth, leading to the suggestion that the soil had been brought in and deliberately dumped rather than accumulated. This transition is often perceived as representing some kind of urban failure whereas instead, if it did occur, it is just as arguably evidence for provincial maturity and self-sufficiency no longer dependent on massive imports. Also, as we saw in chapter 3, house ownership was a complex matter in the Roman world. Just because houses were larger and more widely spaced need not necessarily mean that London's population had radically declined even if the nature of the town had changed. The construction work involved in the new public buildings and defences would have involved large numbers of workers. A rare reference in contemporary texts actually confirms this. An imperial panegyric of about 297 says that *artifices* (skilled workers), 'with whom the provinces [of Britain] were overflowing', were taken to the continent to help work on the restoration of the Gaulish city of Autun. In any case excavations on the wharfs have shown that commercial activities were continuing, though at a reduced level, with imported pottery still arriving at quayside warehouses in the mid-third century.

If the dark earth in London was due to the farming within the town walls we have no actual evidence for it, but two fourth-century houses (*Insula* XII.I/2) in Cirencester were connected by a wall and had a number of associated structures including a possible barn (**51**). Nothing had ever been built on the site before and as the layout resembles a villa it has been suggested that this was a farm perhaps working land immediately outside the town walls. There is also evidence for other trades in late towns, working from houses rather than shops. A fourth-century house in Dorchester (Dorset) seems to have had two separate components. The north wing had a mosaic in almost every room while the south wing seems to have been designed around a trade which involved the removal of water, perhaps fulling (**52**), suggesting a thriving local cloth trade.

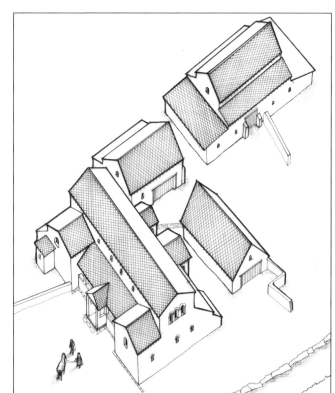

51 *Reconstructed axonometric view of a house in Cirencester (Insula X11.2). This building, closely associated with another nearby, was built in a secluded virgin part of the town between a river and the defences during the latter half of the fourth century (6). Excavation produced traces of metalworking and weaving tools and this along with the out-buildings has led to the suggestion that this was a farm, perhaps working land outside the walls*

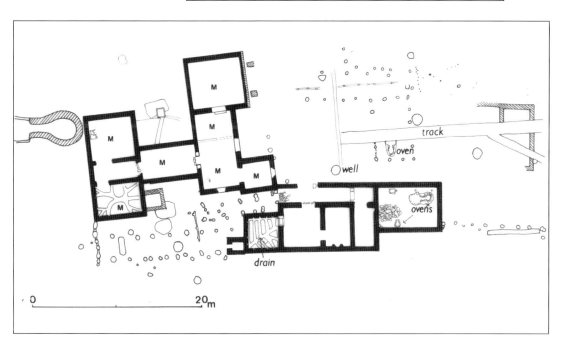

52 *Plan of a fourth-century house in Colliton Park, Dorchester, Dorset. There were two separate wings, one of which was apparently residential with a number of mosaic floors (M), while the other seems to have been concerned with a trade, perhaps fulling and dyeing (provision had been made for water drainage from floors). After Selby*

Conclusion

So the Romano-British towns of the third century and, as we shall see later during the fourth century also, present us with a complicated picture which is difficult to interpret. Like so many aspects of modern archaeology, the old habit of extrapolating broad conclusions based on a few 'key' excavations is rapidly giving way to the more mature recognition that circumstances could vary from house to house, block to block, and town to town. So we cannot necessarily conclude that the whole province and its towns were experiencing a downturn in their fortunes. Stagnation and depression are terms often used to describe the period but it is just as reasonable to interpret what we see as stabilization and transition. London shows this in particular, while a change in function for any one town's basilica may have been no more than a matter of local conditions and convenience. A failure to repair one burnt down is as likely to have been linked to local quarrels about who was going to pay for it, leading to civic inertia, as it is to have resulted from impoverished civic finances.

There has always been a tendency to start with the observation that Roman town life more or less disappeared during the fifth century and work backwards, looking for signs of gradual deterioration from up to two hundred years or more earlier. The truth is that conditions in the fifth century were a great deal different to anything that had gone before. Conditions in the third and fourth centuries may have been different to those in the second century but the towns were still functioning within the unifying and stabilizing influence of the Roman world.

Trapped within the vagaries of archaeological evidence it is very easy to make generalizations which both exaggerate trends and ignore the probability that much of what we see was caused by the actions and decisions (perhaps misguided) of a small number of powerful people in each town. During the first and second centuries the Roman government would have been more influential because the province was being built up. Official policy was being instituted in all the towns, which is why we see a broadly similar pattern of development. Subsequently, as the province became more self-sufficient, and especially during the periods of independence, members of local town governments are likely to have had a more individual and perhaps idiosyncratic influence on a town's development. It is of course a great shame that we cannot know who these people were, but recognizing this possibility goes some way to explaining why we see so many different kinds of urban histories developing out of what was originally a similar origin. Assuming that localised instances of change necessarily reflect a general and protracted pattern of decline may be entirely wrong. Our inability to resolve this kind of problem from the archaeological record is one of the unpalatable realities of studying the period.

5

TRADE, INDUSTRY AND
URBAN ECONOMIES

The population of a town with a thriving economy usually expands and also enjoys an increased standard of living, while a town with an unhealthy economy experiences the opposite. All towns will tend to veer towards one or the other at different times. As we saw in the last chapter, Romano-British towns are sometimes pictured as initially successful before going through a phase of stagnation and then declining, in one case being described as 'administrative villages', prior to being abandoned during the fifth century. But in an economic sense the evidence for this is non-existent apart from a reduction in imports, and the archaeological evidence for decline is at best ambiguous and prone to local variation.

Romano-British towns are a special case because there were none before 43. There is a difference between evidence for a town growing and expanding during a good period, and being built from scratch. Major building works in *civitas* capitals would take place in their early years because otherwise the towns would not have been able to function. Once built, only routine maintenance would be required unless they were burnt down or collapsed through bad design. But, as the buildings no longer exist, apart from footings and foundations, we have no evidence for sustained investment of this kind unless an inscription is found recording repairs, or archaeological evidence is uncovered for renovation. At the other end of the time-scale Romano-British towns cannot be fairly regarded as 'failures' because, by and large, they did not survive as towns beyond the mid-fifth century. The whole basis of society had altered into one in which towns as Romano-British markets and administrative centres had less of a role to play.

Towns theoretically represent a 'surplus' because for every town dweller not working on the land (though some would have been) there are several people (at least) producing enough food on the land to support such a town dweller. This has only ceased to be true in the modern machine age. We don't know what that 'surplus' actually meant because we have no idea of prices related to earnings and the relative wealth of town and rural dwellers as a share of the 'Gross Romano-British National Product', and we do not know how much food town dwellers produced themselves. If we consider the case of the Roman army in Britain we can be sure that it would have taken all that it required, more or less regardless of how that left the farmers. We know from evidence found in other provinces, such as Egypt, that the army had arrangements to pay for supplies with money or credit notes, so it should not be automatically assumed that the army operated in a wholly oppressive fashion. But when food was short, and administration less ethically enforced, military muscle could have been easily brought to bear when necessary. In the same way it may be that towns existed as much as a result of coercion through local taxation in kind as the purchasing power of cash. Equally, we have no idea of what supporting the wealthy part of the community 'cost' the poor – in the nineteenth century for example this inequality was much more pronounced than it is now.

The location of towns certainly seems to reflect this crucial dependence on the availability of surplus food. Towns were distributed widely in the central and southern parts of the province. It can hardly be coincidence that this was also the part which was the most agriculturally fertile, or in economic terms, the least marginal. Here the land was generally good enough to allow the regular production of a surplus. In the north, west and extreme south-west this was not so true, though these areas were more productive than was once thought. Quite apart from that, these more remote areas were relatively unstable and while isolated villa estates existed, like Llantwit Major in Wales or close to Durham in the north-east, nothing matched the density of rural settlement found in, say, the Mendips and Cotswolds.

The villa estates reached their greatest number in the fourth century and many show that they earned sufficient surpluses to pay for the installation of mosaics and other luxury items at this time, though it is very important to stress that in no Romano-British case do we know anything about a villa's economy. Chedworth, for example, lies about 7 miles by road from Cirencester but we know nothing about any of its agricultural products (if there were any), or where they were sold. In fact, very few villas are within a couple of miles or so of a town (London is especially conspicuous in this respect), raising the possibility that quite a lot of farmland close to towns was farmed by the urban population. One case is the villa estate at Gorhambury which lies about 1.2 km (just under 1 mile) from the north gate of Verulamium. Excavation on the site has shown that occupation within an enclosure dated from the Iron Age, and seems to have been linked to the dykes that formed part of the pre-Roman *oppidum*. By the beginning of the second century a stone house had been erected within the enclosure and it remained in occupation until the middle of the fourth century. In this case at least one plausible explanation is that the site belonged to an especially prominent family within the existing local tribal population and its members retained their status, and privileges, throughout most of the period, perhaps dominating the town government. The same probably applied to the owner of the Greetwell villa, located one mile east of Lincoln. With an unusually elaborate series of mosaics, and a prestigious south-facing viewpoint, it must have belonged to someone of considerable prominence in Lincoln but who chose to live in a more exclusive location. It has been very reasonably suggested that the house was used by the governor of the fourth-century province of *Flavia Caesariensis*. Such men could hold status in towns and help control them, but enjoy all the advantages of rural peace. Others, living further away, could retire to the country for the summer, but winter in town while a bailiff managed the country estate.

Even if villas were rarely located very near to towns, the way they generally clustered around major routes between towns makes it difficult to avoid the conclusion that their principal markets were urban populations even if we cannot take if any further. Curiously the fourth century, when villa numbers reached a maximum, was a time when many archaeologists argue that towns had diminished populations with a very reduced level of commercial activity. Of course, the town need not have been the only end-user. In the year 359 the emperor-designate Julian is recorded as having built ships in the Rhineland, and using them to ship grain from Britain to help repair the losses caused in Gaul by barbarian incursions (**53**).

53 *A Roman ship depicted on a sarcophagus. Britain's economy depended on her maritime links with the Mediterranean world. Produce was shipped in and out, and manufactured goods shipped in*

Clearly, as the towns were built and existed throughout the period they served some sort of purpose, and their populations were fed. The archaeological evidence is the only possible source of information but it provides us with instances and examples, not secure foundations for generalizations. It also, of course, necessarily tends to be confined to non-perishables, making the marketing of the most fundamental of all resources, food, largely a mystery. One exceptional instance has been found in London where a room in a building destroyed about the time of the Boudican Revolt had been used to store grain. On analysis the grain was found to have come from a country bordering the Mediterranean or in the Near East. Evidently, Roman London was not entirely fed by the countryside of Britain.

Goods in substantial quantities were shipped across from the continent during the first and second centuries. London has produced the largest amount of evidence but much is paralleled in the other significant towns like Colchester, Cirencester, Silchester and Verulamium. One amphora, from Southwark, bore the painted inscription 'excellent fish sauce by Lucius Tettius Africanus, from *Antipolis*'. *Antipolis* was a port on the south coast of Gaul near Nice. Servandus of the colony at Cologne manufactured white pipeclay figurines of goddesses, and stamped his details on the base. Various examples have turned up in Britain including one from Colchester. Servandus may have relied on a *negotiator* to ship the goods over (see under imported ceramics below). These two examples alone indicate maritime trade routes from Gaul round past Spain and the Bay of Biscay into Britain, and across the North Sea. There are many others. Such trade routes were already functioning before the Roman invasion though for the benefit of a smaller part of the population. Most of the evidence for this survives in the form of ceramics, particularly fine wares and amphorae, deposited in wealthy graves. These routes extended as far as Italy as early as the mid-second century BC.

By the late first century BC a number of *oppida* in south-eastern Britain were receiving a wide range of goods from a number of continental and Mediterranean sources. So in some respects Romano-British trade and commercial activity was an extension of a marketing infrastructure which was already established and into which the new towns were absorbed. As the period progressed this cross-Channel trade became initially more extensive with what seems to have been a one-way trade in manufactured goods to Britain paid for by the exports of raw materials, though by the fourth century the province appears to have become much more self-sufficient in most respects. In economic terms the fourth century presents archaeologists and historians with enormous problems in trying to understand what happened to urban economies; some of the problems are explored in chapter 7.

Population

As individuals the town dwellers of Roman Britain are only known to us through graffiti and inscriptions but these give us no idea of total numbers (**54**, see also **1** & **94**). While we can assume that the urban population was one that largely depended on the surplus agricultural production of the rural population we have no records of either the absolute or relative numbers of either. The only factor that is constantly changing in all this, is the continuous elevation of numbers of known Romano-British rural settlements. In some of the more intensively settled areas, the popularity of archaeology and the arrival of new techniques, as well as the impact modern building and road development, has increased estimated Roman site density by a factor of around ten.

This does not help us much with towns where the numbers of large towns and their approximate sizes has remained fixed, though there are surprises here too. In theory, cemetery evidence ought to help us but excavations and publication of urban cemeteries are few, and often inconclusive (see chapter 6). Marcus Aurelius Lunaris, already mentioned, we know held office in York and Lincoln, but travelled to Bordeaux (**1**). So do we count him as a citizen of York or Lincoln, or both? Just to add to the problems, it is almost impossible to know *when* a burial occurred other than a general assessment based on grave goods (if present), or whether the burial represents a town-dweller, or a rural person whose family selected burial in an urban cemetery (**97**).

The relative numbers of urban and rural populations would be of more value because this would provide a basis for assessing the efficiency of the economy. As far as towns are concerned we have Tacitus' claim that 70,000 people died at London, Colchester, Verulamium and possibly other undefended settlements in the area during the Boudican Revolt. Quite obviously he had no access to accurate records, if any even existed. He wrote around 30-40 years later, and the towns had been destroyed. The governor Suetonius

54 *Fragment of tile from London inscribed before firing with a list of names, perhaps tile factory workers. Here the name Titus is clearly visible, though this may be part of a longer and more common name, Potitus. Actual diameter 47mm. From Billingsgate, London*

Paullinus did not hang around to count either. We have no means of correcting Tacitus apart from looking at the sort of population the medieval towns and cities could support. One basic estimate of medieval urban population density, founded on parish records and other data, is approximately 150 persons per hectare (equivalent to 61 per acre). Roman Cirencester's walled zone covered about 107 hectares, giving us a theoretical population of around 16,000. But since we know areas within the walls remained undeveloped, and that urban housing density varied, we ought to consider a true figure of 8–12,000, which would have varied according to the season and over the years due to economic conditions, disease and migration. As Roman Britain's third-largest city this corresponds with Norwich of the 1520s, then England's second-largest city, with a population that fluctuated around 10,000. Population estimates for the 1520s at Canterbury, Colchester and York which approximated in area to their Roman predecessors, are 3,000, 3–4,000 and 8,000 respectively. At the same date, the city of London had a theoretical population based on its size of around 39,000 but other evidence suggests it was actually as much as 60,000.

It is possible that given the marginally greater likelihood of a Romano-British town having a better water supply and drainage, the ancient populations could have been higher because the death-rate would have been a little lower. Unfortunately there is no reliable data that would allow an accurate figure for life expectancy in Romano-British towns to be assessed. Statistical models based on modern pre-industrial societies do provide a means of calculating a theoretical urban population for the province and these have been used to suggest a figure of around 240,000 plus or minus about 50,000. A recent estimate of about 3.3 million for the rural population is based on the density of known sites and together with an army of about 125,000 (including dependants) suggests a total population of around 4 million. It therefore took something like thirteen or fourteen members of the rural population to support a town dweller, not counting imported food. By way of comparison we can take the Domesday Book data for 1086 that suggests a population of about 2 million, but it was distributed very differently (south Sussex, south-east Kent and central East Anglia being especially conspicuous concentrations). In any case, as more and more sites are found it becomes obvious that 4 million is very rough and the actual figure could quite easily have been half or the same as much again, depending on the time. It is worth remembering that the European Black Death of the fourteenth century eventually reduced England's population of around 5 million to just 3 million. By 1601 it had risen again to 4.1 million.

It would be wrong to assume that people who lived in Romano-British towns always lived there, and had no interests in the countryside, and that therefore rural and urban populations were two exclusive groups. The lack of villas very close to major towns has already been mentioned. The villa at Lullingstone in Kent was a modest but well-appointed establishment in a charming location that would have probably been inadequate for protracted stays. The recovery of two marble busts of obviously cultivated individuals, carved in the late second century, has led to the plausible suggestion that at the time the house was a country home of a man involved in provincial administration in London, which is less than a day's journey away. A writing tablet bearing a text recording a dispute over the ownership of a tract of land somewhere in Kent in 118 has been discovered recently in London. A man called Lucius Julius Bellicus was claiming that the land, *in civitate Cantiacorum*, 'in the canton of the Cantiaci', was his. Of course he may have come to London to sort out the dispute but equally he may have been one of many Roman Londoners who also owned rural estates.

Communications

A town needs to be supplied with food and goods that are not manufactured locally though until modern times, most towns could be fed from, and basics supplied by, their immediate hinterlands. In turn it needs to supply its own products effectively. Verulamium grew up around a road which was one of the first features of Roman life to appear in the valley of the Ver. London was the product of its location and communications. Caistor-by-Norwich was a *civitas* capital built in what amounted to a regional dead-end and therefore could not benefit from through-traffic arriving from a number of different directions. This is almost certainly one reason for its modest development, and later contraction. We do not know the extent to which Roman roads were built along existing tracks, though this certainly occurred. As many towns, particularly the *civitas* capitals, lay on or close to the sites of native settlements it may well be that much of what passes for a Roman system of communications was actually pre-Roman. A series of Iron Age settlements in Lincolnshire, at Ancaster, Navenby, Lincoln, Owmby and Dragonby, lie on the route later utilized as Ermine Street, suggesting that the eternally pragmatic Romans simply made use of what was already there (**79**).

Bridges were built at key crossing points so that traffic could pass unhindered. This did not just mean men and carts. It is important to remember that until modern refrigeration became available, cattle were routinely driven across huge distances to their markets. This is testified right up to and through the nineteenth century in Britain, with cattle being regularly brought from Wales as far as London to service the vast urban population of what by then had become one of the largest cities in the world. London Bridge is the only urban Roman bridge known in detail in Britain. It was built on colossal timber piles, whereas the better-known examples in the north like the military bridge at Chesters, developed into massive masonry structures that rode on vast stone piers. Where the rivers were too deep or too wide, ferries carried passengers and freight across. This much is evident from Ermine Street that headed north through Lincoln right up to the Humber estuary. The road system to York and

Malton picked up on the north bank. The landward route took a diversion north-west through Doncaster.

It is easy to focus on Roman roads and treat them as the exclusive main arteries of Romano-British urban trade, and they probably were for individual travellers, imperial messengers, light freight and cattle. But water was probably far more important in antiquity though it is now almost impossible to assess by how much. Merchants called *negotiatores* are known as we saw in chapter 4 (**44**), and also a very rare regional occupation called *moritex*, thought to mean 'shipper'. The root word for the Latin *mare* ('sea') also supplied the Celtic word for sea, which survives in Welsh as *mor*, 'sea', and *morio*, 'to sail'. The most recently-discovered is Tiberinius Celerianus who seems to have sailed in and out of London (**55**). At York, Marcus Verecundius Diogenes was a *sevir* of the colony of York as well as a *moritex* (though this depends on a recent re-reading of the inscription on his coffin). Like Lucius Viducius Placidus, a trader we have already met, Diogenes will have made his money on the maritime trade across the North Sea and up the Humber and Ouse to York. In 1724 Daniel Defoe could say of York, 'the merchants here trade directly to what part of the world they will … they import their own wines from France and Portugal … and indeed what they please almost from where they please'. The foundations of York's eighteenth-century wealth were laid in Roman *Eboracum*. London's extensive Roman wharfs have been explored in some detail and a great deal is now known about the range of warehouses and other dockside facilities, as well as some of the goods that were shipped in. These included goods from abroad and within Britain, though necessarily most of the traceable remains are ceramic. But by the early eighteenth century the Thames was used for shipping dairy products to London like cheese manufactured in Wiltshire and doubtless had been for generations. The cost and

55 *Southwark, London. An inscription (found 2002) on which Tiberinius Celerianus made a dedication to the Spirits of the Emperors and Mars Camulus. Celerianus tells us he was a citizen of a north Gaulish tribe called the Bellovaci, and also a* moritex. *Moritex is a rare Celtic (?) word of uncertain meaning but is thought to mean merchant seafarer. See appendix 2, part 2 for a transcription though the text awaits full scholarly publication*

difficulty of road transport then meant that Gloucestershire cheese had to go mainly to Bristol and Bath. From this we can quite reasonably infer that Roman Londoners were able to buy perishable goods produced from well within Britain.

Remains of several ships that plied the Thames have been found, including the Blackfriars ship. Flat-bottomed and 16m long, it was clearly designed to cope with the shallows along the tidal reaches of the Thames. Villas strung out along the Darenth Valley in Kent are just one example of rural sites tied into a network of water communications that linked them to towns. The Darenth flows into the Medway, which runs past the town at Rochester and on into the lower reaches of the Thames.

Roman towns undoubtedly in part capitalized on existing trade routes and patterns of local markets. This helps to explain why towns that grew up around early forts sited close to native settlements tended to remain in existence once the fort was given up, instead of their populations following the soldiers. As such they were an adaptation of what was already there, with the forts providing an impetus to move locally because they provided security as well as customers. People are much more likely to come to trade in a place used for generations, than to accept new routes and new markets imposed by a coercive authority. In the military north, the reverse was true. Here there was little or no tribal tradition either of urban-like settlement, or even much interest in adopting aspects of Roman culture. As we shall see at the end of this chapter the small towns that gathered around forts like Vindolanda (**colour plate 19**) and Housesteads were really extensions of the military community and totally dependent on it. When these forts ceased to be used by the Roman army by the beginning of the fifth century, their attendant settlements were abandoned if they had not been already.

Urban markets and trade

Although we know about buildings that acted as markets, mainly the forum and the *macellum* (see chapter 3), it is not surprising that we know almost nothing about the process of trading in the markets themselves. A rare instance is the forum at Wroxeter that was wrecked by a disastrous fire during the second half of the second century (**56**). Subsequent repair work buried the shattered remnants of temporary stalls in the portico where they had fallen. Some of the non-perishable stock was recovered during excavations. This included a substantial quantity of samian ware from East and Central Gaul, both plain and decorated, mixing bowls (*mortaria*) manufactured in Britain and whetstones. The vendor might have been an importer (see below), his agent, or simply yet another middleman in a chain of traders that stretched back from the Wroxeter market all the way to the kiln sites in Gaul.

There is a little colour to paint in from elsewhere. In Rome during the first century BC there was an increasing sense of anxiety about moral laxity and the

56 *Column bases from the portico of the forum at Wroxeter which was damaged during a disastrous fire in the late second century. Although it was repaired it seems to have been disused by the fourth century*

57 *Ostia, Italy. The pretentious architectural façade is that of a granary owned by two freedmen called Epagathus and Epaphroditus. It fronted a street that led to the riverbank. Foundations of warehouses are well-known from behind London's wharves, and their agents would have touted for business in the town's market places*

decline into indulgence. Julius Caesar appointed officials to stand in the *macellum* in Rome to watch out for the sale of illegal luxuries, and impound them for his examination. In Ostia, the port of Rome, one of the forums is now known as the Piazza of Corporations. Seventy different commercial companies had offices here, and outside the entrance to each a mosaic panel illustrated the business and base of every company. In other streets nearby, warehouses accommodated goods (**57**). Ostia also had a *macellum*, which lay next to a major town-centre crossroads. An inscription carved on one of its columns means, 'read this and understand there is a lot of chatter at the *macellum*', a useful reminder that commercial activity was also where political, social and scandalous gossip was exchanged. A man's political reputation could rise or fall on his commercial standing. Ostia was of course of exceptional importance, since this was where Rome's vast requirements were met by imports from across the Mediterranean world, but Britain's markets were probably similar in many respects.

Imported ceramics

Pottery is the most ubiquitous find on any Romano-British site (**colour plate 21**). One of the defining features of the period was the availability of domestic and imported goods (**58**). We know that shipping merchants called *negotiatores cretarii* (literally 'pot dealers') existed, like Marcus Secundinius

58 *Towns acted as magnets for potters, urban, rural and foreign. Householders could purchase wares made nearby or somewhere else in Britain, or imported. Pottery helps archaeologists record the trade routes that supported a town, and along which perishable goods, that do not survive, could have come. Reconstructed display of the first or second century at the Museum of London. Note the square glass bottles, a common utilitarian vessel in Roman towns at the time*

Silvanus who probably shipped goods from northern Europe to York in the early third century. He erected an altar to a goddess called Nehalennia in Holland, probably close to where his continental base was. He actually calls himself a *negotiator cretarius Britannicianus*. The meaning is not totally clear, since this might be a reference to a trade in British ceramics, or trade in ceramics on the British route. But we might imagine that the Wroxeter stall owner had bought his samian from someone like Secundinius Silvanus. Some of the large quantity of samian excavated along the riverfront in London appears to be in 'as new' condition, which suggests (not surprisingly) that this was one of the major ports of entry for the commodity. At least two late second-century ships bringing samian into London seem to have been wrecked on the Pudding Pan Rock of Whitstable in Kent. Nineteenth-century fishermen who dredged up complete vessels named the rock, and took the pottery home to use.

Samian is found almost everywhere in first- and second-century Roman deposits in Western Europe along with other imported wares (**colour plate 22**). Amphorae were almost as common in towns and are found over a longer period of time and were probably distributed in a similar way. The amphora was the universal method in the ancient world of storing foodstuffs and liquids for long-distance transportation. They were usually cylindrical with a cone-shaped base, or spherical in shape, and in both cases had necks and rims and a pair of handles. The base tip meant amphorae could be inserted into holes or frames

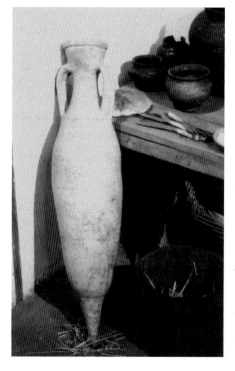

59 *Amphorae.* Left: *'London 555'-type amphora, found in London. Probably from North Africa or Spain, and perhaps filled originally with wine or oil.* Above: *neatly-trimmed base from a kitchenware jar, probably used as an amphora bung, secured with sealant (diameter 83mm). Field-walking find at Ancaster (Lincs), and evidence for amphora use or reuse, to add to sherds of amphorae found nearby*

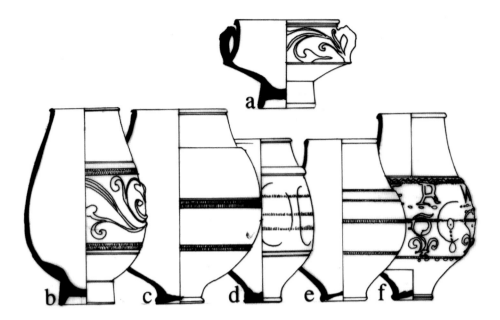

60 *Black-slipped wares imported into Romano-British towns from Gaul and the Rhineland, mainly in the second century. Scale about 1/5*
a–c: Central Gaulish black-slipped wares with barbotine and rouletted decoration. The ease with which sources of these products can be confused is evident by comparing b with **22e**. *About 150-200.*
d–f: Trier black-slipped ware, with f bearing white painted decoration and motto DA MERVM, *'serve unmixed wine'.* After various sources

to keep them secure on ships or while stacked in warehouses. It also meant someone could easily twist an amphora along the ground while gripping the handles. The most common sources for amphorae found in Roman Britain were southern Spain, southern Gaul and Italy and they generally contained (on the evidence of painted inscriptions) varieties of fish products, wine, or oils (**59**). An example from Spain, and found in London, records the contents as being 250 measures of green olives transported by a merchant, whose name is abbreviated to G.L.A., on behalf of someone called Avernus who may have been the owner. Some were still being imported during the fourth and fifth centuries from as far away as Palestine but in much smaller quantities.

There were other sources of imported ceramic goods, for example the cups and beakers manufactured in the Cologne area (**60**), Italian and Gaulish oil-lamps (**61**), and the pipe-clay 'Venus' figurines from Gaul or Germany (**62**). Together with the samian and amphorae they form an enormous body of evidence from the port of Roman London for the massive levels of trade during the first and second centuries. But other evidence exists to show that continental-style industries were established in Britain too. In the mid-first century at Colchester a lamp manufacturer was working on a site in West Stockwell Street, perhaps supplying local demand amongst colonists more

61 *Oil lamps. The upper two are first-century types, made in moulds, and exported into Britain from Italy and Gaul (though a workshop that produced similar examples was found in West Stockwell Street, Colchester). It remains the only known Romano-British lamp factory. The bottom lamp was found in the Thames at Billingsgate. It was wheel-turned, and mica-dusted to imitate bronze. It was probably made in London. Lamps burned oil that had to be imported, usually in amphorae. Lamps are thus usually found in towns and forts. Lengths 94, 114 mm and 81mm (clockwise)*

62 Left: *part of a moulded white pipe-clay female figurine made in Gaul and imported into Britain (a number were found in quayside debris in London). The figure is sometimes described as Venus but may have been a more regional fertility deity. Height when complete about 15cm.* Right: Dea Nutrix, *or mother goddess*

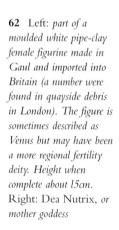

cheaply than an importer could manage. He may even have been a retired military potter. The Black-Burnished kitchen ware industries of Dorset and the Thames estuary shows that within the province throughout the period some goods were being moved considerable distances.

The larger industries supplemented the products of small-scale producers who operated here and there on an individual basis, producing ceramic goods for everyday use for very local markets. The army on the northern frontier seems to have been initially the main source of demand, and indeed may have provided the main impetus for some continental goods arriving via the towns before being shipped north and westwards during the first and second centuries. The Dorset Black-Burnished wares were still turning up on the northern frontier in the fourth century.

During the third and fourth centuries the character of trade appears to have altered radically in favour of 'home industries', reflected in a reduction in the amount of imported ceramics recovered from London's wharfs. Most fine wares in use in Roman Britain at this time were made in the Nene Valley (**63**) and Oxfordshire with lesser sources in the New Forest and in the north at Crambeck. Nene Valley and Oxfordshire goods in particular were moved widely around the province showing that goods could be dispersed to almost anywhere, though there is almost invariably a bias in favour of towns that were easily accessible. The Oxford potteries for example had easy access to London down the Thames, whilst the New Forest industries did not and this is reflected in a much more restricted distribution pattern. The kitchenware potteries at Alice Holt near Farnham came to dominate the market for cheaper pottery in the south whilst Crambeck took a similar role in the north.

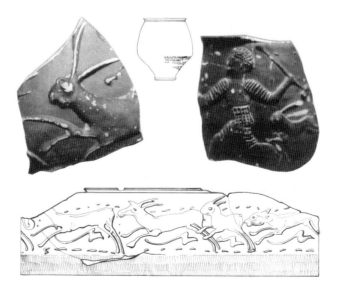

63 *Beakers and 'hunt cups'. The basic form is shown at the top (height about 15cm).*
Left: *fragment of a beaker made in the Rhineland (Nene Valley products were very similar) in the late second or early third century, decorated with an animal scene made by trailing liquid clay on the vessel (barbotine decoration).*
Right: *a more sophisticated design showing a hunter.*
Below: *a 'rolled-out' animal chase design from a late-second, early-third-century Rhineland cup found at the New Fresh Wharf. All are from London*

Coinage

Coinage must be the most unbalanced of all artefacts that turn up from Roman sites in Britain. Roman bronze and copper coins are common, sometimes very common, finds, so the logical assumption ought to be that the Romano-British relied on them as a means of exchange. It was not until the eighteenth century that base-metal 'small change' coinage was used again in such abundance. But in terms of date, the coins are very erratically distributed. The vast majority belong to the late third century, and episodes in the fourth, and a high proportion of these are 'imitations' of official coins, though we have no idea to what extent the copies were condoned. There is some evidence of semi-official striking of copies in urban public buildings.

In the 'old days', levels of Roman activity in towns and forts were often measured against the absolute numbers of coins found. So, if a town site produced a dozen coins of the period *c*.100-150, but twenty times that number from 260-300, that was taken as evidence of intensification of occupation. In more recent years an enormous amount of work has been done to examine the coins stored in hoards (**64 & colour plate 5**), those deposited on religious sites, and those casually lost as single items. This has made it possible to prove that between AD 64 and 154 base-metal coins of certain periods, and sometimes exact years, entered Britain in large consignments (**65 & 66**). Many of these base-metal coins remained in service until at least the late 200s, when the coinage system underwent enormous changes. And, like base-metal coinage across the Roman Empire, these coins very largely remained within Britain. In other words, once dispersed into Roman Britain's coin pool, they stayed there.

This was because in the Roman world, just as in the medieval world, wealth was moved around in silver and gold. Bullion is far more valuable than bronze

64 *Part of the Shapwick (Somerset) hoard of 9238 silver* denarii, *found in a villa close to the road north-west from Ilchester*

65 *A pair of bronze asses of Domitian for the year 86, struck at the mint of Rome. Like* **66** *the coins are unworn. They were struck from the same dies and probably represent part of a consignment shipped directly to London for provincial dispersal. The reverses depict Minerva carrying scales. Actual diameter 26mm*

66 *Bronze as of Marcus Aurelius as emperor designate, struck in the year 154 during the reign of Antoninus Pius (138-61), and of an issue only usually found in Britain. The reverse depicts a figure of Mars carrying a spear. Field-walking find from the small roadside settlement at Asthall (Oxon). The coin is virtually 'as struck' and had probably only just arrived in Britain when it was lost. Actual diameter 24mm*

or copper, it is universally accepted, and a great deal of wealth can be packed into a small volume. The Shapwick hoard was found in 1998 on a villa site close to the main road heading north-west from the Roman town at Ilchester (**64**). A total of 9,238 silver *denarii* were recovered, with the latest belonging to the reign of Severus Alexander (222-35). So, the hoard belongs to the latter part of his reign or some point in the next few years. We know nothing about this individual hoarder, but we can imagine that his commercial activity or business took him to Ilchester, Exeter, or perhaps even Bath and Cirencester. Here he might have been paid in silver on government business, or he or his bailiff could engage in whatever his trade was and, at the end of the day, carry the takings to a money-changer where it was converted into silver. It was rather like paying the takings into a bank account, except of course that the Shapwick villa owner's 'bank' consisted of stacking the coins into rows and rolling them up in cloth or leather, before burying the package below the floor in the corner of a room in his villa.

Some of the silver in the hoard came from Syria and Egypt. Perhaps the Shapwick hoarder had spent time there or, more likely, those coins came with soldiers, officials or traders who came to Britain and who had, in turn, converted their silver into bronze for day-to-day transactions. Moneylenders and moneychangers were a routine part of Roman town life, and they made a living out of charging a percentage on each exchange, or building it into the rates. A silver *denarius* was technically equal to four brass *sestertii*, but a man wishing to turn his change into bullion before returning home would probably find it cost him between four and five *sestertii* to buy each *denarius*. Another way to profit on changing money was making forgeries, and the Shapwick hoarder had twenty-five fakes in his hoard – *denarii* made of copper with a silver skin. He might never have known this at the time. Forgers' equipment of the early third century from the area suggests a contemporary local counterfeiter, perhaps feeding the money-changing trade in the canton of the Durotriges.

Severus Alexander's silver coins are not scarce in Britain or indeed anywhere else. But his base-metal coins are virtually unknown in Britain though they are abundant in Italy and North Africa. When the Shapwick hoarder changed his bronze into silver, he will have handed over mostly worn old coinage, some of which had by then been circulating for more than a century. It was similar coinage that made up almost all the casual losses of coins that archaeologists recover from their trenches and spoil heaps. But it would be completely wrong to assume these automatically reflect day-to-day activity. Thriving markets and other commercial areas are filled with people and children who might pick up coins other people had lost while normal cleaning and sweeping would pick up much of what was left. At Verulamium in the fourth century the theatre had fallen out of use and became a rubbish tip. The *macellum* across the road might have been one of the sources of the refuse. At any rate the rubbish in the theatre included a lot of coins, but displaced and moved about they are really meaningless as evidence for commercial activity.

There is no doubt that coins, especially low-value ones, were favoured as casual votive offerings. They turn up in unequivocally religious contexts like the sacred spring at Bath but we also know from a few literary references, like Lucretius' account of the ceremonial parade of Cybele, that copper and silver coins were thrown into the street as a figure of the goddess approached. Counterfeiting was always an issue but there is a marked difference between the instances of forgeries that turn up as singletons, compared to those found in hoards. Although silver hoards rarely contain forgeries, up to half of 'silver' coins found individually in towns or at temples can turn out to be fakes. One of the gate-towers of the 'London gate' at Verulamium contained what seems to have been a forger's die, or a stolen official one (which would be very hard to explain in Britain), for the reverse of a silver or gold coin of Hadrian. In London a tower on the wall contained clay moulds for producing forged copies of coins of Septimius Severus and his sons, with melted-down base-metal coins found alongside the moulds. At Bath many of even the base-metal offerings were counterfeit. Clearly the Romano-British were discerning about what they lost or gave away, making the pool of coins in active circulation rather different from money used to accumulate savings.

Even if supplies of base-metal coinage were erratic, the fact that the coinage turns up at all, and often in a very worn state, provides us with ample physical proof that they circulated and changed hands far more frequently than silver and gold. The colossal abundance of coin production from the 260s up until the late fourth century (though supply remained episodic), including copies, shows that they must have been needed and had to have played a part in the economy. But we have no idea to what extent. The very fact that we have so many is because they were discarded, either as a result of being demonetized when the coinage went through one of its reform phases, or because their low value meant they were used in change and rapidly discarded due to their inconvenience and the connotations of poverty in being used in large quantities. Today, the American one-cent piece is distributed in billions, and is normally used to make up change after a cash transaction. A high proportion are used just once this way, and then exit the currency pool by being discarded into myriad jars, bowls or sidewalk cracks.

A comprehensive survey of coins found in the sacred spring at Bath has shown that there were several low denomination coin issues that were peculiar to Britain both in terms of type and date. River spoil at Billingsgate in London contained numerous coins of many dates but there was a particular group issued in the middle years of Domitian's reign. A number appeared to have been in 'as struck' condition, and several of these were from the same dies (**65**). Amongst these are the 'Britannia' *as* of Antoninus Pius of 154 and an *as* of Marcus Aurelius as emperor designate (heir apparent) for the same year (**66**) both of which are relatively common in Britain but rare elsewhere. They may represent a consignment of coinage shipped direct from the mint in Rome for official dispersal in London.

Coinage in the late third and fourth centuries

Late Roman coinage is a subject all on its own. Little is known for certain about the names of denominations, or even the hierarchy of values. During the third century a double-*denarius*, which we call the radiate or *antoninianus*, was introduced and it gradually replaced the *denarius*. Produced at a proportionately lower bullion value, people like the Shapwick hoarder spurned it and clung on to the better-quality *denarius*. Eventually the government ceased to issue the *denarius*, but a shortage of bullion and the political and military unrest of the third century led to the radiate degenerating into a coin that was nothing more than bronze with a silver wash (**67** & **68**). The absurd situation then existed where a second-century *sestertius* was 'worth' one-eighth of one of these degenerate bronze radiates, but actually contained ten-times as much metal.

Traders and their customers in the Britain from the 270s on used what coinage there was to hand, and if that meant the last of the 140-year-old *sestertii*, now virtually featureless, mingled with local copies of radiates then so be it. A hoard found at the small town of Alcester, *Alauna*, in Warwickshire had 95 radiates ending with Postumus (259-68) but its earliest coins were four worn *sestertii* of Trajan, by then at least 142 years old. If supply was unpredictable, and 'value' difficult to assess, then barter must also have played an active part in everyday dealing, while we also know from written records in other provinces that 'I-owe-you' dockets could be made out in terms of denominations without any actual money changing hands.

The disparity in face-value and metal content between radiates and the *sestertii* of course drove out the old *sestertius*, since the government and forgers alike could use the old coins to make new ones at a profit. In the third century the basilica at Silchester was being used by metalworkers and this activity seems to have included producing copies of coins of the Gallic Empire's rulers. A mould for a coin of Tetricus I (270-3) was found amongst the metalworking debris (**68**). The location in this instance makes it likely that this was being done with local official approval, perhaps in an effort to supply coin to help keep the urban economy going because official supplies had dried up. There was a fundamental incentive. Base-metal coins could be exchanged for bullion, so it was worth making it, even at the most appalling standard (**68**). Equally, from the government's point of view there was an advantage. Taxes paid in money had to be paid in gold and silver, so ordinary people had to be able to get hold of bullion to hand over to the state.

Making small change even smaller in size of course provoked inflation in an economy where people expected coins to be made of metal equal to their

67 *Bronze coins struck at London and issued during the reigns of Allectus (293-96), and Constantine I (307-37). The Allectan coin bears the mint-mark ML for* Moneta Londinii, *'Mint of London'. The Constantinian coin bears the mark PLN for* Pecunia LoNdinii, *and was struck before 325 when the mint was closed. See also* **colour plate 5**. *Actual diameters 22 and 24mm*

68 *Decline of the radiate.* Left to right: *Gordian III (238-44) on a coin from the Dorchester South Street hoard of 1933, still mostly silver; a base metal radiate of Tetricus I (270-3) similar to the types being produced in the basilica of Silchester during the latter part of the third century; and a degenerate, barbarous, copy from the 270s or 280s*

monetary worth. If the coin was made of low-value metal, and less of it, then its buying power dropped too, and that meant how much gold could be bought for a sack of bronze coins as well as wheat, bread or any other commodity. From the late third century on, continual efforts were made to stabilise the coinage in a series of reforms. Under Constantine I (307-37), at the top was the gold *solidus*, which replaced the old *aureus* (**98** & **107**). To a large extent the *solidus* took over the money-storing, tax-paying and government salary parts once played by both *denarius* and *aureus*. It was in every sense the gold sovereign of its age and it continued in this role until the Middle Ages. Silver was struck only occasionally, based on a unit we call the *siliqua* (**107**). A curiosity of Britain is that the *siliqua* appears to have been unusually favoured for bullion hoards of the fourth century, unlike almost all of the rest of the Empire. Perhaps this represents lower per-capita wealth, or even a historical preference for silver – we do not know.

Late gold and silver issues are recovered in minuscule quantities compared to the reckless abundance of fourth-century bronze coinage found in Britain and abroad. Ranging from the large so-called *cententionalis* to diminutive pieces smaller than a modern fivepence piece, they represent a confusing series of issues, reforms, legitimate pieces (**67**), the products of rebellious regimes (**99**), and the work of forgers ranging from the competent to blundering illiterates. They are common finds in towns and indeed on almost any fourth-century Romano-British site, with a conspicuous climax of coins struck between 364-78 and their copies. Most hoards from the late third century on are made up base-metal radiates, or later bronze issues, quite often in colossal numbers (**colour plate 5**). It seems that most late hoarders of Roman Britain had no choice but to accumulate savings in inconveniently bulky stashes of bronze, and abandoned them when coinage reforms rendered them worthless though it is absurd to suggest that in any one case we know *why* a hoard was not recovered. What makes these late bronze coins most interesting here is the fact that they seem to have been an essential part of life until the fifth century when supplies ceased, copying to make good a shortfall in supply ended, and the use of coinage in Britain diminished radically until it virtually disappeared. We will return to this, and what it meant for town life, in the last chapter.

Mints

In the western half of the Empire the principal sources of coins were Lyons (under Nero and Vespasian) and Rome until the middle of the third century when it became increasingly common for the government to issue coin regularly from other major cities like Lyons and Milan. Some of the major Romano-British towns later served as mints, but only for short periods, and even then London is the single definite candidate (**67** & **colour plate 5**). In

286 the commander of the Romano-British fleet, Carausius, took power in Britain and a small part of northern Gaul. In order to help consolidate and advertise his power he issued coins, some of which carried mintmarks. Initially he seems to have contented himself with over-striking earlier coins with his image. This may only have been for a few weeks and soon new coins were being produced. The mintmark M L must stand for *Moneta Londinii*, 'the Mint of London'. The mintmark C, or occasionally CL, may represent one of a number of places including Colchester (*Camulodunum*) and Gloucester (*Glevum*) or even Silchester (*Calleva*). Both the former mints were kept open by Carausius' murderer and successor Allectus but after the latter's defeat by the Roman forces under Constantius Chlorus in 296 they were closed. The London mint was opened up once again by Constantine I in about 306 (**colour plate 5**) but by 325 it seems to have been permanently closed, though the rebel Magnus Maximus (383-8) may have issued some gold from there but this is unlikely and certainly not proven (**99**). Thereafter, apart from domestic copying, Britain was supplied by mints like Trier, Arles, Lyons or, under the rebel Magnentius (350-3), Amiens.

Industry and trades in towns

Since we mainly depend on the vicissitudes of excavation for evidence of manufacturing it is easy to forget the obvious fact that all towns would have had metalworkers, leatherworkers, blacksmiths, launderers, fullers, carpenters, masons, tilers, potters and so on. The examples mentioned here are just that, and would have existed in some form in every major town and many smaller ones. Towns with a concentration of specialist skills generally supply services not easily provided in the countryside. There were sure to have been itinerant potters, scrap-metal merchants, blacksmiths and the like who toured the countryside seeking business, and some rural estates were bound to have been more or less self contained. But for a craftsman or merchant an urban location allows him to store his tools, equipment and stock and also advertise his presence. A rural customer could visit a town and know that a number of jobs would be dealt with, or commission a trader to come and visit him at home. We might imagine the villa owner or his foreman bringing his produce to sell and taking the opportunity to have a horse's harness repaired, a leaking bronze jug plugged, purchase imported wine and change some money into gold and silver to add to the concealed hoard at home. A weekly or monthly market would also have attracted the travelling tinkers to offer their services. This is not an idle fantasy – towns supply exactly the same sort of services today because without a rendezvous, trade and industry cannot function. Even the most self-sufficient villa estate would have needed an outlet for its produce.

Not all trade of course took place in markets. Until modern times it was just as usual, and sometimes more convenient, for traders to visit customers at home. Towns provide the perfect concentration of demand. In his play *The Pot of Gold*, Plautus described the succession of doorstep merchants who harassed householders for payment: weavers, laundrymen, dye-sellers, cobblers, goldsmiths (**73**), dressmakers, and so on. They perhaps included the oculists who used engraved stone dies to stamp their solid cakes of medicine, which turn up surprisingly often. One from Kenchester names Titus Vindacius Ariovistus and his various products like *chloron* ('green salve') and *anicetum* ('infallible salve'). Distribution of the stamps suggests not only that their owners were itinerants, but also that they had been bought or acquired by secondary users who manufactured proprietary compounds according to well-known recipes and stamped the results to give them commercial credibility. The important point to bear in mind is that an archaeologist might find that a forum or *macellum* had been allowed to fall into disrepair, and assume that the town's economy had decayed. That, self-evidently, might not have been the case at all.

Industrial activities were controlled both privately and publicly by organizations. There is some evidence for the existence of guilds, known as *collegia*, in Romano-British towns, reminding us of the Piazza of Corporations at Ostia. The Chichester temple inscription records a local guild of smiths (*collegium fabrorum*) some time around the middle of the first century (**108** & appendix 2). Other guilds are known from Silchester (**114**) and near Verulamium but these are not specifically associated with any particular craft or trade. It is less easy to know what date these belong to, but the late first century has been suggested for Silchester.

There was a government weaving factory (*gynaecium*) at one of the Romano-British towns prefixed *Venta* (the *Notitia Dignitatum*, a fourth-century document, is not specific). It would have been used during the fourth century to supply the army. Incidentally, weaving is the sort of industry that is very hard to identify or attribute in any settlement apart from artefacts like weaving combs or loom weights. The actual cloth survives only in exceptional conditions, or as impressions in material like gypsum used to pack inhumations. Obviously, it is impossible to know *where* the cloth was made, but when the material was silk (as in a Colchester child's grave in the Butt Road cemetery) it must have been imported rather than made locally. Goods produced for, or by, provincial authorities were bagged up and sealed for security. A small lead seal was clamped over the tie used to close a sack, and was stamped. A fourth-century example from Silchester was marked with a *chi-rho*, then an imperial symbol, and the letters PMC for *Provincia Maxima Caesariensis*, one of the four provinces Britain was divided into by then.

In London tiles were made in the name of the provincial government (**69**). Civic authorities could also directly control some urban manufacturing. After all, there were public buildings to erect and maintain and they needed support

69 *Tile stamps from Romano-British towns as evidence for public and private tileries.* Clockwise from upper left: *PP BR LON, the stamp of the Procurator of the Province of* Britannia *at London, from London (see also* **colour plate 24***); ARVERI, '[tilery] of Arverus', from Cirencester; RPG QQ IVL FLOR ET COR SM, for 'Res Publica Glevensium, (in the year of) the* quinquennales *[civic magistrates] Julius Florus and Cornelius Sim(ilis?)'. The latter seems to be evidence for a city-owned tilery in the* colonia *at Gloucester, administered by elected civic magistrates. The Arverus tiles are well-known around Cirencester but one found near Caldicot (Monmouthshire) shows how far products like this could be dispersed, though Arverus may have travelled to build a tilery there to fulfil a commission*

industries and crafts. The evidence found at the Caerwent basilica suggests that local stone was quarried and brought to the site where decorative features like columns and capitals were carved by masons. The colony of Gloucester manufactured tiles stamped RPG for *Rei Publicae Glevensium* and named the magistrates for the year. One site in London has also produced a number of tiles marked with a stamp of what seems to have been a private concern owned by two men who both had the same first name, Decimus. Their stamp read DMVAL DMP TECVLAR, or 'tiles [*teculariae*] of Decimus M... Val... and Decimus M... P....' Another fragment of tile, inscribed before being fired, may record part of a London tile kiln work roster (**54**). Apart from stamping his product with his name a tiler might manufacture distinctive products like the Medusa terminals from Colchester (**70**).

Metalworking

Other towns featured industrial activities as part of a rather broader spectrum of commercial activity. Verulamium is the best example of a town containing evidence for artisans making a living. This was mainly in the form of metalworking, fortunately the kind of activity that tends to leave identifiable traces in the archaeological record, like fragments of scrap, ceramic crucibles or moulds, and slag. Evidence like this has shown that a gold-worker was running some sort of business in the middle of London close to the later site

70 *Moulded antefix tile from Colchester depicting a head of Medusa. The tile was inserted into the bottom row of roof tiles in order to provide a decorative trim. It was probably made in a local tilery. Diameter 18cm*

of the so-called governor's palace in the Flavian period. Towards the end of the third century the basilica at Silchester seems to have become, at least in part, the workshop of bronze and iron smiths (**68**). Some of these workshops, known as *officina*, stamped their products (**71**). The small town of Castleford in West Yorkshire has produced a unique find of the remains of a manufactory for bronze and silver spoons: over 800 baked clay moulds have been found (**72**).

The small settlements at Nettleton and Camerton on the Fosse Way are known to have had facilities for casting tableware in pewter during the fourth century. There must have been numerous establishments like this in towns all over the province turning out small metal artefacts. Brooches, one of the most common finds from Roman sites, were almost certainly made in town-based factories as well as by itinerant craftsmen though evidence for all this is very limited. An unfinished brooch blank from the small settlement at Baldock points to a brooch-maker working there, while in North Norfolk evidence for isolated brooch manufacturing in a remote rural setting at Old Buckenham shows this kind of work did not have to take place in towns. The Old Buckenham brooch-maker used bronze two-piece moulds and could quite easily have carted his basic tools and equipment around, perhaps setting up in town markets or fairs throughout the year. Indeed, the location of the find close to a Roman road has led to the suggestion that a bag of equipment fell from a cart as it passed. Total speculation of course, but it explains the comprehensive lack of any other material. The discovery of this brooch-making kit shows just how much the evidence we have to hand depends on total chance. Perhaps some brooch-making was franchised at an official level. Some of the brooches made at Castleford, *Lagitium*, were made in moulds marked *Fibula Ex Reg(ione) Lagitiense*, 'Brooch from the Lagitian region'. A distinctive group of brooches with marked catch-plates has been identified recently as being distributed in and around Gloucester, which was probably where they were made.

We can safely assume that almost all towns had some sort of metal industry though we know very little about the individuals. At Colchester an undated bronze plaque has been found which records a dedication to the god Silvanus Callirius by one Cintusmus the coppersmith (*aerarius*). He was probably someone who worked in the town. An actual establishment is testified in the *vicus* at Malton where a building stone, also undated, bore a dedication to the Genius of a goldsmith's shop (**73**). Knives and other utensils were sometimes stamped with a manufacturer's name, for example Basilis who probably made his iron-bladed knives in London. By definition though, finished goods were normally sold and so turn up in places where the customer lost or hid them. A magnificent gladiator-handled penknife found at the Piddington villa (Northants) is exceptional, and we have no idea where it was made. It was, perhaps, a souvenir of a day at the games in a town.

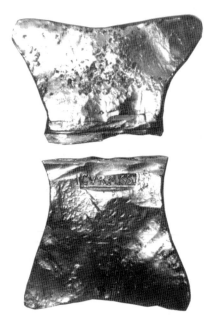

71 *Silver ingot stamped [EX OFF] CVRMISSI, 'from the workshop of Curmissus'. This ingot is from the late/post-Roman hoard of treasure buried at Coleraine (Northern Ireland), and probably booty stolen from Britain. The text can be restored from a complete example found in Kent. Normally originally issued as bullion donatives such ingots were probably manufactured in London or on the continent. Some owners may have given them to silversmiths to produce fine plate*

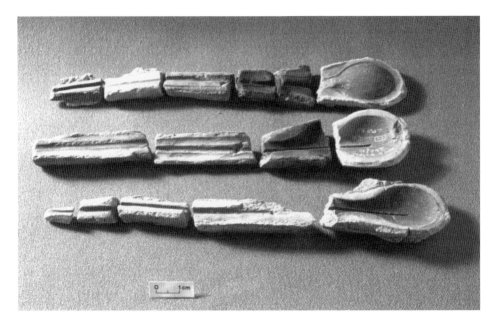

72 *Spoon moulds from Castleford* (Lagitium), *Yorkshire. Part of a unique find of evidence for spoon manufacture.* Courtesy of West Yorkshire Archaeology Service

73 *A building stone from Malton* (Derventio), *Yorkshire, recording a dedication to the Genius of a goldsmith's workshop. It reads:* FELICITER SIT (Happiness be...) GENIO LOCI (...to the Genius of this place) SERVULE UTERE (Young slave be..) FELIX TABERNAM UREFICINAM (...happy in this goldsmith's shop). *The inscription is exceptionally crude, and very difficult to read; the lettering has therefore been electronically enhanced here*

Pottery manufacture

Metal of course retains some sort of value, whatever state it is in. Pottery has virtually no value unless it is complete or an expensive ware, considered worthy of repair. The presence of pottery is one of the most obvious clues to a site of Roman date because of the prodigious amount and range used and its almost complete disappearance during the fifth century. As a result, a vast amount of broken pottery was dumped throughout the Roman period and it can form an excellent, if limited, indicator of the kind of area over which a Roman town might have had an economic influence if the fabric of the pottery can be identified and tied to a kiln source. Although it is often possible to identify fabrics and sources, there are numerous examples of wares that turn up and that defy attribution. Kilns can turn up in almost any context, and vary from single-use versions found in isolation to those found in large clusters belonging to longer-lasting industries. They also vary immensely in type (**74**) and it is worth bearing in mind that basic kitchenwares could be fired in surface bonfires called 'clamps'.

74 *Late first-century kiln, discovered at Sedgefield (Durham). This kiln was found in an exceptional state of preservation as it was abandoned before a firing went wrong and caused collapse (the usual reason for abandoning a kiln). The kiln was built in a specially dug pit and its dome with air vents is almost complete. Inside vessels were stacked on a perforated floor through which hot fumes circulated from the stokehole off to the side (at upper left). Kilns like this would have existed in almost every Romano-British town or village though simpler surface 'clamps' (bonfires) and larger industrial-scale kilns were also used. Diameter of the dome approximately 1.1m*

Almost every settlement in Roman Britain would have had potters working at some time. An example of how small-scale an industry could be is the so-called 'Sugar Loaf Court' potter in London, whose kiln has been found. Working in the late first century, this potter produced a simple range of kitchen-wares for local sale. But some places developed into major industries. Generally these were in rural areas where it was easy to obtain fuel, water and clay but which were also accessible by road or water. The pottery industry known as Black-Burnished 2, for example, consisted of a number of dispersed kiln sites around the Thames estuary. During the first and second centuries some of the major towns like Colchester had potteries situated in their outskirts. The industry that developed here was particularly important and it contrasts with the Romano-British pottery industries that developed in the third and fourth centuries, and which were almost entirely divorced from urban centres. At Lincoln in the fourth century, nearby kilns at Swanpool serviced local needs.

As a colony, Colchester was largely populated from the beginning by people who had romanized tastes, as the West Stockwell Street lamp-manufacturer, and the 'samian shop', demonstrate. Although this would have extended to as much of their way of life as possible, pottery is one of the few means that we can use to identify such habits. A great deal of pottery was imported during the first and second centuries with the fine ware component being dominated by Gaulish samian. However, potters identified a ready market in early Colchester and by the mid-first century colour-coated cups and beakers mostly modelled on examples made in Gaul were being produced nearby.

By the early second century Colchester's local industry had become more adventurous and productive, making a wider range of forms which were them-selves being traded further afield in Britain, even reaching the northern frontier. Much the most distinctive are the decorated beakers but the potters were also manufacturing large quantities of the special kitchen mixing bowl, the *mortarium*. These were transported in large numbers to the military sites in the north until the early third century. *Mortaria* seem to have been made by potters who specialized in their production.

Around the year 160 a group of samian potters from East Gaul appear to have also identified Colchester as a good place to work, since they set up kilns close to the town. Perhaps they were encouraged by a *negotiator* who had lost too many consignments to shipwrecks and en-route breakages. Their mould-decorated products resemble East Gaulish styles, hence the assumption about where the potters came from. But they were unsuccessful because, while a great deal of debris including fragments of more than 400 moulds was found, the samian is barely known outside the vicinity of Colchester. The recovery of pieces of unfired pots suggests a swift termination to potting on the site but this could have been due to anything, perhaps frustration at inadequate clays or resistance from local vested interests, and there need be no sinister conno-tations. Curiously the other well-established parts of the local industry seem to have also had trouble keeping customers and eventually many of their markets (especially the army) seem to have had to buy from Nene Valley potters.

During the third and fourth centuries major pottery industries in Roman Britain were more likely to be rural in location but sometimes an industry was so successful that a major town grew up around the kiln sites, and became more than just an appendage to the industry. The best-known example of this in Roman Britain was the Nene Valley pottery industry that became centred on the town at Water Newton (*Durobrivae*) just to the west of modern Peterborough (**75**). A pottery industry had existed here since at least the beginning of the second century and possibly earlier but it was only of local significance. Throughout this time the fine ware market in Roman Britain was so dominated by the Gaulish samian ware industry that other sources of pottery had only limited success. By the end of the second century the samian ware potteries had entered a period of steep decline and their products gradually disappeared from the Romano-British market-place over the next twenty or thirty years. A few industries in Britain stepped in to fill the gap and the Nene Valley was one of them. They supplied colour-coated bowls and dishes that emulated some samian forms and also a series of drinking beakers, sometimes

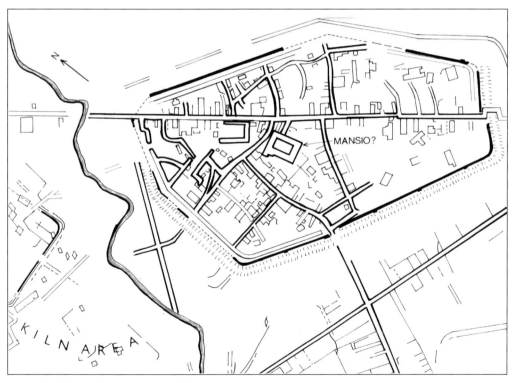

75 *Plan of the town at Water Newton (*Durobrivae*) which grew up largely as a result of the pottery industry in the area, capitalizing on its location on a major road and access to water transport. The sites of what may have been a* mansio *and an earlier fort are marked. After Mackreth*

decorated with appliqué figures of animals known as 'hunt cups' (**63**). *Mortaria* were also made, and on one unique example the potter signed his work and where he had fired it (**colour plate 23**).

The Nene Valley potters were well placed. Although their various kiln sites straggled along the banks of the Nene for several miles, the main road from London to the north (Ermine Street) passed through the area and the town of *Durobrivae* had grown up along it. The river Nene would have almost certainly served for transporting the products to the North Sea where they could be shipped to the northern frontier and southwards to London. Whatever the routes used, they were effective, for Nene Valley products are found widely distributed in Roman Britain. Interestingly, Water Newton is one of very few towns that had several villas in very close proximity. If at other towns laws and urban farming interests controlled town hinterlands, Water Newton can be explained by the townsfolk being primarily engaged in potting and servicing passing trade, with villa owners dealing with farming nearby or even owning and managing some of the potteries.

While *Durobrivae* grew to be a place of some consequence, very few large-scale potteries were located in or near the *civitas* capitals or *coloniae* in the third and fourth centuries. Instead many important pottery centres seem to be almost as far away from towns as possible. The Oxfordshire, New Forest and Alice Holt industries consist of regional groups of kiln sites quite unconnected with the major towns one would have assumed to have been their principal markets (and indeed were). Why? There are all sorts of possibilities and no facts. For example, did the élite in the *civitates* tend to stifle local production (of whatever sort) through their control of movements and taxation? Or, alternatively was access to the Thames (and therefore most of the province) of greater importance to the Oxfordshire and Alice Holt industries? As we know nothing of taxation in Roman Britain or pottery distribution controls it seems rash to make assumptions and generalizations based on the hypothetical effects of hypothetical systems. Instead we must content ourselves with the observation and remember that these possibilities may also have affected other industries like food production, which are much more poorly represented in the archaeological record.

The important point here is the development of the town. Like London, *Durobrivae* was not an official foundation but unlike London it was not apparently elevated to formal status (though we should not ignore the possibility that it was, and that we simply do not know about it). It is clear from aerial photography that the town was never laid out in a regular fashion and probably had no building that served as a basilica or forum though there was probably an official inn (**75**). It was clearly a product of local commerce and industry, much as London had been in the first instance. Nevertheless the town could afford to provide its own earth fortifications consisting of a bank and a ditch. Little is known about the town, but a group of people were wealthy enough here to endow a Christian community in the vicinity with a substantial amount of silver plate in the third century, now known as the 'Water Newton Treasure' (**89**). It seems that the concept and convenience of towns was an idea sufficiently well established in the minds of the local community for them either to develop a town, or to put it another way, not to obstruct its natural growth given the local circumstances.

Glass manufacture

Glass was widely used in Roman Britain (**58** & **76**) but unlike pottery the fabric of the glass cannot usually be definitely associated with a specific place unless the style is peculiar to a region or the glass bears a mark. Even then, the mark is rarely of much use. A bottle found in London had been cast in a mould stamped by 'Briginus, freedman of Ingenuus', but that tells us nothing about where it was made. However, Cologne is known to have been a major source of glassware used in the north-west provinces, and Britain probably received a lot of glass from here but attribution of individual vessels is usually derived from probability rather than certainty, and is usually based on much larger numbers of similar finds in the Rhineland. A tiny 'gold-in-glass' bead found in a late third-century context in London's New Fresh Wharf belongs to a class believed to have been made in the Black Sea area, on the other side of the Roman Empire.

76 *Not surprisingly, Roman glassware scarcely ever turns up in urban contexts other than in a thoroughly smashed state, making the vessel type sometimes very hard to identify. Most complete vessels have been found in cemeteries where they were deposited as grave goods. This example of a small globular jug is from Winchester and is dated to the late fourth century. Usual height for this type is between 10 and 12cm*

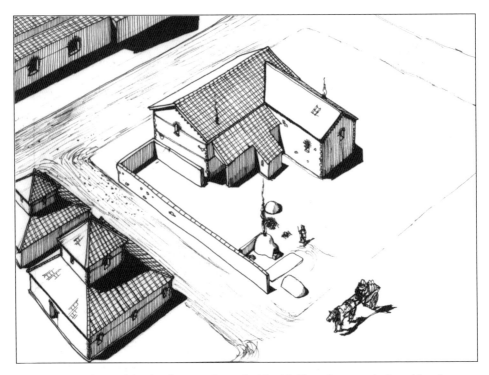

77 *Reconstructed view of the glass factory at Caistor-by-Norwich* (Venta Icenorum). *Several hearths were found along with debris from glass manufacturing*

Manufacture could take place in towns or in a rural location, depending on availability of fuel and reasonable access to markets. These considerations, and the risk of breakage, would favour a town-orientated industry but it is clear that glassware was used widely in the countryside, perhaps made by itinerant craftsmen. At the Lullingstone villa in Kent, some 25km (16 miles) from the nearest town, fragments of several hundred glass vessels were found. Glass used for windows was thicker, cruder, and more easily made. It was much more likely to be made widely across Britain than fine table glassware as an obvious matter of convenience, with production having to meet steadily increasing demand from the second century onwards in towns.

Glass manufacturing has been identified in Wroxeter, but a first-century date means that it might have belonged to the legionary fortress, rather than the *civitas* capital that followed. At Caistor-by-Norwich a glass manufacturing workshop consisted of a main L-shaped building divided roughly into two, with an access corridor from a partially enclosed courtyard. In the courtyard were the glass furnaces, presumably to minimize the risk from fire (**77**). Of course we have no idea of where the products were sold but we might assume that this took place on the premises and perhaps in the forum, with a certain amount being re-sold locally by merchants. Other traces of glass manufacture are known, for example at London, Mancetter and Silchester, but owing to the nature of the product it is virtually certain that all major towns would have had a glass production factory at some time. Typical finds from a glass-working site are piles of waste glass called cullet (which of course could be recycled), hearths and ceramic crucibles.

The mosaic industry

The mosaics that were laid in Romano-British country houses in the fourth century belonged to what was by then a well-established tradition (**34**, **43**, **78**, **colour plates** 1, 9 & 12). As early as the mid-first century some exceptional country houses, particularly Fishbourne, were having mosaics installed, probably by mosaicists brought in from Gaul or even Italy. In time, a domestic industry would have developed and studies of mosaics have usually concluded that regional industries and traditions grew up centred on major towns, called 'schools', much in the same way that the style of a major artist of the Renaissance can be seen reflected in the work of his students and associates. Mosaics have the added advantage to archaeologists of not being mobile, though of course mosaicists were. The work is based on tracking the distribution of mosaics in similar styles in rural villas clustered around towns. It has been generally assumed that these distribution patterns, for example the Orpheus-type mosaics around Cirencester (*Corinium*), may be evidence for individual workshops in the towns in this case attributed to the early fourth century. In other words a master craftsman, or men, with assistants, worked from a town where he would be commissioned by villa owners to work in

78 *Low Ham (Somerset) villa. The mythical Roman hero Aeneas depicted out hunting on a large celebrated villa bath-suite mosaic that illustrates scenes from Virgil's famous* Aeneid. *Low Ham was one of many villas that clustered along the roads radiating from the town at Ilchester,* Lindinis. *Its owner, and the villa's economy, will have been dependent on, and influenced by, urban markets and services. The floor is thought to have been laid by mosaicists from Ilchester or Dorchester (Dorset). Fourth century*

their houses, possibly preparing complex panels in the workshop and then transporting them. However, there is no satisfactory way of distinguishing style-copying from original work.

In fact, the number of mosaics attributed to any one 'school' is fairly limited, about 14 being associated with the so-called *Corinium* 'Orpheus school' of which one is in London, one in Silchester, one in Dorchester and at least one in south Wales. While the workshops may have existed as 'schools' there is no convincing evidence for this being a town-based industry and it is hard to see what the advantage of a town location would have been unless this was where prefabricated panels were manufactured. We may be looking at regional fashions as much as school styles and even if there were 'schools' with master mosaicists working from towns they would actually have done most of their work at the villas. As with many aspects of Romano-British archaeology good ideas and theories have a habit of turning into facts: no actual town workshops have been identified. The urban mosaic industries are thus better regarded as phenomena tied to one man or his family, who happened to be based in one town and which depended on his personal reputation and the capacity of his firm to supply demand. As a high-class luxury product exclusivity was probably of more importance than availability, so mosaics can never be treated as an industry comparable with metalworking, potting and other basics.

The 'small' towns

There were many 'small' towns that defy easy categorization because despite their size little is known about them except that they were not towns with formal status. A number of these, like Alcester, Ancaster and Mancetter, have already been mentioned. The *civitas* capitals and the colonies were relatively early foundations. Most seem to have been in existence by the end of the first century. The small towns took rather longer to develop and apart from their relatively small size the only consistent feature is that a major road usually ran through the centre (**79**). Buildings were laid out in a haphazard fashion resembling medieval villages and towns with winding streets. In fact this is how some *civitas* capitals started life. The difference is that the 'small towns' stayed that way.

At Sandy (Beds) excavations showed a series of houses built gable-end-on to a road, perhaps to maximise the number of establishments with a street frontage. This is found elsewhere, for example at Catterick and early London. The overall impression, as at most other small towns, is a lack of co-ordinated or supervised town development. Burial within the settlement at Sandy seems even to have been tolerated, in spite of the fact that it was theoretically prohibited by law. Very few small towns, for example Dorn (Glos) and Kenchester (Herefs), had defences. There are exceptions, Alchester (Oxon), for example, lies a little way from a major road and also had a regular street grid.

IMPC
FL·VA
CONSTANTINO
P·F·INV·
AVG
DIVI
CONSTANTI
PII AVG
FILIO

79 *Ancaster (Lincs), milestone. Milestones were erected throughout Roman Britain's road network, but they seem to have been frequently and erratically replaced. Most surviving examples belong to the third and very early fourth centuries. The majority were carved with just the emperor's name and titles, so that they could be used anywhere. Details of the distance to the next town were probably painted on. This example carries the name of Constantine I (307-37), and states that he was the son of Constantius I. It was found 0.5km north of the small Roman town at Ancaster, which sat astride Ermine Street, the main road from London to Lincoln. Height 71cm*

Some small towns may originally have grown up around forts, for example at Wall (*Letocetum*) in Staffordshire (**45**) but it is just as likely that the forts were sited close to traditional gathering places so it is perhaps more likely that the majority had some basis in pre-Roman Britain. This was certainly the case where towns like Baldock (Herts) and Great Chesterford (Cambs) were concerned. Even where the small town developed close to, rather than on, the site of a late Iron Age centre this was likely to be where the latter was not located in a place suitable for a road to run through. It had therefore been by-passed and thus the nucleus of settlement was likely to drift. Like the *civitas* capitals the reasons were likely to be more than one in any individual case, with a fort, and then a *mansio*, for example playing key roles at different times.

Catterick, for example, had a substantial *mansio*. Although it seems to have been demolished in the third century it seems not to have affected the rest of the settlement's survival, even to the extent that in the fourth century the settlement was equipped with defences.

It can hardly be coincidence that the small and major towns generally lie in places between 16 and 32km (10 and 20 miles) apart along roads. This sort of distance was roughly equivalent to a day's journey on foot or by cart. Passing trade would have therefore influenced the development of small towns at sites in an appropriate location, such as Crayford and Springhead that lie on Watling Street between London and Rochester, at a day's journey or thereabouts from a major town. Along and around these roads in the fertile south and some parts of the north, villas and their attendant villages clustered (**colour plate 19**). Towns depended on villa estates for food, while the villa estates and villages depended on towns for markets and specialist services. Catterick, for example, had leather-workers and unusually this is even testified by a late-first-century document from Vindolanda that mentions how one load had been suspended due to the state of the roads.

Local self-sufficiency for basics was just as important because long-distance river and road traffic and trade was almost certainly confined to a period between April and October, as it remained until modern times. During the winter small settlements would have played a vital role in serving the needs of outlying farms and houses whose occupants would have been unable to travel far. At Sandy evidence for small-scale trade and industry came from the metalworking debris that had accumulated in a stream that ran through the little town.

There were many small towns that seem to have depended on the existence of local specialist industries or the extraction of resources. In the Roman world the majority of mines were owned by the imperial government and adminis-tered on its behalf by a procurator who acted like a kind of small-scale governor. He controlled all activities on the site even to the extent of restricting services like shoe-making to approved concessionaires. Mines were also controlled by the army in the initial phases of a conquest and subsequently could be leased to private entrepreneurs, though a fixed proportion of metal remained government property. Naturally mines required a considerable amount of labour and this was usually slave or forced. Can we really call a mining settlement a town? In the true sense of the word, probably not but the communities themselves would have come to resemble small straggling villages with many of the various activities associated with town life.

At Charterhouse in the Mendips lead mines were in operation as early as *c.*50. Lead was a vital commodity because it was the only substance known at the time that could be readily manipulated and hammered into a variety of shapes. In other words it served some of the functions that are now fulfilled by plastics. It was essential for the manufacture of piping and waterproofing, and was also the main component of pewter. Pewter became particularly popular in the fourth century as an economical form of plate, since when new and polished it resembles silver. As we saw above the small settlements at Camerton and Nettleton on the Fosse Way both became manufacturing centres. Lead in an impure form contains silver and this was an added attraction of its exploitation. We know that British lead was considered valuable enough to be exported. A cistern found at Pompeii seems to have been made of British lead. Charterhouse was an extensive settlement though very little is known about its buildings. These however included a small amphitheatre constructed from earthen banks, probably once fitted with wooden seats. It might have been more accurately a cock or bear pit though it could have been associated with an as-yet undiscovered temple, and been used for religious festivals.

The small town at Brampton in north Norfolk appears to have developed as a result of specialization in pottery and production of iron and lasted from the first century at least until the end of the third. It is particularly interesting that the settlement had a wharf, giving it access to the river Bure which meets the coast in the vicinity of the third-century shore fort at Burgh Castle and another site nearby at Caister-on-Sea (now identified as a possible fort or fortified port rather than a conventional civilian settlement). This makes it virtually certain that Brampton's products were traded over some distance. The presence of iron-works is proved by the large quantities of slag found, with some buildings apparently being used by metalworkers. Pottery production was mainly in the form of straightforward kitchen wares though some potters seem to have concentrated on making flagons and *mortaria*, which require more skill, and were generally made by specialists.

Between London and Verulamium the small settlement at Brockley Hill, *Sulloniacis*, was a major production centre for *mortaria* and flagons. The *mortaria* potters stamped their names on their products, which have as a result been identified over a wide area, but especially in the south-east. Sited on a main road, it was well placed to make the most of the main markets in London and Verulamium, both of which were only a day's journey away (**80**).

There are many other examples of small towns that seem to have more or less entirely depended on the existence of specific specialist industries. They included Droitwich in the west Midlands, called *Salinae* indicating its connection with salt. A considerable amount of evidence in the form of buildings, storage containers and by-products, has been found for the extraction of salt from salt-bearing springs. The town at Middlewich in Cheshire seems to have had a similar industrial base. The one consistent factor is that these small industrial towns never really developed into anything particularly significant. Largely anonymous in the ancient record, we often do not know their former names and they rarely produce structural evidence for anything other than simple buildings – though they have in the past been the subjects of minimal archaeological attention.

80 *Potters' name-stamps on* mortaria *(mixing bowls) provide useful evidence for the transport of goods around Britain. Near London the small town of Brockley Hill,* Sulloniacis, *grew up in the late first century around potteries. Finds on the site have produced evidence for kilns and the potters who worked there. Left to right: Marinus, c.70-110; Doinus, c.70-110, from the Thames at London; Iunius, c.100-140, field-walking surface find from Brockley Hill. See also* **colour plates 21 & 23**

The perceived slow development of small towns has been linked to a hypothetical change in taxation from gathering of tax in cash to a more localised collection of goods in kind, such as crops. This would have reduced the stimulus to obtain cash by selling produce or services in a market; but we should be wary of such a sophisticated explanation when the available evidence is so limited. Alternatively, we could imagine the *civitates* reaching maturity in the third century, having benefited from early investment and therefore exhibiting less evidence for development at this time. The small towns may have benefited from the development of the countryside, perhaps supplying services and markets to the increased number of more affluent villas in the third and fourth centuries, though even at the largest and most developed the small towns were hardly impressive expressions of Roman urban life. Of course, the small towns in reality consisted of many dozens of different settlements each with a unique set of factors lying behind both beginnings and sustained growth. We have to recognize this and accept that only in a very few cases can we suggest reasons for their existence. Water Newton was one but there were also the towns that grew up around the site of a shrine. Bath is the best known but there were also others such as Ancaster and Springhead. These are discussed in more detail in chapter 6.

The vicus

The word *vicus* is normally applied to settlements that grew up outside forts. Those that developed outside legionary fortresses were called *canabae*, 'the hutments'. Usually described by us as 'civilian', in reality they probably contained populations made up of soldiers, ex-soldiers, military families, traders, prostitutes, and others whose livelihood depended on helping troops spend their pay or providing essential services.

Earlier on we saw how the presence of forts may possibly have played a role in promoting the development of towns, but in all the cases mentioned the forts like that at Cirencester were given up at a relatively early date, leaving the civil settlement to survive on its own merits. The northern and western part of the province remained a military zone throughout Romano-British history with a number of forts being consolidated in stone and becoming permanent features. In these cases the civilian settlements remained suburbs of the forts around which they had grown up. Whether we can really regard them as towns is a problem but it is likely that they functioned as local centres and markets of a sort. Most such settlements are known from aerial photography, for example at Old Carlisle in Cumbria, or outside many of the forts on Hadrian's Wall, and probably date from around the middle of the second century.

At Vindolanda, where the fort *vicus* is one of the very few to have been excavated, the circumstantial evidence of coin loss suggests that the *vicus* may have fallen out of use long before the fort was abandoned by the end of the fourth century. However, it is probably safe to assume that the *vici* would have continued to exist in some shape or form as long as the fort existed. Unlike the short-lived *vici* in southern Britain it is not so easy to see an association between an existing native settlement and a fort. In the north they were rather more likely to be a direct consequence of the fort alone and as such, considerably more dependent. Some gained a semblance of formal identity. The *vicani Vindolandesses* name themselves for us on an inscription from the fort at Vindolanda. Another, of second- or third-century date, from near Vindolanda records a dedication to a goddess called Sattada by the senate (*curia*) of the 'Textoverdi'. These were almost certainly the inhabitants and government of the immediate area, with a centre in the *vicus* at Vindolanda (**colour plate 19**) or more probably a few miles away at Corbridge. So even if Vindolanda's *vicus* was a consequence of the fort there may already have been something of an established tribal community in the area. However, it is equally likely that people were also drawn from the general vicinity of a fort, attracted by the obvious captive demand.

Most military *vici* consist of fairly simple buildings straggling along the roads leading to the fort though in the most elaborate instances an independent street pattern grew up. Like more conventional small towns these are usually irregular. The buildings tend to resemble the early commercial strip-house properties found in the major towns of the first and second centuries though occasionally more elaborate courtyard structures resembling inns have been identified. In a number of instances, Old Carlisle and Housesteads being two of the most conspicuous, field boundaries and terraces can also be seen and this creates an impression of forts which, together with their civilian annexes, were probably largely self-sufficient though obviously we do not know to what extent agricultural land was farmed by the soldiers. This would have had obvious advantages – the unique collection of writing tablets from

Vindolanda's late first-century fort shows that supplying an outpost with food and goods was a complex and arduous task. By the third century there may not have been a clear distinction between military and civilian interests and it is probably better to see these forts and their *vici* as single units, especially in the third and fourth centuries, where soldiers lived with families in the civilian settlements. It ceases to be possible to differentiate groups of finds from fort or *vicus* and in reality there had probably come to be no practical distinction. Their sons probably went on to join the unit while the fathers retired to the *vicus* to carry on an established family business or smallholding. In time, as garrisons were denuded in the fourth century and a climate of insecurity took over, the *vicus* communities probably withdrew into what were by then rather rundown fort compounds.

6

RELIGION IN TOWNS

Religion in Roman Britain is one of the best-testified activities, but it also presents some of the most difficult problems. Identifying cult activity from artefacts alone is a notoriously suspect activity, unless the context is definitive. A good example of such a definitive context is a temple precinct, but a small bronze statue of a god or goddess found amongst the general debris of a metalworking shop might have been there for scrap, or displayed as a guardian of the trade.

Inscriptions present us with a more reliable source of material. Of all the inscriptions that survive from Roman Britain, the majority are linked in some way with cult activity or burial. Most are offerings or dedications that name a deity, but often little else apart from the name of the donor. However, about eighty-five inscriptions from Britain specifically refer to buildings, and of these about thirty-seven are concerned with temples, shrines, or the entrances to religious precincts, the best-represented class of all. Many of the actual buildings referred to do not survive, making these invaluable records. Unfortunately the majority of inscriptions in general, and those referring to buildings in particular, come from the military zone though a useful exception is the third-century altar from London that mentions a temple of Isis (**112**). But there is plenty of structural and artefact evidence that helps build up a picture of religion in Roman Britain's towns. In chapter 3 the importance of the theatre and amphitheatre to religious ceremonies was touched on, and it emphasises how religion was so integral to Romano-British and Roman town life that it could significantly affect the appearance and layout of a town and perhaps even define its existence.

The Roman town was where official religion was on public display and for the most part sat easily beside unofficial private cults. The Roman calendar was built around a series of religious festivals, and at the heart of each was the relentless observation of ritual according to prescribed formulae. On the last day in May, for instance, townsfolk walked their city's boundaries in the *Ambervalia*, a ceremony that had its origins in a rural purification of crops. Accurate repetition, or so it was believed, was the key to the effectiveness of these rites, and the preservation thereby of Rome's interests and future. So, the state's interests were inextricably merged with religion and because of this public status and office included the holding of priesthoods.

That was the theory. In practice, Roman religion was also an excuse for riotous entertainment integrated into the sequence of celebrations. On 15 February in Rome was the festival of the *Lupercalia*, which had remote origins in the legend of Romulus and Remus. It had evolved into an event when two young noblemen ran through the city, almost naked, and marked with the blood of sacrificed goats. They whipped anyone they could with strips of skin from the goat and young women who wanted to become pregnant leaned out to be struck. We have no idea if such an event took place in Britain, but the occasion illustrates the combination of primeval traditions, ritual, and the involvement of an urban community in a day of celebration, which eventually became the Christian festival of the Virgin Mary's purification. In Britain, prehistoric festivals must have been integrated into the urban cycle of religious events, especially as many Romano-British temples overlie Iron Age ritual sites.

Emperors and provincial politicians alike recognized the importance of funding games and fairs that could take place in towns or at country shrines. For example, on 21 August and 15 December the games called *Consualia* were celebrated. The name Consus was derived from the Latin word *condere*, 'to store', and referred to the storage receptacles for grain. Consus had become identified as another manifestation of Neptune. It was very easy for the Roman public to be beguiled by the prospect of entertainments and lose sight of the religious origins of the festivals. In time, Christian writers like Tertullian found it equally easy to castigate these occasions as exemplifying the pagan world's love for shameful idolatrous capers masquerading as religious events.

Power over fate

One of the most mature features of Roman government was the ability to accommodate provincial religious beliefs and customs. This was all part of ruling by exploiting existing ways of life. In any case, the Roman government was keen to appropriate any benefits to itself that a new god might provide. The basic practice of attributing good and bad events to the actions and whims of gods was common to Celtic and classical cults in any case. It was a mentality built around superstition and omen. Despite its pagan origins it survived intact into the Christian era and exists today in the form of astrologers' charts, fad cures for ailments, and 'systems' devised to win lotteries or at the races. Nothing is more guaranteed to provoke more widespread interest in superstition than the onset of disasters like plague or earthquakes. In his *Journal of the Plague Year* (1722), Daniel Defoe described London in 1665 but he perfectly summed up the role of superstitious hysteria in the context of an urban crisis:

> These Terrors and Apprehensions of the People, led them into a
> Thousand weak, foolish, and wicked Things ... this was running about

to Fortune-tellers, Cunning-men, and Astrologers to know their Fortune … this Folly made the Town swarm with a wicked Generation of Pretenders to Magick … this Trade grew so open, and so generally practised, that it became common to have Signs and Inscriptions set up at Doors; here lives a Fortune-teller; here lives an Astrologer … I need not mention, what a horrid Delusion this was … but there was no remedy for it, till the Plague itself put an end to it all.

Defoe pointed out that the 'fortune-tellers' had a vested interest in perpetuating a fear of the plague to keep themselves in business. In many respects, Defoe could have been describing the Roman world, especially a shrine town like Bath. The upshot was that the Romano-British who faced a world of unknown forces sought to influence a god's behaviour by offering gifts at shrines. It was almost a kind of contractual arrangement based on a promise, 'if you will do me this service, then I promise that I will offer up such and such a gift at your shrine', though much of this was probably part of day-to-day casual superstition rather than devoted faith (**81**). One of the other options was to leave funds in one's will to make an offering that might ease passage into the afterlife. This way Publius Oranius Facilis of Colchester left a small legacy to cover the cost of dedicating a *sigillum* (statuette) to Jupiter, recorded on the bronze plate attached to the idol. It would be a mistake though to believe that everyone believed in this sort of process. There is plenty of literary evidence to show that in the Roman world some people were extremely sceptical about

81 *Altar from York recording a dedication to the god Arciaconus (an obscure local divinity) and the spirit of the emperor (Numen Augusti) in the third line by a centurion called Mat… Vitalis. The letters V S L M in the fifth line are a standard abbreviation for* votum soluit libens merito. *This means that he was 'freely and deservedly fulfilling his vow' to the god. In other words Vitalis had promised the god an altar if he was granted a favour. Since the latter was a private arrangement with the god there was no need to specify it*

religion in general, treating it variously as a cynical way of keeping ordinary people under control, and as a mug's game.

In Britain the merging of existing cults with classical gods meant that the abstract deities of the Celtic world were represented as humans and were often associated with a similar Roman god. Mars, for example, became allied with a number of Celtic hunter-warrior gods like Cocidius. Celtic cults were not usually centred on temples but instead the focal point was more commonly a tree, a spring or a hill. These often had temples built on or near the site in the Roman period, for example at Harlow, but temples in towns were unlikely to have such origins for obvious reasons, unless the town itself grew up around the centre of a cult. The most famous example is Bath, *Aquae Sulis*, but there were several smaller settlements with similar backgrounds. Temples have been found all over Roman Britain but it is only in towns that we find examples of all the different aspects of Romano-British religious life including state cults, individual temples, which we might regard as centres of social or community cults, and domestic religion.

Romano-Celtic and classical temples were often associated with theatres and amphitheatres, discussed as structures in chapter 3. Public auditoria played a very important part in sacred ceremonies where performances and displays were put on as an integral part of religious festivals. Often, a parade would start at the theatre or amphitheatre and carry on down a prescribed route to the temple. In addition, annual bouts of public games, gladiatorial displays or beast hunts were usually part of a religious festival. So public religion and entertainment were closely linked in a way we often overlook because we tend to regard amphitheatres as places where gladiatorial bouts and other bloodthirsty entertainments took place.

State cults

Despite religious tolerance provincial communities across the Empire were obliged to pay lip-service to official religion. In about AD 12 the townspeople of Narbonne in southern Gaul dedicated an altar inscribed with a record of their vows to worship the spirit of Augustus for ever. Pliny the Younger, as governor of Bithynia and Pontus, wrote to the Emperor Trajan in 112 to confirm that he and the provincials had fulfilled their annual vows to pray to the gods for the emperor's health and safety. He also personally welcomed the privilege of becoming a priest, which was a normal component in the life of a man of status.

Similar events took place in Roman Britain though with so few inscriptions the evidence is not widespread. The town senate of Chichester recorded a vow for Nero's health and safety in the year 59, interesting not just because of early date for an imperial dedication but also because it states the existence of a formal local government body (**109**). Chichester's other dedication of a temple to Neptune and Minerva (and the imperial house) by a guild of smiths, in the name of the client king Togidubnus, was as much a political statement as it was a religious one (**108**). It was important that the spiritual identity of corporate bodies be firmly tied to the state through the mechanism of cult though, as so often with Britain, our inscription evidence is biased to groups likely to be immigrants or soldiers. At such an early date, the Chichester smiths were probably foreigners and at Silchester a *collegium peregrinorum consistentium Callevae*, 'guild of foreigners in residence at *Calleva*', was named on three inscriptions from statue bases found in a temple (**114**). The guild appears to have approved the donation of what were probably statues to Mars, Victory and Pax, through the efforts of an unnamed member. A good case has recently been made that these guild members were using the word *peregrinorum* to mark themselves out as resident aliens neither of Roman citizen, nor Atrebatic citizen, status in the Atrebatic capital. This guild was subscribing to the normal Roman urban habit of observing, serving, and contributing to mainstream cults, as a powerful cohesive force in the town community.

In truth, a religious and a political motive were totally indistinguishable. We have already met Marcus Aurelius Lunaris, the *sevir Augustalis* (**1**). Serving in this capacity was an important part of an aspiring citizen's portfolio of offices, and it mirrored the emperor himself who was *pontifex maximus*, 'chief priest'. Tiberinius Celerianus, the shipper from northern Gaul, made his dedication at London to his personal choice of Mars Camulus but prefixed it with a protocol-conscious dedication to imperial spirits (**55**).

As we saw in chapter 1, one of the earliest formal developments in Britain was the building of a temple to Claudius in Colchester. To begin with it might have been dedicated to his victories, but after his death in 54 and promotion to a god it was dedicated to *Divi Claudii*, 'to the Deified Claudius'. By 60 the structure was sufficiently far advanced to act as the centre of the colonists' resistance to the Boudican Revolt. The temple foundations were used in the eleventh and twelfth centuries as the base for the Norman castle keep and what remained of the superstructure was cleared away. However, it is certain that the temple was an impressively sized building in classical style (**12**). It lay inside a substantial walled precinct and a large altar stood in front of the temple (see cover). The building's dedication to Claudius had probably made much of his successful conquest of Britain, perhaps in the form of carved reliefs. In Canterbury an irregular *insula* facing the theatre on one side and the forum (?) on the other seems to have formed a substantial temple precinct. The building itself has not been located but its central location and imposing precinct make it very likely that this was an important classical temple that was almost certainly associated with a state cult. Fragments of carved stonework that clearly came from a classical structure reinforce the impression. Other similar fragments point to lost classical temples at other cities, for example Leicester and Lincoln (**82** & **colour plate 27**). Bath's classical temple is the best-known (**82** & **92**).

82 *Classical temple architecture in Britain: Corinthian capitals (not to scale).* Left: *massive capital from Leicester,* Ratae Corieltauvorum, *probably from a temple portico.* Right: *column capital from the Temple of Sulis-Minerva at Bath,* Aquae Sulis *(74cm diameter at base), late first century.* Centre: *capital from the Baths of Diocletian at Rome showing the approximate original appearance of the Romano-British versions (from* The Parallel of Architecture, *translated by John Evelyn, 1707)*

Most Roman towns elsewhere based their local state cults in temples that formed integral parts of the town centres. The Romano-British forums and basilicas are largely distinguished by the absence of these temples except possibly for Verulamium and a small temple added to the forum at Caerwent. The Verulamium temples lay on the south side of the forum, but there is great uncertainty whether these three buildings were all temples. They were built at different times, and one at least may actually have been a council chamber. So whether or not these were dedicated to the Capitoline Triad made up of Jupiter, Juno and Minerva, and the imperial cult, common elsewhere in the Empire, is unknown. It is curious that Roman Britain seems to have had so little of this kind of town centre classical state cult. Perhaps after the Boudican Revolt state cult temples were considered by the government as unnecessarily provocative – in the decades following the Revolt (which was when many of the forums and basilicas were being built) there might have been a very real fear of a re-emergence of armed rebellion in the south, though there is no evidence for that. Nevertheless, Britain was very nearly lost in 60.

Classical temples of any form were always rare in Roman Britain, and the cults of purely classical deities just as scarce. In later years we do have some instances of dedications to Jupiter Optimus Maximus ('the Best and Greatest') and variants like Jupiter Dolichenus, especially in the north where his cult was a routine part of military religious observations and statements of loyalty to the emperor (**83**). In towns there are a few instances of what we call 'Jupiter columns'. These were columns normally erected in a public place, such as a forum, with a plinth recording the dedication to Jupiter by some local worthy, or a provincial governor. Examples are known from Cirencester (**100** & appendix 2) and Great Chesterford.

Celtic, synthesized and oriental cults

The majority of urban temples were built in a simple style called by us 'Romano-Celtic' because it predominantly appears in the 'Celtic' provinces of the Roman north-west. These temples consisted of the *cella* (a square central chamber where the cult statue was stored), and a surrounding square ambulatory (**84**). Like most temples, and unlike churches, public cult activity took place outside in the precinct, a sacred enclosure called the *temenos*. It was surrounded by a wall that marked out the precinct as a distinct area from everywhere else. It was entered through a gate or arch that symbolized the transition from one zone to another (**colour plate 28**).

The only structural evidence that we have for the superstructure of a Romano-Celtic temple (a well-preserved example survives at Autun in France) suggests that the central chamber was tower-like and the ambulatory had a lean-to roof. Variations on this theme include circular and octagonal examples, but all retain the principle of concentric chambers. No Romano-British urban examples survive above their footings so we know nothing about internal decorations.

The precinct could take any form and this usually depended on the layout of the town. At Verulamium the so-called 'Triangular Temple' occupied an awkwardly shaped *insula* created by the entry of Watling Street from London at an angle at variance to the grid (**8** & **85**). On the other side of the middle of the town the much larger, rectangular, *Insula* XVI acted as a precinct and was much more symmetrical as a result. Lying right next to the theatre it was

83 *Section of frieze from a classical-style temple in the military town at Corbridge and probably dedicated to Jupiter Dolichenus (Dolichenus was an eastern god associated with Jupiter). The mounted figure is Apollo and the figure leading another horse is either Castor or Pollux. Third century*

84 *Late urban Romano-Celtic temple at Caerwent. This structure was built c.330 and was still in use in the late fourth century. Some urban communities in other provinces are known to have actively resisted the state's anti-pagan laws. A remote town like Caerwent might have found it relatively easy to flout the law, especially if local officials were sympathetic*

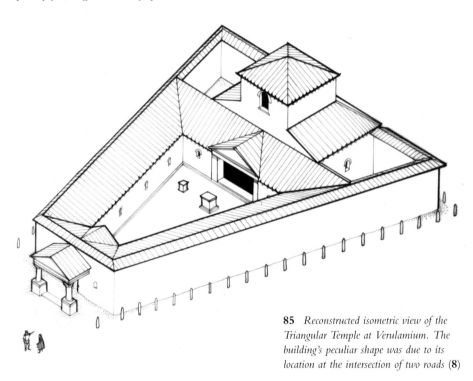

85 *Reconstructed isometric view of the Triangular Temple at Verulamium. The building's peculiar shape was due to its location at the intersection of two roads (**8**)*

probably set aside as a town-centre religious zone from the outset but unlike the theatre the temple was in commission by the late first century, and may have followed even earlier religious activity of Roman date on the site. Although it was walled, an entranceway allowed movement between the temple precinct and the theatre next door when it was built in *c*.140 (**30**). Unfortunately, there is no evidence at all for the nature of the cult. The theatre's auditorium faced Watling Street on the other side, and from here another road led north-east out of the town and straight to the remarkable mid-first-century extra-mural burial and temple site at Folly Lane, where a nearby baths suite seems to have been another feature of the complex.

At Silchester a small trapezoidal precinct beside the town walls on the east side contained three temples, and made up a whole *insula*. It was right next to the east gate and was linked by road to the amphitheatre (**17**). The theatre at Canterbury is known from traces of walls and was almost certainly accompanied by a major temple of unknown style within a substantial colonnaded precinct across the main street, underneath which was an Iron Age shrine. Colchester's theatre was immediately next door to the Temple of Claudius. Curved masonry found at Bath might come from a theatre connected with the cult of Sulis-Minerva (though a circular temple has also been suggested).

Urban temples were not always within the main area of settlement. Recent excavations in London revealed possible traces of an octagonal Romano-Celtic temple just to the west of the city walls. However, the temple seems to have been built about 170, roughly fifty years before the defences were erected. It may therefore have lain within a suburb that was subsequently excluded from the enclosed area.

Even small towns could have room for temple precincts, perhaps as many as two or more. Indeed, the temple might even have played a major part in helping to sustain a small town. At Godmanchester, a minor town on Ermine Street with a possible military origin, a small temple precinct was established at least as early as the first half of the second century beside a building identified as the *mansio*. The temple, which had at least two structural phases, was probably dedicated to Abandinus – a votive feather found in a filling from a building nearby refers to the god, who is not known anywhere else. The town also had another temple precinct that occupied a prominent position beside Ermine Street, but little is known about it. Interestingly a substantial Neolithic complex of banks, ditches and wooden obelisks dating to the third millennium BC has recently been discovered in the area. It has been identified as a temple connected with astronomical predictions (this is a common archaeological explanation for sites like this, but very difficult to prove). If so, there may have been something of a local religious significance and tradition about the place though of course coincidence is just as plausible an explanation.

Throughout the first four centuries AD the Roman world became increasingly interested in cults originating in the eastern part of the Roman Empire.

Quite why we cannot be sure, but there seems to have been a widespread desire to seek more spiritual explanations for life and its meaning, especially as Roman power waned. The formality of state cults might have made them seem ponderous and irrelevant to those who wanted something more intense. The towns were crucial to the spread of these religions because they were centres of communications and trades and therefore new ideas. So it was here that people already familiar with the cults were likely to establish temples. Not surprisingly London, as a major port, has produced the most evidence for such cults in Britain. As early as the late first century we know that London had a temple to the Egyptian goddess Isis because a flagon has survived bearing a graffito that refers to it. The cursive inscription says *Londinii ad fanum Isidii*, which means 'At London, by the Temple of Isis' (**86**). In a way the inscription is of more interest than an otherwise unidentifiable building; unless it is ancient fraud we can be sure that there was an Isis sect active in early Roman London. That cult, or another like it, was functioning nearly two centuries later when a governor

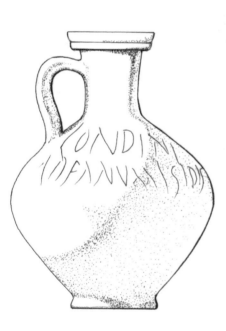

86 Left: *flagon from Southwark, London, bearing a graffito recording an address* Londini, ad Fanum Isidis, *'London, by the temple of Isis'. First century, though of course the inscription could be later.* Right: *wall-painting from Herculaneum depicting priests of Isis performing the Water Ceremony. Similar rites would have taken place at the London temple*

87 *York, inscription from the fortress and colonia recording the erection of a temple to the Egyptian god Serapis by Claudius Hieronymianus, commanding the* VI Victrix *legion. Style dates this to the end of the second century or very early third. It cannot be later since the VI legion's commanding officer was made a full governor of northern Britain by Septimius Severus (193-211)*

called Marcus Martiannius Pulcher arranged for a temple to Isis in London to be repaired (**112**). Artefacts found in London show that other eastern deities, for example Cybele and Atys, enjoyed the attentions of Roman Londoners. A vase from a grave at Dunstable seems to refer to a Verulamium-based cell of Atys adherents, and a temple of Serapis (a late Egyptian deity) was built at York (**87**).

The cult of Mithras was concerned with a complex myth based on good versus evil and centred around the killing of a bull that released the essence of life. Exclusive to men, the cult had attractions to the military and is best known in military areas. However, it was also popular in ports or towns with a military presence (London had a fort and soldiers were seconded from the legions to the governor's staff). Unlike more conventional temples where ritual was enacted outside the building a Mithraeum acted as a stylised 'cave', emulating the one in which Mithras had killed the bull. The buildings were either subterranean or had sunken floors and would not have had windows. Inside the devotees could proceed with their initiation rites and other ceremonies in an atmosphere suitably heightened by darkness and skilful use of artificial light. These conditions made the cult a self-contained and unobtrusive one.

London has the only certain Romano-British urban example of a Mithraeum. Its discovery in 1954 was accompanied by the finding of a number of cult statues that had been concealed by the followers (see below). Like most Mithraea it was built in basilican form because this suited the congregational aspect of the cult, something equally applicable to Christianity so it is no coincidence that both used the same existing building type. It was put up some time between 200 and 250 on the banks of the Walbrook stream on top of nearly two centuries worth of urban rubbish and spoil. Despite this down-market location it contained marble and limestone sculptures of considerable quality. It is certain that a Mithraic relief found in the vicinity in the nineteenth century came originally from the temple. It was dedicated by a veteran of *II Augusta* and had been carved from marble at Orange in France, an important reminder of how large a part the military played in the Roman identity even of Britain's civilian settlements (**88**).

The temple's proximity to the stream seems to have resulted in flooding and this caused structural problems. In the fourth century the temple appears to have become a focus of local hostility for it was seriously damaged and left to become derelict. However, the sculptures and ritual equipment were carefully buried beforehand, which suggests that the cult was being deliberately suppressed. By this time London was one of the Romano-British towns with its own bishop (see below) and it is reasonable to suppose that the London Christians were directly opposed to the presence of a cult which had features they regarded as insultingly similar to their own.

Christianity was an established urban cult by the fourth century. At the Council of Arles in 314 bishops from London, York and possibly Lincoln were present. These bishops would have had churches but where those were located is another problem altogether. At Water Newton the chance discovery of a group of silver pieces marked with Christian motifs and slogans dating to the third or possibly fourth century is certain evidence of an active local Christian fellowship which may have had a church in the town; however, the fact that they secreted away and never recovered their valuable goods suggests that the group was not popular (**89**). This does not necessarily mean an intolerant pagan state. Christians often suffered most from other Christians who disapproved of variations of theological themes. In the fourth century one of the greatest issues was Arianism. Arians did not believe in Christ's divinity, though they still believed he was the Son of God. Arianism was popular in the East but reviled in the orthodox West. It led to violence and persecution. The pagan-like elements of the Water Newton treasure could easily be linked to

88 *London, Mithraic relief. Found close to the site later identified as a temple of Mithras. This piece was carved for the benefit of Ulpius Silvanus, veteran of* II Augusta, *who may have joined the cult at Orange* (Arausio) *in Gaul*

89 *Part of the Water Newton Christian treasure. Some time probably in the third century a small Christian sect in the town buried a cache of silver plaques and vessels, some of which bear unequivocal references to Christianity. The larger plaque (height 15.7cm) bears a simple chi-rho monogram, repeated on others. One (right) bears a pagan-style record of a fulfilled vow by someone called Amicilla (width 10cm). The use of such plaques was traditionally a pagan custom and the find is an interesting conflation of conventional religious practice with what was still a relatively new cult*

some variation of Christianity that had provoked the wrath of a bishop who got to hear about it.

The fourth-century 'church' at Silchester is an enigmatic building that cannot be attributed to any religion with certainty (**90**). No evidence for religious activity was recovered and it is possible that small meetings of magistrates and councillors were transferred here from the basilica. Another problem is that the building seems to face east rather than west. However, it is very difficult to explain the structure as anything other than a church, and at the time orientation and arrangements of churches were still far from exactly defined. That Verulamium's Christian activity was centred on the martyrium of Alban is more definite, but the building lies somewhere under the Abbey church. At Colchester a church-like building was found in the middle of an extramural cemetery. Here the east-west orientation of the graves makes it likely that this was a church for the use of mourners, perhaps on or near the site of the grave of a particularly notable local Christian, maybe a martyr (**91**). Another possible candidate has been identified from a geophysical survey in the middle of Wroxeter where an aisled building with an apse is visible. However, none of these examples have either revealed artefactual evidence like the Water

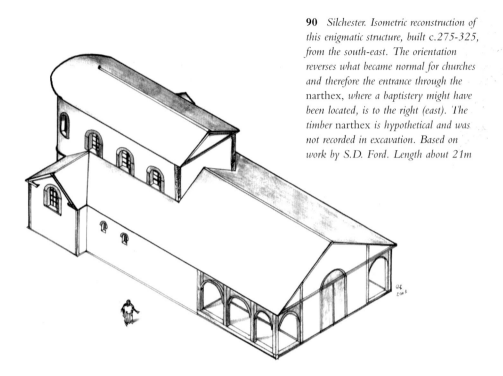

90 *Silchester. Isometric reconstruction of this enigmatic structure, built c.275-325, from the south-east. The orientation reverses what became normal for churches and therefore the entrance through the narthex, where a baptistery might have been located, is to the right (east). The timber narthex is hypothetical and was not recorded in excavation. Based on work by S.D. Ford. Length about 21m*

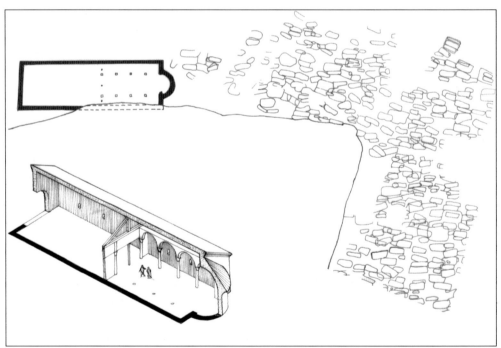

91 *Colchester. Plan of the Butt Road church and cemetery outside the south-west corner of the walls (after Crummy). The church was built c.320-40, but the apse was not built until c.380. Note the east-west orientation of the graves, marking this as a Christian-period burial ground. Insert shows a possible cutaway restoration of the church structure*

Newton treasure or wall-paintings like those from the Lullingstone villa. So while we know that Christianity existed in Romano-British towns, and was organized with an episcopal hierarchy, we have no idea of the extent to which Christianity was popular amongst the Romano-British public.

Shrine towns

In major towns like colonies or *civitas* capitals, temples were developed as the towns themselves developed. There may have been pre-Roman religious activity, as there had been at Canterbury, but even then that represented an additional component of the Iron Age settlement. In a few cases a town, or at least a town-like settlement, grew up around a sacred place. At Wycomb (Glos) the central feature of the small town seems to have been a temple precinct, probably containing a temple of Romano-Celtic style. Finds indicate a range of gods, including Mars and the *genii cucullati* (an obscure Celtic triad of unnamed hooded figures). Close by, traces of curving and elaborately carved masonry have been tentatively identified as remains of a theatre but there are problems because apart from the curve there is nothing else to confirm what it was. Wycomb is interesting because the temple's prominent location suggests that the town itself may have grown up around the shrine, rather than vice versa.

There are other cases where the only pre-Roman activity seems to have been religious. If such a place subsequently found itself on or near a Roman road, it could become the focus of new settlement and thereby help generate a town. Bath is probably the prime example. Springhead, *Vagniacis*, was a roadside settlement in Kent on Watling Street. The little town was always modest in size and almost nothing is known about the several temples that existed during the Roman period other than that they were Romano-Celtic in form. The place was probably regarded as sacred because of the spring, but at the site today it is clear that a small perfectly-formed hill immediately to the north is a very dominant and pronounced feature that may have had some importance. Perhaps rather more crucial to the settlement's development was its prime location on the main road up from the Kent coast to London and therefore to the rest of the province also.

Lying on a major route seems to have been a feature of most town-like settlements that grew up around shrines and suggests that town-like services were provided there. Quite what the process of development was we cannot know but we could envisage an important Celtic shrine attracting a military presence to a place traditionally associated with gatherings of the local population. In places where it was both appropriate and desirable the subsequent or contemporary laying out of roads would then put the shrine on the map. Thereafter its custom was more or less guaranteed, especially if it had a reputation for healing. While there are plenty of places where this didn't happen, for example the unsuitable hill-top temple at Lamyatt Beacon, it can hardly be coincidence that the Fosse Way has a number of settlements which seem to have developed around shrines. For travellers this would have made the site convenient as a place to make vows, offer sacrifices and stay a night. These shrines were also bound to have had appeal as recreational and interesting places to stay.

At Nettleton, on the Fosse Way between Bath and Cirencester, a small fort of uncertain date overlooked the narrow valley, suggesting that there was a good reason to be there. This may have been the presence of a Celtic shrine to a little-known god called Cunomaglos which needed policing (shrines might act as focal points of local resistance), and a possible Late Iron Age settlement. The fort was probably disused by the early second century at the latest and by the third century the valley came to contain not just a magnificent octagonal temple built in Romano-Celtic style (though by an architect of dubious competence) but a significant number of other buildings which included other temples and a water-mill. It is obviously difficult to form a conclusion about a settlement like this. Unlike Springhead the physical geography makes the site very restricted and it is unlikely to have spread far beyond the area covered by the archaeological excavations. However, the impression is of a self-contained settlement with an obvious source of income sited on a major route. Of more significance is the way in which, following the temple's collapse, the site remained in occupation by people who were engaged in the manufacture of pewter. This suggests that Nettleton's population had not been entirely restricted to those concerned with administering the cult(s).

Nettleton owed its development to the fact that traffic between major towns was bound to pass through it. That traffic need not have been just commercial and social. Pilgrimages to major shrines were regularly made, and a thriving industry existed to service pilgrims with souvenir badges, brooches, statuettes, and other religious items. People en route to Bath to take the waters, and visit the shrine of Sulis Minerva, could spend a night at Nettleton and enjoy the aesthetic pleasures of a small rural religious settlement. Bath had been under major development from the Flavian period when water-healing was in vogue, and possibly even before. Eventually it developed into a site that earned a reputation across the Empire as a recreational cult and healing centre. It would be naïve to assume that this was purely based on devotional considerations. The 'healing' waters that gushed from the ground, and were associated with the Celtic deity Sulis, were just as obviously a profitable commodity. There is good evidence for an early military presence, and soldiers continued to be patrons of the healing complex, so there is a real possibility Bath was originally devised as a military spa of a type known on the continent, and was managed in part thereafter for the benefit of troops.

For people visiting Bath the experience must have been exciting, entertaining and probably expensive. The temple and baths complex came to dominate the centre of what would later be the walled town (**92**). But excavations around the settlement have shown that Roman Bath extended along the roads that radiated out of the town in all directions, especially to the north-east towards Cirencester and north-west. Trade was never going to be confined to morose individuals with severe problems or grudges. Afflictions, real or imagined, were serviced by doctors and quacks alike, while others will have come purely for rest, recuperation and recreation. A handful, as we know from an inscription recording the repair work by a centurion, occupied themselves by vandalising a sacred spot. Other inscriptions show that visitors included soldiers from the legions stationed in Britain. One of the tombstones commemorates Gaius Murrius Modestus, a soldier of *II Adiutrix Pia Fidelis*, a legion in Britain from *c.*70 to 85 which was stationed at Lincoln and Chester. Although he could have been at Bath in a professional capacity it is quite possible he died while receiving treatment at Bath soon after or during its development.

Bath's development began in the 60s and 70s by erecting a retaining wall around the spring to create a manageable pool. Sluices and drains allowed excess water to be drained off into the river, which stopped the spring flooding

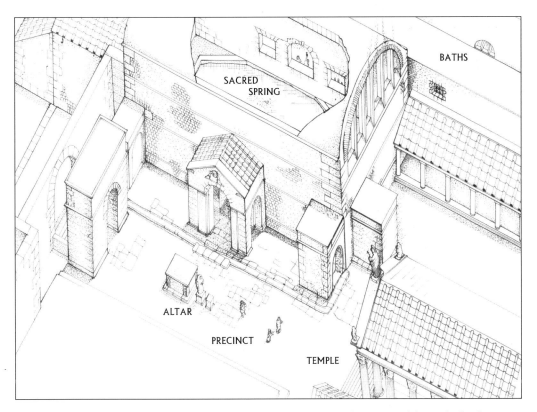

92 *Reconstructed view of the congested temple precinct at Bath as it may have appeared during the fourth century. In the foreground the Temple of Sulis-Minerva overlooks the precinct with its altar. Behind the altar is the sacred spring enclosed by its vaulted cover building. The cutaway roof shows pilgrims throwing offerings to the spring through three special windows.* Based on views by S. Gibson but adapted

the vicinity. This allowed the ground to dry out so that major buildings could be erected, like the cult temple and the baths. The pool acted as a focal point for the cult centre by giving pilgrims somewhere tangible into which they or the priests could (and did) throw their offerings (**93**). It also created a head of water that was run off into the bath complex built immediately to the south. To the north, the main cult altar was sited in a temple precinct. Part of the spectacle was the interpretation of the entrails of sacrificed animals, and here indeed we have the only Romano-British example of a soothsayer who 'read' the offal, the *haruspex* Lucius Marcius Memor. Commemorated on a statue base here, Memor made his predictions of doom, gloom or better days to come, apparently to a bemused local crowd. The abbreviation HAR on the plinth had to be extended to HARVSP, presumably because not many people knew what it meant.

The tetrastyle classical temple of Sulis–Minerva was conventional in basic form, but with sculptures that were a mixture of Celtic and classical motifs. In the early fourth century the whole complex was radically altered by enclosing the spring pool in a vaulted cover building, and adding some sort of ambulatory to the temple (**92**). The cover building's buttresses seem to have had sculptures decorated with references to the sun, and was balanced by a little known structure to the north, embellished with sculptures of the Four Seasons and a pediment depicting Luna. Not very much is known about the rest of the settle-

93 *Religion at Bath.* Left: *curse tablet from the sacred spring. Written backwards on a sheet of lead, the text lists a number of possible culprits responsible for 'carrying off Vilbia' and devouring her, and asks that the guilty become respectively 'as liquid as water' and 'dumb'.* Right: *altar from Bath to the Suleviae, an offering from Sulinus the sculptor, son of Brucetus. This same man made an almost identical offering at Cirencester. Such altars were gifts to the gods in return for the sort of services requested in curse tablets*

ment but on the site of the medieval abbey there may have been a further religious complex possibly built in the second century under Hadrian. This is where the possible theatre was located. It is evident from the enormous number of finds made in and around the baths and temple complex (including the partial excavation of the sacred spring) that the site was very popular and attracted visitors from all over the province and from some other parts of the Empire.

Does all this mean Bath really counts as a Roman town? In many respects the settlement resembled a town, albeit a small one even if it was much larger than a place like Springhead. It had substantial buildings, houses, walls, extra-mural settlements and cemeteries. However, it apparently had no public administrative buildings and the dominant feature was the cult centre that was about a third of the width of the whole site. It was also not a *civitas* capital, and the altar that mentions a 'centurion of the region' makes it possible it was administered as an imperial estate (see chapter 1). But it is difficult to imagine that Bath did not serve many of the functions of a town, and may even have had some sort of delegated administrative role. It would have acted as a market for people who lived in the outlying countryside and it lay on a major route (the Fosse Way). So for practical purposes it can be regarded as an unusual town that grew up from an unusual origin, even if it did not enjoy official status.

Private religion

Bath's particular appeal to pilgrims must have been a combination of many things. The site had a marvellous natural setting, surrounded by hills. There was the mystical appeal of a natural hot spring, and it lay on a major route. Visitors sought the services of Sulis-Minerva, though other gods like Mercury and Loucetius Mars are recorded here too. These ranged from healing to arranging for some disreputable person to have his or her comeuppance. Sulis-Minerva was contacted by throwing inscribed lead sheets into the spring and these tell us what the various 'customers' wanted. If the deity fulfilled their wishes, or simply needed encouraging, gifts were donated to the spring as well, such as jewellery, plate and coins. These are the ones that survive. It's clear from literary references to cult activity at other shrines in the Empire that most of what went in was probably food and drink in different forms. Several skillets were found in the spring and all were worn or damaged. They had probably been used for pouring libations in, but were accidentally lost over the course of time.

We do not have the same kind of written evidence from Bath at other Romano-British urban religious sites but we do have a number of instances where offerings were obviously being made over long periods of time (**93**). At the 'Triangular Temple' in Verulamium the modest enclosed precinct surrounded a number of small pits containing animal bones, presumably sacri-fices (**85**). There were also miniature pots that may have contained liquid offerings or libations. Coins were a very common gift at sacred sites probably because they were cheap (the vast majority found at sacred sites are very worn examples of low denominations). The few places where we know, or assume, that state cults were observed are not accompanied by such finds and this is an interesting feature of Romano-British religious life on a day-to-day basis. In other words, official state cults were subject to formal observation by the corporate entity of the town and its officials, but ordinary people expended their energy (and money) more selectively.

Religious activity 'at home' in towns is less easily identified. The pagan canon of gods was infinite and there was a deity for anything and everything. Door components had their own spiritual guardians, while the concept of the *genius*, literally 'spirit' or 'being', could be qualified in any context. The *Genius Loci*, 'Genius of this Place', was the most adaptable and turns up on many altars, especially from the military zone. Building a house meant beginning with a foundation deposit. We have only Roman literature as detailed evidence for this, but it is clear that digging a pit and depositing food, drink and even turf altars were routine. It is equally clear that little or none of this might survive for any archaeologist to find, and even if it did, there would be a real problem distinguishing it from a rubbish pit. Similar offerings were made throughout a house's history to celebrate festivals or commemorate family events. Within the house itself, a small cupboard-like shrine (the *lararium*) displayed selected representations of a family's ancestral spirits. One house in *Insula* XIV at Verulamium seems to have had its own underground shrine. An underground corridor was entered down a ramp from the street and ended in an apse where a statue was probably once displayed. Niches in the walls housed lamps to light the way. Oddly the corridor was not accessible from the house, so it may have been some sort of public shrine used by the owner's retainers or clients as they exited the basilica across the road. At street corners throughout the town and along the roads outside little shrines decorated the way and afforded individuals the opportunity to indulge in ritual observances if they were so inclined.

Death and burial in Romano-British towns

All towns had burial areas that were set aside specifically for the purpose. In theory these were outside the area of settlement, something that was enforced by law, and were demarcated by a boundary. In cases where cemeteries are located within a Roman town this is usually because they belong to an earlier and smaller phase in the town's history. However, it is clear from some small towns and recovery of bodies within some larger towns that burial was by no means always excluded from the area of settlement.

In general, cremation was customary during the first two centuries AD. Thereafter inhumation became normal but in neither period was the dominant practice exclusive. Cremations took place in or near the cemetery. The pyre was placed over a pit to allow a supply of air to be sucked through the fire, and followed a funerary meal. Next the ashes of the deceased were gathered up and placed in a container, usually a pottery or glass urn, and buried along with several other vessels containing libations and offerings such as a brooch and coins. The quantity and quality of grave goods reflected the status of the deceased, or at any rate the preferences and wealth of those organizing the burial. The choice of grave goods also reflected the date and the habits of the time, or even the occupation of the deceased. Brooches, for example, were popular very early on but by the late first century had become a rarity. One of the mid-first-century burials found at Stanway, close to the pre-Roman and religious zone of Gosbecks outside the colony at Colchester, was exceptional in this respect. It contained a gaming board, and a set of surgical instruments, as well as a suite of pottery vessels including an amphora. The surgical instruments must mean the dead person had worked as a doctor presumably at Colchester.

The group of vessels was occasionally enclosed in a miniature chamber made out of wood, tile or stone. Usually a pipe of some sort was inserted into the covering soil through which further offerings to the deceased could be passed. The individual graves were marked either with some sort of timber structure, which only survives in post-hole form, or a tombstone. When inhumation became customary the wealthiest families paid for expensive decorated stone or lead coffins buried in mausolea. Those less well-off probably used wood coffins or constructed cists out of tiles or slabs of stone whilst the poorest were probably buried in nothing more than a shroud. Wood coffins naturally rotted away and traces are hardly ever found except for the iron nails used in their construction (**97**). In exceptional instances, for example in a cemetery to the north-east of Winchester, lead lining was used for a wood coffin. Shrouds present similar problems but the gypsum graves at York (where the bodies were surrounded with a gypsum packing) preserve the impression of the shrouds and sometimes fragments of the cloth.

Evidence from cemeteries around Verulamium have led to the suggestion that lower social classes were packed into the graveyards clustered around the town, while the ruling classes were buried away from the town on their rural estates. Where a cemetery has been extensively examined it sometimes appears that graves were grouped according to different burial practices, such as the type of grave goods, alignment of the body, or the use of chalk packing in the coffin. In the first and second centuries it was also quite common to accumulate a group of cremations in a zone enclosed by a ditch, often with one of the graves being more prominently endowed with grave goods. In the late-Roman Poundbury (Dorchester) cemetery a small number of mausolea were located in amongst the surrounding inhumations, at least two of which were decorated with painted wall-plaster. These must represent the graves of prominent individuals, surrounded by the graves of their families or retainers.

Such practices may represent extended family groups, or larger zones of ethnic groups. We know from inscriptions found elsewhere in the Empire that a man might offer places in his family plot to his freedmen and their families too. It is not unknown for contemporary inhumations to be found scattered in ditches marking enclosures to cremation groups. Usually lacking any grave goods, we can only guess who they were, but slaves of the household are a possibility. The only practice we can specifically associate with any particular social sub-division is the nominal 'Christian' practices of orientating inhumations east–west and not using grave goods, which started to appear in the third century. Even that is not a fixed rule. Some of those new to Christianity, or reluctant to abandon old habits, continued to bring food and offerings to the grave. This earned the opprobrium of Christian writers who provide the evidence by condemning the practice. Without tombstones or written grave markers, there is simply no possibility of getting any further apart from educated guesswork. One of the most frustrating aspects of Romano-British cemeteries is that tombstones almost without exception do not turn up in association with the graves, and even then cremations are of little use in trying to associate data on the stone with the physical remains of the deceased.

Evidence of dead bodies does not automatically mean a cemetery has been found, even in a town context. In London, up until *c.*160, a number of skulls of young males were thrown into the Walbrook stream (a tributary of the Thames which passed through the town) and other waterlogged locations. This has been linked with the Celtic veneration of the decapitated head. The head was thought to retain the spirit of the deceased and to have special powers such as foretelling the future, especially if the person had been held in great esteem. Certainly the London heads show evidence of having been left out on view before they were thrown into the water. The rest of the body was probably cremated in the normal way. Similar evidence from the ditches surrounding the early fortress at Colchester has been interpreted as skulls of tribal enemies posted on the fortress walls.

Cemeteries ought to be a useful source of factual evidence for the nature of the urban population though even this assumes, probably incorrectly, they were confined to the urban population. Cremation burials give us little physiological information for obvious reasons but tombstones can supply some factual material about the kind of people who were buried in any one place. So, from London we have Aulus Alfidius Olussa who was born in Athens but died in London when he was seventy. At Cirencester, Philus from the Besançon region in Gaul died when he was forty-five. At Lincoln Claudia Crysis reached the magnificent age of ninety (**94**). The trouble is that tombstones usually belong to people who are otherwise unknown and hardly ever carry information that allows them to be dated (**15** is an extraordinary exception). Instead we have a name, and if we are lucky an age, possibly town of origin and occasionally further details of kin who were either buried there too or who were responsible for erecting the stone.

94 *Tombstones (not to scale), computer-generated emulations of the originals.* Left: *tombstone (diameter 61cm) found at Silchester before 1577, and the only complete example from the town. The text means 'To the memory of Flavia Victorina, Titus Tammonius Victor, her husband, set this up'. Tammonius is restorable from a religious dedication found in Silchester erected probably by a kinsman. His name is distinctly Celtic, but Latinized into the* tria nomina *of a citizen. Her name is wholly Roman and it is impossible to say whether she was British and a daughter of someone who had adopted a Roman name, or the daughter of an immigrant or soldier.* Right: *tombstone (diameter 76cm) from Lincoln. The text means, 'To the Spirits of the Departed, and to that of Claudia Crysis. She lived 90 years. Her heirs arranged the burial'. The name Crysis was more usually spelled Chrysis, and had connections with Apollo and gold as a colour. It was probably given to people with blonde hair, thus 'Claudia Golden-Hair'*

But of course, tombstone texts only tell us about people who were inclined to pay for permanent grave markers. Those that tell us what the deceased were or where they came from, show that soldiers dominate the record, even in towns. Many of the rest are women and children (some of whom are stated to be military dependants, and others who probably are), and foreigners. Towns with little or no military phase or population tend to produce virtually none. So, 360 years of Silchester as a Roman town has produced just one surviving complete tombstone. Here Titus Tammonius Victor erected a tombstone for his wife Flavia Victorina but tells us nothing about her age or where she came from (**94**). His name appears to be a British one 'latinized' into a Roman form, and since one of the few other legible inscriptions from the town is a religious dedication by Titus Tammonius Vitalis, it rather seems they were probably kinsmen and from a family with the means and inclination to commission inscriptions, unlike most other residents of *Calleva*.

Titus Licinius Ascanius, apparently a civilian in London, made his own tombstone 'in his lifetime'. Since Ascanius was a place in Asia Minor, and the name of a son of Aeneas, he is unlikely to have been British and therefore brought with him both the inclination to epigraphy and the ability to do it himself. Foreign origins definitely apply to three of the four civilian tomb-stones from Cirencester, including Philus mentioned above, and a woman called Casta Castrensis, whose name originated in Gaul at Lyons. Verulamium and Winchester have produced not a single legible tombstone, and Wroxeter has three for its time as a legionary fortress and a fourth for a woman and a boy. At Bath, of eleven tombstones where the deceased can be identified, six are soldiers or veterans. Of the remainder, two are of women, two baby girls and one was an octogenarian decurion from Gloucester. Either this means soldiers were the most frequent visitors to Bath, or simply that they were more likely to be commemorated with inscribed slabs. Tombstones are rare enough in Britain anyway, but the demonstrably indigenous Romano-British urban population is miserably under-represented even in what we have. Correspondingly, tombstones from the rest of the Empire, where inscriptions are far more common, commemorating Britons who were soldiers or civilians are virtually unknown. Aelius, the Dumnonian who served with the *classis Germanica* (the fleet in Germany) at Cologne, is an exception.

So tombstones are interesting, but of limited value. Elaborate tomb sculptures add to our picture of the character of urban burial practice but tell us nothing about the deceased. The sphinx from Colchester and a stone bust from York may have come from two that were subsequently broken up (**95**, **96** & **colour plate 30**). What can an archaeologist do with the anonymous evidence

95 *Stone sphinx from Colchester, probably from a funerary monument. Height 84cm*

96 *Stone female head with a mid-third-century hairstyle from a cemetery at York. It may have come from a mausoleum, and probably had detail (like the eyes) painted in. Height 18cm*

from graves? If a cremation includes datable grave goods, such as samian pottery or coins, then an estimate of the burial's date can be made. These observations made throughout a cemetery will clarify its general period of use, or phases of use as the cemetery extended. Occasionally a cremation container carries an inscription. A particularly explicit hand-inscribed one on a lead urn from York says that it contained the ashes of Ulpia Felicissima aged eight years and eleven months, though another from the London/Verulamium area on a jar says simply 'SATTONIS', meaning '(the ashes) of Satto'. But this tells us nothing about who this girl was, or when she lived.

The tombstone problem is just as relevant to inhumation cemeteries but it is at least possible to gain from skeletons some sort of idea about the genetic characteristics of people from the same community, the reasons for and age at death and the various conditions from which they suffered during their lives. Two of the best known cemeteries are at Cirencester (Bath Gate) and at Poundbury by Dorchester. The archaeological effort involved in systematically examining hundreds of graves is enormous and not surprisingly very few such cemeteries have been paid such attention. A single grave can take several days of methodical work to extract (**97**).

At Colchester more than 700 burials from a single cemetery were examined in the late 1980s at the Butt Road site, just outside the south-west corner of the town walls (**91**). A few were aligned north-south and were generally accompanied by grave goods, normal for pagan burials of Roman

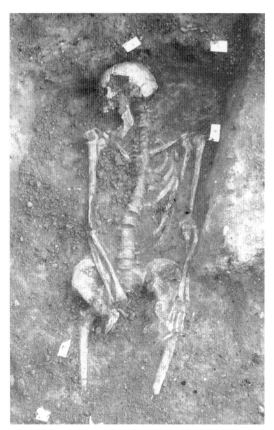

97 *Bath. Roman adult male burial found close to a road to the north of the Roman town in what is now public parkland just below the famous Royal Crescent. As is more normal for inhumations there is no surviving tombstone or other evidence to identify the deceased, and just to complicate the issue no datable grave goods either. The north-south orientation indicates a pagan burial of the third century or later (perhaps even post-Roman). The white tags mark the location of nails from the now-rotted wooden coffin. It is not yet clear whether this was a burial in an occupation site, or a proper cemetery*

date. By the early fourth century, however, a change seems to have taken place: burials were now orientated east-west and far fewer had grave goods. These later burials were associated with a rectangular structure with an apse at its east end. This has been plausibly interpreted as a cemetery church though nothing was found which bore any kind of Christian motif. Examination of the Colchester skeletons showed that most were buried in wooden coffins on their backs with hands crossed and wrapped in some kind of simple shroud, one of which seems to have been made of Chinese silk (a remarkable instance of long-distance trade). Grave goods were mostly everyday personal ornaments such as hair-pins, brooches, necklaces and armlets though occasionally they were also equipped with sandals and pottery or glass vessels containing food and drink for the journey. Confirming the criticism that some Christians clung on to pagan customs it is interesting that grave goods were found in some of the east-west 'Christian' graves. It shows how a long-established tradition can endure even when its ostensible purpose has disappeared.

One of the most interesting features of these inhumation cemeteries is that they ought to form the most comprehensive evidence for an urban population in the fourth century. This was a period for which archaeologists have tended to argue for diminished urban populations. However, a large cemetery excavation can present a beguiling, but misleading, picture to archaeologists anxious to make good the lack of documentary information about population size, and distribution according to age, sex and genetic type.

In fact, it is very easy to show in a variety of ways just how unrepresentative the evidence from cemeteries can be. When the eighteenth- and nineteenth-century crypt burials were cleared at Christchurch, Spitalfields, in London the opportunity was taken to test archaeological methods of assessing age at death, since the ages of the deceased were known from the coffin plates. The results were alarming. In many cases, estimates based on skeletal development tended to equate minimum age reached by death with actual age at death. The true figure was in a number of cases twenty to thirty years later than that estimated. Only dental forensics, based on the steady progress of tooth wear, produced more accurate estimates. At a stroke many of the measurements derived from archaeological excavations of cemeteries, Roman, prehistoric or post-Roman, were called into question and this remains an issue since correcting the problem would involve re-examining every skeleton previously published.

The fourth-century Bath Gate cemetery at Cirencester provides us with more examples of problems. Here male inhumations, for instance, appear to exceed female burials by a margin that cannot possibly represent the original population. Of 337 skeletons where the sex could be determined 241 (71 per cent) were males. This must represent different practices for men and women. However, the bias to males has been noted elsewhere so it may be for more general reasons that urban cemeteries had more men. Perhaps men were more likely to gravitate to towns looking for work in government service, in household staffs or as labourers, or simply were more likely to benefit from the necessary expenditure. Another possibility is simply that men were more likely to have made arrangements for organized burial, perhaps paid for by membership of professional bodies like guilds. Finally, there is at some ages, particularly early adulthood, some skeletal ambiguity between males and females so there is a possibility that the proportions are not entirely accurate though this would only slightly modify the discrepancy rather than demolish it.

Of course there is an obvious problem with the total number in the first place. Since we do not know exactly when any of the burials were made, we cannot possibly assess the rate of usage. Were, for instance, the 241 male burials at Cirencester's Bath Gate cemetery made at a rate of ten per annum over around twenty-five years, or were they all buried within a year or two? It ought also to be obvious that the burials represent a minute potential proportion of Cirencester's population considered over, say, the third and fourth centuries when inhumation was common. Prior to the plague of 1665, London's population of around 400,000 suffered a death-rate of around 14,000 per annum or about 3-4 per cent. If we recall the suggested population figure for Cirencester in chapter 5 of 8,000-12,000, it is clear that the 337 Bath Gate burials represent around one year's worth of possible deaths for the town, or one two-hundredth of all the deaths across the two centuries during which inhumation was the norm. Even that is an exceptionally large sample to have available.

One estimate of all the Romano-British graves excavated is about 20,000, equivalent to about 56 for every year of the Roman period in Britain. At a death-rate of 3.5 per cent in a population of 4 million there ought to be 140,000 deaths per annum, of which the 56 represent 0.04 percent of those deaths. In other words 139,944 annual graves are not represented. Even if we assume a totally implausibly low death-rate of one percent (40,000 deaths), our 56 annual burials still only represent 0.14 per cent of those who died. If the death-rate was higher, then the proportion of the original population represented drops even further.

In other words any meaningful statistical assessment of an urban population is going to be affected by factors we cannot measure. It is not until the appearance of documentation like medieval parish registers and the Bills of Mortality used to record cause and age of death in London from the sixteenth and seventeenth centuries on, that any sort of useful measurement of population can be made and even those records are notorious for their inaccuracies. Unfortunately excavating graves does not provide a substitute. Instead, the value (which is considerable) lies in providing evidence for burial practice, congenital defects, disease, injuries (accidental or violent), and surgery. For example, a number of the Cirencester skeletons exhibited evidence for gout, apparently a unique concentration for Roman Britain, and it has been noted that amongst the modern local flora is a plant that contains a chemical called colchicine, traditionally used to treat the condition.

But even then, extrapolating any conclusions about the general urban population cannot really be justified from such tiny samples. Likewise, anything else, like age at death, sex bias, and date of burial is prone to far too many variables to be of statistical use though they do help create a general impression. What ought to be clear, though, is that we have no way of knowing how accurate that impression is.

7

THE PASSING OF
ROMAN TOWNS

During the third and fourth centuries, literary references to Roman Britain diminish in quantity and quality, making even the basic process of events difficult to reconstruct. Inscriptions, never numerous, dry up during the third century and only milestones continued production until the reign of Constantine I (307-37). Only a very few can be attributed to a later date. Ironically, Britain's towns occasionally featured prominently in the history of the known world. In 211 York was where Septimius Severus died, and a century later in 306 Constantius Chlorus died there too. The immediate proclamation of his son Constantine as emperor in York (he did not secure elevation to the rank of Augustus until the following year) was a major international event that changed the course of history in Europe forever.

This was a time of mounting insecurity in Europe. Between about 342 and 370 tribal incursions from northern Britain and across the sea from northern Europe created a renewed climate of fear. The Roman government was also showing further signs of disintegration. Constantine I died in 337 and although he left the Empire to his sons, Constantine II (the far west including Britain), Constans (the centre), and Constantius II (the East), by 340 Constantine II had been killed by supporters of Constans. A decade later, Constans was killed by the forces of the rebel Magnentius, leaving just Constantius II as the sole legitimate ruler of the Roman world (**98**). Magnentius was said to be at least half-British and he seems to have enjoyed a lot of support in Britain, perhaps in part because he was accommodating to paganism. There were further complications. Constantius II was an uncompromising Arian, and the West was predominantly Orthodox.

When Constantius II defeated Magnentius in 353, the repercussions in Britain were very serious. He sent an imperial secretary called Paul to weed out supporters of Magnentius. Paul was ruthless in the extreme, imprisoning and disinheriting landowners and other wealthy men. These will have included men who sat on town councils and helped administer, and endow, the *civitas* capitals of Britain, and perhaps had a catastrophic effect on some communities. Other rebellions followed, and also ended in defeat. In 383 and 407 soldiers in

Britain called Magnus Maximus (**99**) and Constantine III respectively led similarly disastrous rebellions that denuded Britain of troops, but which probably gained their initial support in Britain from the upper-classes that had given up on the legitimate Empire to protect them from barbarians.

Unfortunately none of this can be directly linked to the towns because there are no useful literary references and urban inscriptions have not survived (if they existed). We know that after the major barbarian incursion of 367 the general Count Theodosius was sent to Britain by Valentinian I (364-75) to reconstruct the province. He based himself in London, and 'restored the *civitates* and the forts', according to the historian Ammianus Marcellinus.

During the first and second centuries all the evidence gives us a reasonably clear impression of major towns being developed in fairly homogeneous form. London, the *civitas* capitals and colonies were all equipped with the various

98 *Magnentius (350-3), bronze* centenionalis, *and gold* solidus *of Constantius II (337-61). Constantius' ruthless suppression of the Magnentian Revolt had major repercussions in Britain where members of the ruling class were arbitrarily imprisoned and had their estates confiscated. Actual diameters about 21mm*

99 *Bronze coin of Magnus Maximus (383-8) who took control of Britain, Gaul and Spain. Actual diameter 22mm*

facilities required to fulfil their functions as administrative, economic and social centres. These varied a little from place to place and the timescale was also protracted and not necessarily contemporary but it appears that a broadly similar pattern of development was taking place. This was certainly guided at the very least by official provincial administration, rather than being purely local in instigation and planning, and backed by motivated and high-ranking members of the communities. Even the small towns show a common and gradual, albeit modest, degree of romanization based on their location or some kind of local industrial specialization. The indirect evidence of inscriptions suggests that in Britain few of these individuals recorded their personal efforts, or that development was more commonly directed through local bodies and guilds.

In the third century, apart from the building of town defences, there is less impression of a provincial urban pattern. Instead regional factors seem to have played a more influential role, with some towns showing signs of sustained investment, for example Canterbury's theatre or the reconstruction of the temple precinct at Bath. At other towns a change in circumstances was manifested in the different functions of public buildings like Silchester's basilica, or industry-based towns capitalizing on the change in the economy in favour of domestic production – Water Newton is the best example.

The changes in urban economies during the Roman period are hard to understand, and particularly so in the fourth century. London has provided the largest quantity of evidence for urban occupation and economic development even if its individual buildings have only been traced with difficulty. This has been due to the enormous numbers of small-scale rescue excavations since the 1960s. As we saw in chapter 4, interpreting the so-called 'dark earth' layers has led to a variety of, and even contradictory, interpretations. On one hand, it looks like evidence for agriculture within town walls and in some cases this seems certain (**51**). On the other hand it could be dumped soil brought in to consolidate and level the ground surface on ruined plots to support undetected, and now undetectable, timber buildings. Either way the dark earth represents change, but to what?

Some of the towns have also produced evidence for a change in the way in which they were administered in the latter part of the period as shown by the demolition of London's basilica in the early fourth century and the occupation of Silchester's basilica by metalworkers from the mid-third century on. But what this really means is less clear because we can hardly accept the notion that if a basilica ceased to function then civic justice and government of the tribal cantons also ceased. The result would have been urban anarchy or collapse during the fourth century and this is not something there is evidence for in the archaeological and historical record, especially as in the fifth century the episcopal hierarchy of the church was still functioning in 429. London, for example, was issuing coins in the name of Constantine I and his sons until at least 325 (**67**) and may also have been used by Magnus Maximus to strike gold between 383-8. It was known as *Augusta* throughout most of the fourth century, and that implies that it was still functioning as the provincial capital, though whether it had any formal urban status is still unknown.

In some other towns the basilicas appear to have remained in use for a while, for example at Caerwent and Cirencester. Nevertheless, Caerwent's basilica was demolished by *c.*390 and even then seems to have spent the last forty years of its life being used as a blacksmiths' workshop. Cirencester's forum was altered during the fourth century by having a dividing wall built across the piazza. This has been linked to the town's late status as a provincial capital, perhaps making provision for a governor's residence. Certainly the forum seems to have endured considerable wear on its flagstones during this time which makes it likely that civic activity of some sort was still going on, though this may have been commercial rather than administrative. A fourth-century inscription from Cirencester, very rare for this date in Britain, records the presence of a governor here of *Britannia Prima*, of which Cirencester seems to have been the capital. This is the only epigraphic evidence we have for such an office-holder in late Roman Britain and for any sort of public work, so it is a pity we can only say it must date at least to after 296 around when the four provinces were created (**100**). At Exeter the basilica was even equipped with a new floor, late enough to seal a coin of Valens (364-78) beneath it. But by the end of the century the whole site had been demolished and cleared, with metalworking being amongst the activities moving in. The apparently organized removal of the structural debris implies some sort of centralised control of the town even in the context of taking apart its public buildings.

The extensive fourth-century extramural cemeteries, discussed in the previous chapter, are surely proof that there was still an organized urban society even if their statistical value in other ways is very limited. Some late fourth-century repair work on Hadrian's Wall seems to have been performed by gangs working in the names of several of the *civitates*. One from Cawfields

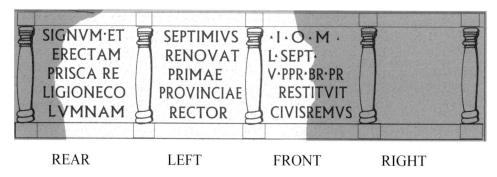

REAR   LEFT   FRONT   RIGHT

100 *Computer-generated reconstruction of the Cirencester column base, recording its restoration by Lucius Septimius, rector and praeses of the province of Britannia Prima, one of the four provinces of Britain created in 296. Fourth century. See appendix 2 for a translation*

101 *Stone from Hadrian's Wall (near Milecastle 42 at Cawfields) recording a section of wall repaired by the Durotriges tribe from Ilchester in Somerset. The C in the first line stands for* Civitas *followed by* DVRTRG *for the tribe. The town name of* Lindinis *is written as* LENDINESIS. *The crude style indicates that it is likely to be of late date, recording repair work in the late fourth century*

milecastle credits the canton of the Durotriges at *Lendiniensis* (Ilchester) (**101**), another from the fort at Carvoran mentions the *civitas Dumnoniorum* whose tribal centre was at Exeter. The Brigantes were named on a stone now lost from Blea Tarn. These are very interesting because if they have been correctly attributed to the fourth century then it appears that the various provincial authorities were working in concert (perhaps at Theodosius' behest) to encourage or oblige the tribal communities to contribute to the reconstruction, a vital part of Britain's security.

The implication of this is that the canton governments based in towns were still able to mobilize their communities and must therefore have had the motivation, resources and facilities to do so. If they could do this then it is equally likely that they could maintain their towns in a centralized way, insofar as it was necessary. But had the towns just become fortified compounds? The finds of late metalwork in Germanic style in town cemeteries, for example at London, Caistor-by-Norwich and Dorchester-on-Thames were traditionally taken to be evidence for the presence of Germanic mercenaries, the *foederati*, employed by towns for their own defence (**102**). This is an ambitious assumption to base on the evidence of buckles that were also standard issue for the Roman army. They might be evidence merely for the presence of individual soldiers in transit or residence. Today it is recognized that even the early imperial army was a good deal less regimented in its use of equipment than

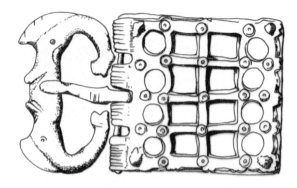

102 *Buckle from Dorchester-on-Thames of a type sometimes associated with the presence in towns of mercenaries of Germanic origin in the late fourth century. However, they are now considered just as likely to be standard military issue for the period. (Length 10cm).* After C.S. Green

was once thought. Helmets, armour and fittings were drawn from stocks accumulated over decades, and it is no longer possible confidently to date a military presence purely on the basis of brooches or buckles. In the late Empire, uniformity was even less of an issue when the army was made up of disparate types of irregular units operating alongside imperial cavalry field armies. However, whether the buckles are evidence for garrisons of Roman soldiers or for mercenaries makes no difference to the implication that civic government was still operating and that there was something worth protecting.

If the evidence for late urban administrative activity is ambiguous so is that from other public buildings. None of the amphitheatres of Roman Britain seem to have been repaired or specifically maintained during the fourth century. At Silchester extensive robbing of the amphitheatre wall took place, which would fit a fourth-century date when anti-pagan measures proceeded apace, but this may have been post-Roman activity (**32**). Structural alterations at Cirencester limited access to the arena though what this means in terms of function is not very clear. It may have become an assembly area for more mundane administrative functions. At Wroxeter the public baths seem to have been largely ruinous by the end of the fourth century and the same fate had befallen Verulamium's theatre, by now a rubbish tip. Yet even at Wroxeter the collapsed columns and other stonework in the baths exercise hall bear ruts worn by wheels which suggests a considerable amount of day-to-day traffic – hardly a sign of a dead town, but instead a different one.

Many urban defences were strengthened during the fourth century by having external bastions added to them (**49** & **104**), or in some extreme cases gates were blocked up (**103**). This may have been part of Theodosius' programme of reconstruction, a quite plausible scenario in terms of the time-honoured tradition of preparing for the war that has just finished but the evidence is only circumstantial. Blocked gates could just be a matter of convenience, when usage patterns changed. In a few cases, like Verulamium, bastions were apparently part of the original late third-century design but for the most part they seem to have been built during the second half of the fourth century. They may represent a change in style, reflecting the preference for defensive

103 *Caerwent. The late blocking inserted into the south gate has remained intact since antiquity, perhaps preserving evidence for enhanced urban security, especially in a part of Britain particularly prone to seaborne raiders in the fourth and fifth centuries*

104 *Portchester, the south wall of the Saxon Shore fort. Many of the towns of Roman Britain presented this sort of image to approaching visitors in the late fourth century, especially London where the landward wall presented a huge stretch of wall reinforced with bastions*

artillery mounted on external bastions, but many show signs of having been erected with reused stonework.

Such changes could have followed, or anticipated, a 'crisis' leading to hasty demolition of convenient structures, but it is equally possible that if some public buildings and temples had been allowed to run down then there would have been reasonable quantities of stone lying around on derelict sites. Cemeteries were favourite sources and several bastions in London have been found to contain sculptures and inscribed stones from tombs including parts of that belonging to the first-century procurator Classicianus (**15**). At Kenchester, a remote town possibly acting as a subordinate cantonal centre for the Dobunni, an elaborate fourth-century gate and tower were built partly out of stone taken from a building of some architectural pretension. Considering that the 'Saxon Shore' forts were built in this style it is more likely that the urban authorities took it upon themselves, or were ordered, to 'update' their defences to conform (**104**). A late fourth-century gate in the lower part of Lincoln contained one piece of temple entablature upside down in its plinth suggesting that it was a handy block, rather than that the temple had been demolished for that express purpose (**colour plate 27**). It might even be misleading to differentiate towns and forts. In some respects towns might have been undergoing these changes so that they essentially functioned as part of the same defensive system as the coastal forts. Collectively the coastal forts and towns could have protected civilians, commerce and garrisons as and when needed. London's late riverside wall would have certainly had the effect of converting into something more like a very large fortified compound than a commercial city, resembling the sort of place the shore fort at Richborough had become.

By the end of the fourth century, and more particularly during the early part of the fifth it becomes clear that what we regard as the archaeological definitions of a town site being 'Roman' were fading away. While life of a sort was evidently going on in the towns it is much harder to define because there is, literally, very little to define – coinage was no longer imported and pottery production in any kind of organized form ceased. Even building in towns, apart from occasional traces of timber structures and possible churches, had apparently stopped.

Understanding what happened after about 400 is much more difficult for these archaeological reasons. St Patrick, who lived during the fifth century, had a father who was a decurion, which implies that the political and administrative organization of some towns was at least nominally intact. The existence of a fifth-century water-pipe in Verulamium, overlying a demolished hall which itself overlay a house which was not built before 370, is often quoted as evidence for sustained organized community life though this does seem rather a lot to read into a single pipe. In fact, this instance is a typical example of how a single site becomes the foundation for a whole teetering edifice of speculation and entirely fails to take into account the possibilities of what might have been found (or not found) on unexcavated plots nearby. The Lower Thames Street bath house in London fell into ruin during the first half of the fifth century (**50**). A Saxon brooch was dropped amongst the roof tiles and while this could be argued as evidence for a ruined city with scavengers rooting through the derelict remains it is also evidence for people still living there.

Continuity of sorts is much more likely than total termination, even if that meant relocating settlements and leaving old streets and buildings to rot away (**105**). In London a number of excavations in recent years have shown that there was an extensive seventh- to ninth-century settlement to the west of the former Roman capital, centred on a part still known as the Aldwych (literally 'old *wic*', *wic* being an early English corruption of *vicus*). Finds from a site in Covent Garden showed that the settlement was engaged in trade and industry. In 731 the monastic historian Bede described London as an international trading centre. It seems unlikely that it could really have ceased to exist in this sense for a long period in between, though for the moment the fifth and sixth centuries have yielded few finds in London. Critically, London's Roman street grid seems to have been almost entirely ignored by the medieval city, suggesting it really had fallen out of use. But another reference of Bede's, this time in the *Life of St*

105 *Not Roman Britain, but the ghost town of Bannack, Montana, in the north-western United States. Despite the arid conditions, constant maintenance is needed to keep the structures intact for modern visitors. Even so, the decay is apparent everywhere and is a reminder of how quickly towns can physically disintegrate when the population moves away especially when so many of the structures are timber. It is also worth remembering how Tacitus grandly described the public buildings at Colchester before the Boudican Revolt in 60: Bannack was once Montana's state capital*

Cuthbert, describes the saint's visit to Carlisle in 685 where he saw a fountain in working order. As ever, the picture changes from place to place, reference to reference, site to site, and trench to trench. We cannot generalize.

Towns which were built on in the medieval period have almost invariably had their sub- and post-Roman levels so damaged by later development that building up any kind of accurate general picture is impossible, though recent work at Canterbury has identified the presence of circular huts with sunken floors containing Saxon-style pottery thought to belong to the mid-fifth century. The same area yielded an exceptionally rare Visigothic gold *tremissis* struck in South Gaul about 480, and a burial has also produced a gold *solidus* of the Byzantine emperor Zeno (474-91). Much the most convincing physical evidence for the existence of a fifth-century urban community (as opposed to isolated instances of occupation evidence) has been found at Wroxeter, though work elsewhere is beginning to widen the picture. Wroxeter is now in largely open fields and this has made systematic examination of late- and sub-Roman levels possible.

Lincoln presents an interesting case because many Anglo-Saxon cemeteries of the fifth century onwards are known in the region, thanks in part to its enduring rural and undeveloped nature. There is evidence of early church development in the sixth, and possibly the fifth, century within the city. By the late fourth century 'dark earth' levels were accumulating in some areas. Local archaeologists have made a good case for this being brought in and deliberately dumped, possibly to level up ruinous Roman building plots, so that new (and barely detectable) timber buildings could be erected on them rather than having to teeter around amongst derelict stone walls. If, in Lincoln's case, that was true then it suggests an already significantly decayed urban environment.

The main problem is tracking occupation and dating it, since pottery and coins – those two staples of Roman sites – start to vanish from the record at the beginning of the fifth century. Despite this, a case has been made for occupation of Silchester's *Insula* IX carrying on into the fifth century. But it is impossible to know when that occupation tailed off, other than to say the town has never produced any Saxon material and its abandonment is evident to anyone today. Urban settlement in the area relocated to Reading, but there are some traces of post-Roman activity. In 1893 this same *insula* produced a reused Roman column that had been carved with an ogham inscription and converted into a memorial stone. Ogham was an early form of twenty-letter alphabet associated with Ireland, and manifested as strokes carved on either side of a base line. Examples tend to turn up in Ireland, south Wales or England's south-west, where Irish influence was strongest, which makes the Silchester stone very difficult to place in context. It could date to any point from the end of the Roman period up to around 800. The Silchester stone was found in one of a series of pits cut into the ground in and around a long-derelict Roman house. Mysteriously, most contained what were by then very old pieces of Roman pottery. These included complete beakers, evidently selected for the purpose, and presumably either removed from elsewhere (perhaps a Roman graveyard) or preserved as heirlooms or curios. It is anyone's guess as to what these pits meant, and who dug them. The ogham stone appeared originally to have been a tombstone, but the pit it was found in was no grave. After a re-reading it is now interpreted as a property marker. The mystery of the post-Roman activity in *Insula* IX is likely to remain just that, despite the suggestion by the excavator that it represented one family's formal closure of their ancestral home. An attractive idea, and even a moving one, it is totally hypothetical.

Other Roman towns that are still open fields have usually suffered from early excavation work. This tended to ignore the minimal traces of building activity in the fifth century. Silchester is the best (or worst!) example, though more recent work has shown that here as at Verulamium both have yet to fulfil their archaeological potential. As we saw earlier, Caerwent's basilica seems to have been built for a town that until then was scarcely worthy of the name. A modest roadside settlement of timber buildings, it seems to have been subjected to a major piece of official investment to create a community. If so, it hardly seems to have stuck. The modern excavation work in the town has provided evidence for a remarkable amount of activity right on into the fourth century, including a new town-centre temple. Even in the first few years of the fifth century parts of the then ruinous basilica were still in use. But once the Roman period ended, so apparently did Caerwent. It literally ceased to be until the Middle Ages. It is interesting that so many Romano-British town defences escaped wholesale demolition even if their buildings did not. This suggests that the wall circuits still had some sort of defensive role to play. The sixth-century chronicler Gildas describes them as fearful places where the population indulged in pagan ritual activities, which implies that they were not wholly abandoned.

At Wroxeter an extensive range of timber buildings were put up about this time. They included what have been identified as shops and a larger structure similar to a winged corridor town house in plan. No-one knows what function this building performed but its prominent location suggests it was more than just a house. The Wroxeter buildings were erected in and around the ruins of the baths-exercise hall, in a manner still to be seen in a number of the former classical cities in North Africa, Turkey and Greece where ruined buildings of Roman date contain modern shops built into ancient walls and vaults. One theory is that the new structures were the headquarters of a chieftain warlord, similar to the tribal chiefs of the pre-Roman period, but in a kind of quasi-classical idiom.

The ideas about Wroxeter may be much closer to the truth for many town sites once the centralized influence of provincial government had disappeared. The tombstone of Cunorix, found outside Wroxeter's walls, probably belonged to an Irish warrior chief who lived there during the fifth century. However, it is impossible to tell whether he was there at the invitation of the local community, or was part of a group that had taken control of the settlement by force. Perhaps the best evidence for urban continuity in a form that went beyond the mere presence of individuals lies in Christianity. Another idea is that the new Wroxeter buildings might even have been the residence of a bishop.

The one administrative system we know survived the formal end of Roman Britain was the Christian church and it may have played a vital role in holding some urban communities together in the 400s. In the year 429 the church in Britain asked for help from Gaul to help suppress the Pelagian heresy in Britain, recorded by historians of the period. There are extremely few instances of structures of Roman date that can convincingly be argued to have been churches (**90 & 91**). But there are a number of cases where churches of later date were almost certainly built on or out of churches that had been founded in the Roman period, even if the earlier structure has not been identified. Bede says that St Augustine established himself in Canterbury in a church built during the Roman period on the east side of the town. The most likely candidate is the church of St Pancras, the ruins of which are still visible. At Verulamium, the settlement moved away from the former Roman town and gathered around the *martyrium* of St Alban, which probably lies under the medieval abbey church (**106 & colour plate 29**).

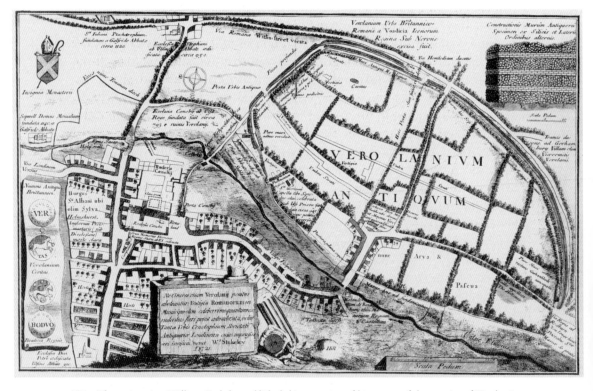

106 *The antiquarian William Stukeley published this engraving of his survey of the remains of Verulamium in 1721. On it he noted features like* umbra strati, *'shadows of streets', and* pars muri, *'part of a wall' (see* **colour plate 20***), but he had no knowledge of any of the town's public buildings or houses apart from depressions he could see in the fields*

There are also instances of medieval or sub-Roman churches being built in the ruins of a forum or basilica. At Lincoln a sub-Roman church with burials of possibly fifth-century date has been found in the forum, though there is nothing definitive from the site that pins it to the Roman period. In addition, a surviving Roman public fountain by Lincoln's south gate, adapted into a baptistery, is thought to have been the possible basis for a pair of churches at St Peter at Arches though these do not predate the seventh century. By the mid-fifth century, the site of Exeter's demolished forum and basilica had become a cemetery. In London the medieval church of St Peter on Cornhill lies in the middle of the basilica site. At York the headquarters building of the legionary fortress attached to the colony, which survived intact for several centuries after the Roman period, now lies under the medieval Minster. If Roman buildings were being reused this was only sensible. We know that the practice could extend to using old temples as churches because Pope Gregory advised this in a letter written in 601 to avoid presenting Christianity as a destructive force. This in itself suggests that a number of urban pagan temples were both intact and functioning and that communities still existed.

Towns were of course a product of trade and a thriving economy. They depended on being part of a system. After various military reorganizations and withdrawals of troops culminating in the rebellion led by Constantine III (407-11), Britain's *civitates* were finally told to take care of their own defence in 410 by the Emperor Honorius, though it is evident that this was only formalizing a break that had already taken place (**107**). It confirmed the end of military assistance, and all the administrative and financial structure that went with it. If the towns were going to survive they would have to do so in their own right, rather than functioning within the delegated hierarchy of Roman imperial administration and the broader economy of the Roman Empire.

The rich villa estates, which were such a conspicuous feature of the fourth-century countryside in central and southern Britain, must have relied on urban demand for their produce. By the fifth-century the villa houses seem almost without exception to have been given up, though circumstantial evidence in a handful of cases, like parish boundaries and church estates, is thought to point to the survival of the estates as single units (for example at Withington in Gloucestershire). At Orton Hall Farm near Peterborough and Frocester (Glos) there is some evidence for continuing cultivation on into the fifth-century, though as yet there is no evidence for the earning of the significant surplus wealth that financed the fourth-century villas.

The material that we rely on to detect economic activity declines and virtually disappears in the first few decades of the fifth century. The potteries at Alice Holt, a mainstay of London's fourth-century kitchenware market, simply fell out of use like all the other major pottery industries. Water Newton, a town with an economy based on pottery, had no reason to continue. Pottery in general virtually disappears, perhaps to be replaced by home-made wooden

107 *Coinage at the end.* Left: *Honorius (393-423), ruler in the West on a gold* solidus *struck at Milan. His reign was afflicted by constant assaults on the frontiers. In 410 he is said to have instructed Britain's* civitas *capitals to take care of their own defences. Roman Britain's towns, or what was left of them, were on their own. The Hoxne hoard contained a number of coins of this issue.* Right: *Two silver* siliquae *of Julian II (360-3), struck at Arles. The one at far right has been 'clipped' during the fifth century when new Roman coinage was no longer officially available in Britain*

and leather vessels that, for obvious reasons, are unlikely to survive. Coinage, which had been prolific in the fourth century, was in increasingly short supply to Britain after 378 and in 402 ceased altogether except for some silver struck between 407-11. There is a real curiosity about this because in a few places, and the shore fort at Richborough is the most prominent, bronze coins of the period 388-402 were apparently available in abundance while elsewhere they are scarce. This proves that coins were still arriving in Britain but copiers did not step in this time to produce substitutes on a grand scale.

Things had changed. After 402 and 411 the Romano-British had to use the existing pool of coinage. Since virtually no coins after these dates arrived, this makes it very difficult to work out exactly when coinage became redundant. Obviously, existing coins could have been used for several generations but if they remained that useful we might very reasonably suppose that copies would have been manufactured. Silver *siliquae* were favoured for bullion hoards in Britain at this time, but many show traces of having been clipped down (**107**).

This practice often arises when bullion coin is in short supply. Clipping was widespread in the seventeenth century until the great re-coinage of 1696 made silver more widely available again.

But this time there was no re-coinage. The disappearance of coinage must represent a huge change in how people traded and exchanged goods, paid servants, and bought services. One of the reasons was that once Britain was separated from the Empire it was no longer possible for anyone easily to go to a moneychanger and convert his bronze into silver or gold. Money-changers had nothing to change, or if they did they could charge exorbitant rates. There was no need to pay imperial taxes in silver and gold, and no soldiers or officials being paid in silver and gold. Those who had what silver and gold was left, clung on to it, and it turns up occasionally in hoards like the extraordinary one found at Hoxne (Suffolk) in 1992. With more than 14,800 coins (as well as plate), including 14,205 *siliquae*, its latest coins are two of the very last to reach Britain: a pair of *siliquae* of Constantine III (407-11). If there was no purpose in earning bronze coins with which to buy bullion, there was no point in going to market to get them, and there was no reason to manufacture copies. Best bury what one had, along with any other handy silver and gold plate. There is a marked rise in hoards of gold and silver in Britain deposited in or after the first few years of the fifth century. With them, the history of coinage in Roman Britain virtually comes to an end.

While towns do not depend on coins to exist, they do depend on acting as focal points of commercial activity. If that had changed, then so must have the towns themselves. Although the traditional name for this period, the 'Dark Ages', is now regarded as a little old-fashioned it is none the less true that we cannot accurately discern the nature of society in post-Roman Britain. Such evidence as has been gathered in recent years and described briefly above shows that we cannot draw any kind of general conclusions. Instead it seems likely that local circumstances were far more influential and these dictated the fate of each town. This may have been as simple as the presence of, or lack of, a single dominant individual. A powerful and effective bishop could, for example, have galvanized the remains of an urban community and acted as very much more than just a priest. A place like London was very unlikely to be abandoned and instead its nature probably changed gradually over a number of generations, though it would have remained a trading centre. At other places like Silchester or Caistor-by-Norwich the Roman settlements were eventually more or less given up but the presence of medieval churches within both may point to a low level of, and consequently not always archaeologically discernible, continuity.

Whatever the efforts at carrying on, nothing changes the fact that by the early years of the fifth-century Romano-British towns as components of a unified complex trading, economic and governmental framework started to disappear from the record available to us. This tantalizing state of affairs is unlikely to alter but some of the evidence discussed above suggests that the process of decline need not have been especially protracted. But ultimately the towns, as Roman towns, faded into archaeological obscurity because they no longer served their purpose as extensions of the Roman government, and because the insecurity following Roman rule prejudiced the economic surplus on which they depended. Few are likely to have been abandoned entirely, but the world had almost turned full circle for Britain. In time though many Roman towns re-emerged as major settlements in the medieval period when their key locations in a newly-unified type of state and revived international economy made them relevant once more. In those capacities many remain so today. London speaks for itself, while York remains the premier city of the north. Bath with its natural curiosities and elegance, in both function and popular appeal, has scarcely changed. Others, like Silchester, belong to a different age and have had no urban purpose since antiquity. But in their names and physical form, whether ruinous or vibrantly modern, the towns of Roman Britain bear witness to the fundamental role they played in Britain's first historical period as a single political, social and economic entity.

APPENDIX 1:

WRITTEN EVIDENCE FOR TOWNS

Evidence from Roman route maps like the Peutinger Table and Ravenna Cosmography is not included, and the reader is advised to consult A.L.F. Rivet and C. Smith, *The Place-Names of Roman Britain* (Batsford 1979) for full details (referred to as *PNRB* below). I have endeavoured to include here references in classical authors and inscriptions on stone, tile or military diplomas that help us with the status or nature of towns in Roman Britain. I have included the latest discoveries, but it will be clear that our picture is still very incomplete.

Coloniae

COLCHESTER (*Camulodunum*)
49 and 60: Colchester is testified by name as *colonia* by Tacitus (*Annals* xii.32, xiv.32)
Undated: inscription from *Nomentum* naming Gnaeus Munatius Aurelius Bassus, onetime *censitor civium Romanorum coloniae Victricensis Camulodunum quae est in Brittannia Camaloduni*, 'Censitor of Roman citizens of the Victricensian colony at *Camulodunum* which is in *Britannia*'. *ILS* 2740
Undated: tombstone from London of G. Pomponius Valens of Colchester, providing part of the town's full ceremonial name as above. *JRS* lii (1962), 191, no. 1

GLOUCESTER (*Glevum*)
Undated: tombstone, recording an anonymous *dec(urio) coloniae Glev[ensis]* who had died (presumably) at Bath. *RIB* 161
Undated: tombstone from Rome naming Marcus Ulpius Quintus, a soldier of *VI Victrix*, then serving as a *fr(umentarius)*, as a member of the Nervian tribe from Gloucester. This is taken to suggest that Gloucester was instituted as a colony during the brief reign of Nerva (96-8), or perhaps under Domitian and afterwards renamed. *ILS* 2365
Undated: numerous tile stamps from the colony and environs are stamped RPG (*R(ei) P(ublicae) G(levensium)*). The stamps, some of which give abbreviated names for the annual *duoviri iure dicundo*, will have allowed batch and production controls as well as discouraging theft. *RIB* 2486-8

LINCOLN (*Lindum*)

237: the existence of a colony at Lincoln is also stated on the altar erected at Bordeaux by M. Aurelius Lunaris in 237 (see York below). *JRS* xi (1921), 102 (**1**)

253-9: *R(es) P(ublica) L(indensis)* is named on a milestone of Valerian found originally in Lincoln High Street. *RIB* 2240

Undated: a dedication from Mainz to Fortuna by M. Minicius Marcellinus of Lincoln, for the eagle of *XXII Primigenia*, is said to be evidence of Lincoln's conversion to a colony by 90. If Domitian was responsible, Nerva will later have been credited, since Domitian was subjected to *damnatio memoriae* after his death in 96. *CIL* xiii.6679

LONDON (*Londinium*)

161-9, or 177-80, or 198-211: dedication to *Numini Augustorum* and Mars Camulus by Tiberinius Celerianus, 'citizen of the Bellovaci' and *moritix*, referring to *Londiniensium*, 'of the Londoners' indicating that London may have had no formal status. *B* xxxiv (2003) (**55**)

314: described variously as *civitas Londiniensium* and *colonia Londiniensium* in different versions of the *acta* of the council of Arles of this year, when naming the bishop Adelphius. *PNRB* 49ff

YORK (*Eboracum*)

237: York is named as a *colonia* on an altar erected at Bordeaux by M. Aurelius Lunaris. The date of York's foundation as a colony is unknown, though suggestions have included the aftermath of the victories of Antoninus Pius in 154, and also the Severan campaigns of 208-11. Unlike other colonies York remained a legionary fortress; the military and civilian sites lay side by side. *JRS* xi (1921), 102 (**1**)

Undated: York is stated, or probably stated, to be a colony on various undatable tombstones or sarcophagi. *RIB* 648, 678; *Brit.* xviii (1987), 367, no. 5

Municipia

VERULAMIUM (St Albans)

60-1: the only recorded instance of a *municipium* in Britain is that of Verulamium during the Boudican revolt of 60-1. The status may have been that at the time, or when Tacitus was writing about thirty years later; nevertheless he does state quite specifically that the *municipio Verulamio* fell to the rebels. The Agricolan forum inscription may or may not have named the *municipium* (see *Catuvellauni* below). Tacitus (*Annals*) xiv.33; *JRS* xlvi (1956), 146-7

Civitates

Belgae (central southern England)
110: diploma naming M. Ulpius Longinus, *Belgus*, of *cohors I Brittonum*. *CIL* xvi.163
238-44: milestone of Gordian III from Bitterne (Hants), naming the *R(es)
P(ublica) BI(= Bel(garum)?)*. *RIB* 2222
238-44?: milestone of Gordian III? from Wonston, Worthy Down (Hants),
naming the *R(es) P(ublica) B(elgarum)*. *Brit.* xvi (1985), 324, no. 3
Undated: tombstone of Julius Vitalis of *XX Valeria Victrix* and *natione Belga*, 'of
the Belgic nation' – not necessarily the British *Belgae*. *RIB* 156

Brigantes (northern England, except extreme north-west)
Undated: centurial stone from Hadrian's Wall, found between Castlesteads and
Stanwix, recorded as naming the *civitat(is) Bricic*, probably for *Brig(antum)* or
Brig(ant)ic(ae). *RIB* 2022
Undated: Nectovelius, *nationis Brigans*, but a soldier in *cohors II Thracum* on a
tombstone from Mumrills. This is an exceptional instance of an auxiliary's
tomb giving a place of origin as well as his unit. Whether the fact that they
differ was also exceptional, or common, is unknown for this reason. But the
tribal name *Brigantes* is known outside Britain (*PNRB*, 279) so perhaps
Nectovelius was not a British Brigantian at all. *RIB* 2142

Cantiaci/Cantii (Kent)
118: *in civitate Cantiacorum*, 'in the canton of the *Cantiaci*', appears on a wooden
writing tablet from London referring to a wood called *Verlucionium* in the
canton, and said to be owned by Lucius Julius Bellicus. This find is interesting given Ptolemy's assertion (see above) that London was a city of the
Cantii (sic), though the location of the property is unknown. *RIB* 2443.19,
revised at 2504.29
Undated: recorded on a sandstone base dedication at Colchester by Similis,
ci(vis) Cant(iacus), 'citizen of the *Cantiaci*'. It may be assumed he was visiting
or had moved. *RIB* 192 (and see *Brit.* xxv (1994), 302, no. 34)

Carvetii (north-western England, Carlisle area)
259-68: milestone pillar of Postumus (259-68) found near Brougham, dedicated
by the *R(es) P(ublica) C(ivitas) Car(vetiorum)*. *JRS* lv (1965), 224, no. 11
Undated: possibly recorded on the tombstone of Flavius Martius, named as a
sen(ator) of C CARVETIOR which can be expanded as *c(ivitas)* or *c(ohors)
Carvetior(um)*. *RIB* 933 (Old Penrith)

Catuvellauni (Herts, Berks, Middlesex and Cambs)
79/81: forum dedicatory inscription from Verulamium. The stone is very fragmentary but enough may be read to attribute it to the governorship of

Agricola (named) during the reign of Titus in 79 or 81. At least two restorations of the last line, which names the organization responsible, are possible:

[civitas Catu]ve[llaunorum], or

[municipium] Ve[rulamium]

Thus, either the *Catuvellauni* are named, or the town of Verulamium. *JRS* 46 (1956), 146-7

Undated: building stone naming Tossodio, of the *civitate Catuvellaunorum* on Hadrian's Wall from near milecastle 55. *RIB* 1962

Undated: tombstone from South Shields of Regina, *liberta et coniuge*, 'freed-woman and wife', of Barates the Palmyrene (Syria). Aged 30 she was *natione Cat(u)vallauna*, 'a Catuvellaunian by tribe'. *RIB* 1065

Corieltauvi or *Corieltavi* (East Midlands)

Undated: tile from Cave's Inn names *[ci]vitatis Corieltauvorom* (sic), altering the formerly-accepted *Coritanorum* for *Coritani*. *RIB* 2491.50

Undated: lead seal from Thorpe in the Glebe (Notts) bearing *C(ivitas) Cor(i)el(tauvorum)*. *Brit.* xxiv (1993), 318, no. 18

Corionototae (Corbridge area)

Undated: recorded by Q. Calpurnius Concessinius, prefect of an unnamed unit of cavalry, on an altar. The stone celebrated his victory over and slaughter of this otherwise-unknown tribal group. As the altar was found at Corbridge, *Coria*, it seems likely their territory was close to the northern frontier. The stone is now only known from an eighteenth-century drawing so there is little opportunity to date it on style. *RIB* 1142

Cornovii (West Midlands, Welsh Marches)

129-31: forum dedicatory inscription from Wroxeter, recording *civitas Cornov[iorum]*. The stone is damaged but the date can be restored as between 129-31 in the reign of Hadrian, depending on whether the 13th or 14th year of tribunician power is meant. *RIB* 288 (**24**)

300s: *cohors I Cornoviorum* at Newcastle (unusually, a unit apparently stationed in the province in which it was raised). *ND* xl.34

Undated: tombstone from Ilkley names Ved[.]ic[...], of *c(ivis) Cornovia*. *RIB* 639

Dobunni (Gloucestershire Cotswolds, Hereford and Worcs, Oxon)

105: diploma from *Pannonia* recording *Lucconi Treni F(ilio) Dobunn*, 'Lucco the Dobunnian, son of Trenus', then serving with *cohors I Britannica*. *CIL* xvi.49

283-4: milestone from Kenchester with an abbreviation restorable as *R(es) P(ublica) C(ivitatis) D(obunnorum)*, erected during the reign of Numerian (283-4). *RIB* 2250

Undated: tombstone from Templeborough of Verecunda Rufilia, *coniugi karissima[e]*, 'beloved wife', of Excingus. Aged 35 she was a *cives Dobunna*, 'citizen of the Dobunni'. The unit testified at the fort is *cohors IIII Gallorum* (see chapter 2). *RIB* 621

Dumnonii (Devon and Cornwall)

Undated: Aemilius, *civis Dumnonius*, recorded on his tombstone at Cologne as having served with *classis Germanica*. *AE* 1956.249

Undated: centurial stones from Hadrian's Wall between Carvoran and Birdoswald, naming *civitas Dum(no)ni(orum)*. *RIB* 1843-4

Undated: tombstone of [....] Carinus, *civi [D]om(nonio)*, 'citizen of the Dumnonii' from Dorchester (Dorset). The former restoration as a citizen of Rome is now rejected. *RIB* 188 (see *RIB95*, note to *RIB* 188, p.760)

Durotriges (Dorset and Somerset)

Undated: centurial stones from Hadrian's Wall (near Cawfields mc 42), naming *c(ivitas) Dur(o)tr(i)g(um) [L]endin(i)e(nsis)*, 'the *civitas* of the Durotriges at *Lindiniae* (Ilchester)'. *RIB* 1672-3

Silures (south-east Wales)

pre-220: explictly named at Caerwent as *civit(atis) Silurum* dedicating a statue to T. Claudius Paulinus, then commander of *II Augusta* at nearby Caerleon. By 220 Claudius Paulinus was governor of *Britannia Inferior* (*RIB* 1280), which means that this dedication must precede 220. *RIB* 311

Vici *and others*

Vicus was a semi-formal rank awarded to towns which were considered worthy of self-government. In reality this extended from significant, even walled, towns like Water Newton to the villages which straggled along the roads outside forts. Nowadays the term is frequently applied to any settlement outside a fort though in reality only a small number are officially testified to have been of this status. The practice of self-government ranges from the high end at Brough, where the sole *aedile* from Roman Britain is testified, to simple bodies of *vicani*, 'villagers'.

vicus Durobrivae (Water Newton)

Undated: mortarium stamps reading *Cunoarda vico Durobr(ivis)*, 'Cunoarda [made this] at the *vicus* of *Durobrivae*'. Said to be of third/fourth century date. See also **colour plate 23**

vicus Petuariensis (Brough-on-Humber or North Ferriby)

140-61: named as *vici Petu[ar(iensis)]* on a slab found at Brough-on-Humber commemorating the gift of a new stage to the *vicus* of *Petuaria* by the *aedile* Marcus Ulpius Januarius during the reign of Antoninus Pius. The findspot is difficult to reconcile with the military archaeology. North Ferriby, 4km

(2.5 miles) to the east, has been suggested as the slab's original home. *RIB* 707 (**28**)

curia Textoverdi

Undated: on an altar to the goddess Sattada from, or from near, Vindolanda, named as *curia Textoverdorum*, 'assembly of the Textoverdi'. *RIB* 1695

vicani castello Veluniate

Undated: named on an altar to Jupiter Optimus Maximus at Carriden as *vikani castello Veluniate*, 'The *vicus* dwellers at the fort of Velunia'. *JRS* xlvii (1957), 229-30, no. 18

vicani Vindolandesses

Undated: altar from Vindolanda is a dedication to Vulcanus and the Numina Augustorum by *vicani Vindolandesses*, 'villagers of Vindolanda'. *RIB* 1700

vicani ('villagers') of unnamed vici

Undated: named on a dedication from Old Carlisle to Jupiter Optimus Maximus and Vulkanus (sic) for the welfare of Gordian III by *vik(anorum) mag(istri)*, 'masters of the villagers'. *RIB* 899

Undated: dedication from Housesteads reputedly records the *d(ecreto) vica(norum)*, 'decree of the villagers'. The very incomplete and unparalleled nature of the text means that the restoration of *decreto* is dubious. A name is as likely. *RIB* 1616

APPENDIX 2:

INSCRIPTIONS FROM TOWNS

There are very few inscriptions from Roman towns in Britain that tell us anything factual about their history. Some of the most important, also referred to in the text, have their full restored texts given here in chronological order along with a brief commentary. A number of the inscriptions are recreated here and throughout the book in computer-generated images. It must be emphasized that these are approximations of the originals, not exact representations, though every effort has been made to present the lettering as accurately as possible. Darkened areas indicate lost parts. Inscriptions can usually be restored from other similar examples, but the Roman epigraphers were very adept at cramming letters together (see **44** for instance) in ways that make arguing for one thing or another on the basis of a rigorous layout potentially wrong.

1. *c.*50-80 CHICHESTER, *Noviomagus Reginorum* – a town temple (**108**)

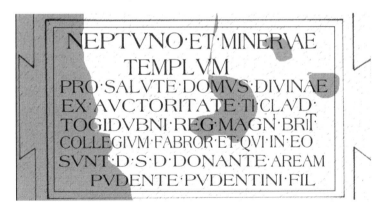

108 *Chichester temple inscription*

'*To Neptune and Minerva, for the welfare of the Divine House, by the authority of Tiberius Claudius Togidubnus, Great King in Britannia, the guild of smiths, and those who belong to the guild, give a temple from their own pockets. The site was donated by Pudens(?), son of Pudentinus.*'

This inscription has provoked much debate over the precise status of the client king Togidubnus/Cogidubnus, who ruled over the Regini/Regni in southern

Britain following the Roman invasion. The restoration shown here is that of J.E. Bogaers. However, in this context the most interesting point is that a local guild of smiths (*collegium fabrorum*) had donated funds for the building of a temple to Neptune and Minerva with Cogidubnus' permission. It was built on a site dedicated by someone whose name is missing, but was a son of one Pudentinus. Given the date and the context, the smiths were probably immigrant craftsmen.

(*RIB* 91; see *Britannia*, x, 1979, 243-254)

2. *c*.59 CHICHESTER, *Noviomagus Reginorum* – a dedication to Nero (**109**)

NERONI
CLAVDIO·DIVI
CLAVDI·F·GERMANICI·CAES
ARIS·NEPOTI·TI·CAES·
AVG·PRONEPOTI·DIVI·AVG
ABN·CAESARI·AVG·GERM
TR·P·IV·IMP·V·COS·IV
S·C·V·M

109   *Chichester Neronian dedication*

'For NERO Claudius Caesar Augustus, son of the divine Claudius, grandson of Germanicus Caesar, great-grandson of Tiberius Caesar Augustus, great-grandson of the divine Augustus, tribune for the fourth time, declared general for the fifth time, and in his fourth consulship, the vow was deservedly fulfilled by order of the Senate.'

This records a vow of loyalty to Nero in 58 or 59. SCVM stands for *Senatus Consulto Votum Merito*, 'by the Senate's decree the vow was deservedly [fulfilled]', and shows Chichester had its own town government by a very early date. Known only from an antiquarian drawing, it has some errors. The 'fourth' consulship is probably a mistake for the third. (*RIB* 92)

3. *c*.61-69 LONDON, *Londinium* – the procurator of the province

For the Latin text, see **15**

'To the Spirits of the Departed, and that of Gaius Julius Alpinus Classicianus, son of Gaius, of the Fabian voting tribe, [from Augusta Treverorum, *prefect of the Fourth cohort of Gauls, tribune of the Second legion* Augusta, *prefect of the Indianan cavalry*

wing,] procurator of the Province of Britannia, his wife Julia Pacata Indiana, daughter of Indus, erected this.'

Tombstone of the procurator Gaius Julius Classicianus found in two parts (1852 and 1935) reused in a bastion on the city wall. Tacitus mentions Classicianus as playing an instrumental part in the reconstruction of Britain after the Boudican Revolt (*Annals*, xiv.38) and the tombstone's location suggests that the provincial government was now working from London. The restoration of the fourth and fifth lines is totally hypothetical and is the work of R.S.O. Tomlin, using other evidence available about Classicianus and the family into which he married. (*RIB* 12 and *Britannia* xxxiii, 2002, 43ff.) (**15**)

4. *c.*79 VERULAMIUM, St Albans – a Flavian public building (**110**)

IMP·TITVS·CAESAR·DIVI·VESPASIANI·F·VESPASIANVS·AVG
PM·TR·PVIIII·IMPXV·COSVII·DESIGVIII·CENS· PATER·PATRIAE
ET·CAESAR·DIVI·VESPASIANI·F·DOMITIANVS·COSVI·DESIGVII
PRINCEPS·IVVENTVTIS·COLLEGIORVM·OMNIVM·SACERDOS
CN·IVLIO·AGRICOLA:LEG·AVG·PR·PR
CIVITAS:CATVVELLAVNORVM:EXORNATA

110   *Verulamium basilica-forum inscription*

'To the Emperor TITUS Caesar Vespasian Augustus, son of the divine Vespasian, chief priest, declared general fifteen times, in his seventh consulship, designated for the eighth time, censor, Father of the Country, and Domitian Caesar, son of the divine Augustus, in his sixth consulship, designated for the seventh time, principal youth [= prince], and all the colleges of priests, through his propraetorian legate, Gnaeus Julius Agricola, the civitas of the Catuvellauni having adorned this building.'

Records the dedication of probably the basilica at Verulamium in *c.*79 during the reign of Titus (79-81) and the governorship of Gnaeus Julius Agricola. Its restoration is an interesting exercise in the standardized formulae of imperial Roman inscriptions but so much is missing there is no guarantee it refers either to the basilica or forum or even the body responsible. Moreover, a current theory is that the fragments may actually come from *two* entirely separate inscriptions.

5. 129-30 WROXETER, *Uriconium Cornoviorum* – a Hadrianic public building

For Latin text, see **24**

'To the Emperor Caesar Trajan HADRIAN Augustus, son of the divine Trajan, conqueror of Parthia, grandson of the divine Nerva, chief priest, in his fourteenth tribuneship, his third consulship, Father of the Country, the civitas of the Cornovii did this'.

This inscription records the dedication of (probably) the forum of the town in 129-130 to Hadrian by the community of the Cornovii. The building is not specified but the inscription was found near the main entrance to the forum. (*RIB* 288)

6. 140-61 BROUGH-ON-HUMBER, *Petuaria* – an *aedile* dedicates a theatre stage

For Latin text, see **28**

'For the Honour of the Divine House of the Emperor Caesar Titus Aelius Hadrianus ANTONINUS PIUS, Father of the Country, consul for the third time, and to the Spirits of the Emperors, Marcus Ulpius Januarius, aedile of the vicus of Petuaria, presented this stage [and columns??] from his own resources.'

Records the dedication of a new stage (*proscaenium*) by an *aedile* of the town of *Petuaria*, Marcus Ulpius Januarius, about 140-61 during the reign of Antoninus Pius. The gesture was made in honour of the imperial 'Divine House' and the 'Imperial Spirits'. Similar texts from elsewhere in the Empire suggest that the missing section referred either to the addition of an orchestra or architectural embellishments like columns as restored here and on **28**. Januarius' names indicate that he or his father received his own citizenship during the reign of Marcus Ulpius Trajanus (Trajan, 98-117). He was possibly of military descent. (*RIB* 707) (**28**)

7. *c.*213-15 CAERWENT, *Venta Silurum* – a town honours a legionary legate (**111**)

Inscription from a statue plinth recording that the government of the *civitas* of the Silures decreed that presumably a statue of Tiberius Claudius Paulinus be set up. He was legate of the legion at nearby Caerleon but subsequently became governor of *Britannia Inferior* (see chapter 4) in about 220. His name can be fully restored from an inscription found on the fort at High Rochester, which dates that office. This stone therefore predates that one by several years. Line 7 is a particularly good example of the epigrapher's art in compressing abbreviations. Expanded, the line reads LEG AVG PR PR PROVINC. (*RIB* 311)

'To Tiberius Claudius Paulinus, legate of the II Augusta *legion, proconsul of the province of* Gallia Narrbonensis *(sic), the emperor's propraetorian legate of the province of* Gallia Lugdunensis, *by decree of the* ordo, *the administration of the civitas of the Silures erected this.'*

111 *Caerwent plinth*

8. Second or third century, LONDON, *Londinium* – a shipper

For Latin text, see **55**

'*To the Spirits of the Emperors and Mars Camulus, Tiberinius Celerianus, from the civitas of the Bellovaci, principal shipper of the* Londinium *[guild of shippers, dedicated this slab?].*'

Found in 2002 in Southwark, this highly important inscription awaits full publication and interpretation. Celerianus evidently came from the Bellovaci tribal region of northern Gaul, but held status as a shipper amongst Londoners. The most remarkable thing is that unlike the Marcus Aurelius Lunaris altar (see below), the text provides a word for Londoners as an adjective, but nothing about London the city or its status. This suggests that London may have escaped formal status altogether. (*Britannia* xxxiv, 2003) (**55**)

9. 221 YORK, *Eboracum* – a trader's gift of an arch

For Latin text, see **44**

'*To [Neptune?], the Genius of the Place, and the Spirits of the Emperors, Lucius Viducius Placidus, son of Viducius, with his home in the civitas of the Veliocasses in the province of* Gallia Lugdunensis, *[priest and] trader in pots, gave the arch and entrance on behalf of himself and his family, during the consulship of Gratus and Seleucus.*'

This slab can be partly restored from another by Viducius Placidus at a shrine on the mouth of the River Scheldt. However, two versions of the text have been published showing how tentative restoration can be, even with the legible letters. *IANV(A)M* ('entrance') in line 6 has also been read as *FANVM* ('shrine'), for example. The text illustrated here combines the elements from both versions that fitted best. The Veliocassian region was around Rouen. (For the two published versions see *Britannia* viii, 1977, 430 and Lactor 4.)

10. 237 YORK, *Eboracum* and LINCOLN, *Lindum* – a priest of the colonies at Bordeaux

For Latin text, see **1**

'*To the Guardian goddess Boudiga, Marcus Aurelius Lunaris,* sevir Augustalis *of the colonies of* Eboracum *and* Lindum *in the province of* Britannia Inferior, *promised solemnly this altar on sailing from* Eboracum. *He willingly and deservedly fulfilled his vow in the consulship of Perpetuus and Cornelianus* [237].'

This extremely important altar provides several key pieces of information. It helps define the extent of *Britannia Inferior*, it shows that one man could hold priesthoods in two cities, and it tells us about his voyage. The stone itself is

'*In honour of the Divine House, Marcus Martiannius Pulcher, of senatorial status, propraetorian legate of the emperors, ordered the restoration of the temple of Isis, [with rededication?], which had fallen down due to its antiquity.*'

112 *London Isis altar*

made of Yorkshire millstone grit, so had been evidently brought along for the purpose. Lunaris was almost certainly a trader, and as a *sevir Augustalis* would have been a freedman. The pair of consuls allow the altar to be dated exactly since consular lists are largely extant. (**1**)

11. Third century, LONDON, *Londinium* – a temple of Isis restored by the governor (**112**)

Altar from Upper Thames Street, London found used as filling in the late riverside wall. It records that Marcus Martiannius Pulcher, possibly governor (or deputy governor) of *Britannia Superior* in the third century rebuilt a temple that had collapsed. The altar was shattered into two, with severe damage to the sixth and seventh lines. The reference to 'with rededication' is thus totally hypothetical but is based on similar examples found in other provinces. The date is based on the style. There is nothing else to confirm it though the reference (AVGG) to multiple emperors means it cannot precede the joint reign of Marcus Aurelius and Lucius Verus between 161-9. The next periods of joint rule are: 177-80 (Marcus Aurelius and Commodus); 198-212 (Severan); 218 (Macrinus and Diadumenian); 238 (Balbinus and Pupienus); 247-9 (Philip I and II); 251-3 (Trebonianus Gallus with Hostilian, then Volusian); 253-60 (Valerian I and Gallienus). The most likely date for this altar is one of the third-century phases.

12. Fourth century, CIRENCESTER, *Corinium Dobunnorum* – a pagan column restored

For the Latin text, see **100**

'To Jupiter Optimus Maximus, Lucius Septimius, a man of perfection, praeses *of Britannia Prima and citizen of Reims, restored this. Septimius, rector of the Prima province, restores the statue and column erected according to ancient religion'.*

Three sides of a column base carry this slightly confusing text which repeats information in different ways. Lucius Septimius is described as both *praeses* and *rector*, different terms for a governor, of *Britannia Prima*, which came into being in the fourth century. That this was a pagan monument means it was either done during a period of pagan revival, perhaps during the reign of Julian the Apostate (360-3). But it could also date to a time when paganism was tolerated, for example under Magnentius (350-3) or simply be a snub to the Christian emperors in a province where paganism proved remarkably durable in the fourth century. (*RIB* 103) (**100**)

14. Third or fourth century, OLD PENRITH, a *quaestor* (**113**)

D M
FL MARTIO SEN
IN C CARVETIOR
QVESTORIO
VIXIT AN XXXXV
MARTIOLA FILIA ET
HERES PONEN
CVRAVIT

'To the Spirits of the Departed
and that of Flavius Martius,
senator *in the civitas of the
Carvetii, and former* quaestor,
*who lived 45 years. Martiloa,
his daughter and heiress,
arranged the burial.*'

113   *Old Penrith* quaestor

Martius is an exceptionally rare instance of a Romano-British *civitas* councillor whose rank and name we know. He will probably have worked in the *civitas* capital of the Carvetii at Carlisle (*Luguvalium*). It is most likely this man served in the civilian government of his region in the third century or possibly the fourth. Unfortunately, the stone is lost (*RIB* 933).

15. Undated, SILCHESTER *Calleva Atrebatum* – a *collegium* (**114**)

R
SIGNVM VICTo
RIÆ COLLATIONIBVS
COMMISSVMSIBACN
LEGIOPEREGRINORvM
CNSISTENTVMCALLEVÆ
DONVM·D·S·D

'a statue of Victory
...with contributions, he
gave from his resources this
gift, a matter entrusted to
him by the guild of
foreigners living at
Calleva'

114   *Silchester guild*

This is one of three inscriptions found in and around the temple in *Insula* XXXV at Silchester in 1907. The original published restorations of the text conjecturally introduced the word *sine*, 'without', between *Victoriae* and *collationibus* ('contributions'). However, it becomes impossible to reconstruct the text in a plausible manner with this word in place as it literally does not fit. It has therefore been omitted, changing the meaning from 'without contributions' to 'with contributions'. The upper part is lost so we have no idea how the text started, or the donor's name, but he was probably responsible for the two other inscriptions, thought to record donations of statues of Mars and Peace respectively. (*RIB* 70, and see *Britannia* xxxiii, 2002, 167-75)

APPENDIX 3:

WHERE TO VISIT ROMAN TOWNS IN BRITAIN

Most of Roman Britain's major towns have some sort of visible remains but these are mainly confined to fragments of the defences. This list refers to the most significant examples of buildings that can be seen. Would-be visitors are advised to check in advance that sites are accessible, especially during the winter. The most satisfying sites are Bath, Caerwent, Lincoln, Verulamium and Wroxeter but places like Cirencester, Colchester, Corbridge, London, Leicester and York all have outstanding museums that make up for less immediately impressive structural remains. Unavoidably, most are in central and southern England. Phone numbers and website addresses are given here (where available), but the reader should note that websites are notoriously subject to change and some museums are liable to be closed for refurbishment, removal to new locations and so on. All websites given here were checked before going to press (March 2003).

The best guidebook is Roger Wilson's outstanding *Guide to the Roman Remains in Britain* (Constable, 2002, fourth edition). It contains full descriptions of visible remains at every site, as well as how to find places, phone numbers, grid references, and so on. It is indispensable and the would-be visitor to Roman towns in Britain is strongly advised to purchase a copy.

Aldborough, *Isurium Brigantium*, North Yorkshire (SE 405661)
Sections of wall and two mosaics in situ, plus site museum. Defences accessible any time, mosaics (**43**) and museum summer season only. Access from the A1 is close, but fiddly. English Heritage (01423 322768).

Ancaster, Lincolnshire (SK 983436)
Sections of the southern defences of this small roadside town are visible beside the traffic lights on the junction between the B6403 (Ermine Street) and the A152 about 5 miles north-east of Grantham (**46**). The area enclosed by the defences is now an open field beside the main road through Ancaster. Posts around the village mark a Roman trail, including stone sarcophagi found under a modern cemetery on the west side (walk through the churchyard and turn

right along the path at the other side). Finds from Ancaster including a milestone (**75**) and Mother Goddesses are visible in Grantham Museum, St Peter's Hill, Grantham (01476 568783).

Bath, *Aquae Sulis*, Somerset
An outstanding site. The baths and sections of the Temple Precinct are accessible from the Roman Baths Museum in Stall Street along with a museum containing some exceptional finds (open daily), including items found in the Sacred Spring, tombstones, altars, and temple masonry. (01225 477791; www.romanbaths.co.uk)

Caerwent, *Venta Silurum*, Gwent (ST 469905) (**25**)
The town defences are particularly striking on the south, including the gate. Two town houses are visible in Pound Lane (western part of the town off main road). There is a temple on the north side of main road in the middle of the town, and just behind is the basilica and part of the forum – the only Romano-British example now visible. Access at any time. (no official website, but the following has pictures and details:
www.theheritagetrail.co.uk/roman%20britain/caerwent.htm)

Caistor St Edmunds, *Venta Icenorum*, Norfolk (TG 230035)
A few miles south of Norwich (head east from the Ipswich Road, A140), the *civitas* capital of the Iceni survives as fields today but the ramparts are visible almost the whole way round. A small car park is provided just south of the church. Along the south roads still protrude from the field showing that the town was bigger before the walls were erected. A bastion stands alone on the west side. Finds from the town can be seen in Norwich Castle Museum. (01603 493625; www.norfolk.gov.uk/tourism/museums/museums.htm).

Canterbury, *Durovernum Cantiacorum*, Kent
The city wall forms part of north wall of St Mary Northgate. The disappointing fragments of theatre in St Margaret's Street are no longer really accessible except at no. 38. The Roman Museum is in Butchery Lane (off the eastern half of the High Street) and has the remains of a town house as well as many finds, including fragments of monumental masonry thought to have come from a major town-centre classical temple (closed Sundays except in the summer and autumn when it is open in the afternoon).
(01227 785575; www.canterbury.gov.uk/cgi-bin/buildpage.cgi?mysql=114 or www.canterbury.gov.uk and search under town museums).

Carlisle, *Luguvalium*, Cumbria
Like Corbridge (below), Carlisle was a military town that was closely linked to the world of Hadrian's Wall, and which started life as a first-century timber

fort. Virtually nothing is visible, but the Tullie House Museum (open daily) has a huge selection of finds from the town, and nearby sections and forts of Hadrian's Wall. (01228 534781; www.tulliehouse.co.uk)

Carmarthen, *Moridunum*, Carmarthenshire (SN 416214)
Part of the amphitheatre lies about 1.5 miles west closer to Carmarthen. Museum (daily except Sundays) in the old Bishop's Palace by a roundabout on the A40 on the east side of town.
(01267 231691; www.carmarthen-museum.org.uk)

Charterhouse-on-Mendip, Somerset (ST 500565)
Nothing survives of this mining settlement except earthworks, including the remains of an amphitheatre.

Chichester, *Noviomagus Reginorum*, West Sussex
Togidubnus/Cogidubnus' inscription on view outside Assembly Rooms in North Street. Amphitheatre off Whyke Lane, a turning from the A259 just east of the city wall. Small fragment of mosaic in the cathedral. Museum at 29, Little London (closed Sundays and Mondays).
(01243 784683; www.chichester.gov.uk/museum)

Cirencester, *Corinium Dobunnorum*, Gloucestershire
Cirencester's medieval and Georgian past has left it with so many listed buildings that excavation in Roman Britain's third-largest city is now almost impossible. Nevertheless, there is still plenty to see. Defences visible in Corinium Gate off London Road just by junction between A417 and A429. Amphitheatre: leave town centre to south-west up Querns Hill, the earthen banks of the amphitheatre visible off Cotswold Avenue. Corinium Museum in Park Street is outstanding (closed Sundays, and Mondays as well during the winter), and contains numerous finds including outstanding mosaics, and sculpture. (01285 655611; www.cotswold.gov.uk/museum/ – note that the museum is closed until September 2003 for a major refurbishment)

Colchester, *Camulodunum*, Essex
Most of the city walls visible on west, north and east. The Balkerne (west) Gate is accessible, as is Duncan's Gate in the north sector. The Butt Road church has been exposed for display just outside the SW corner of the town defences a short walk from the Balkerne Gate. The excellent museum is in the Norman Castle, including the vaults to the Temple of Claudius (weekdays, and Sunday afternoons in the summer), and has finds from the town's origins as a legionary fortress as well as its later periods as a major *colonia*. (01206 282931; www.colchestermuseums.org.uk/CM_html/default_castle1.html)

Corbridge, *Coriosopitum*, Northumberland (NY 982648)

A former fort that grew into a town close to the northern frontier and was linked socially and economically with Hadrian's Wall. A street with aqueduct, water-tank (**115**), drains, granaries, temples and former fort buildings is accessible on a large site to the west of the modern town along with an excellent museum. Open all year. English Heritage. (01434 632249)

Dorchester, *Durnovaria*, Dorset

Probably, but not certainly, tribal capital of the Durotriges (which it seems to have shared with Ilchester). The amphitheatre, adapted from a Neolithic henge monument, is just outside the south side of Dorchester in Weymouth Avenue (**31**). Townhouse foundations and mosaic, as well as an impressive window jamb visible in Colliton Park beside County Hall (**52**). Dorset County Museum in High West Street has various finds from the town including mosaics. (01305 262735; www.dorset.museum.clara.net)

Exeter, *Isca Dumnoniorum*, Devon

Exeter began its life as a legionary fortress, probably for *II Augusta*, before it became a *civitas* capital. But nothing of its extraordinary legionary bath house (which lies underground immediately in front of the cathedral's west front) or any of its later buildings are now visible, except for fragments of the city walls.

115 *Corbridge waterworks. Water supplied by a conduit running in from upper right continuously filled the streetside water tank visible in the centre. Note the heavy wear from people washing clothes and leaning over the edge. The run-off flowed away down the drains visible in front of the tank. This is the only visible example of Roman town water supply in Britain today*

However, the Royal Albert Memorial Museum (closed Sundays) in Queen Street has finds from the fort and town (**colour plate 13**). (01392 665858; www.exeter.gov.uk)

Gloucester, *Glevum*, Gloucestershire
East gate visible outside Boots store in Eastgate. Museum in Brunswick Street (closed Sundays) with an excellent collection of carved stone material from the legionary fortress, the colony, and other sites in the region. (01452 524131; www.gloucester.gov.uk/libraries/templates/page.asp?URN=464)

Great Casterton, near Stamford (Lincs), Rutland TF 002091
Only the defences on the northern side can be seen off a lane from the B1081 heading north out of Stamford, signposted to Ryhall.

Hull Museum
The East Riding and Hull Museum (open daily except Sunday mornings) contains the inscription from nearby Brough that records the gift of a theatre stage. The museum has a substantial collection of Roman material from the area, including the Rudston and Brantingham mosaics (**colour plates 1 & 9**). (01482 613902; www.hullcc.gov.uk/museums)

Leicester, *Ratae Corieltauvorum*, Leicestershire
Museum and Jewry Wall (part of the baths) accessible from St Nicholas' Circle on the inner ring road. The Jewry Wall and baths foundations (**colour plate 18**) are accessible in the grounds of the museum (open daily, except November to March Sunday afternoons only). The museum has an excellent display of finds from the town, including painted wall-plaster, mosaics, monumental architectural fragments and evidence for a military period (**82, colour plates 10 & 11**). (0116 247 3021; www.leicestermuseums.ac.uk)

Lincoln, *Lindum*, Lincolnshire
Lincoln has the most upstanding remains of any Roman town in Britain. The north gate is visible at the top of Bailgate and is the only Roman gate through which wheeled traffic still passes (**colour plate 7**). The south-west gate is in the car-park of the Municipal Offices in Orchard Street (**colour plate 27**). The rear wall of the basilica, known as the 'Mint Wall' is behind a hotel in Westgate (**colour plate 6**) and nearby the foundations of a late- or post-Roman church are laid out in the forum piazza next to an early, possibly military, well-head. A new city museum is planned for opening in 2005.

London, *Londinium*
Various sections of wall, best on the north side of Tower Hill and within the Tower of London. Fort wall junction with town wall visible in Noble Street

close to the Museum of London that contains the most outstanding collection of finds from a Roman town (closed Mondays), including the replicated Gresham Street water-lifting device. Some also at the British Museum in Gt Russell Street (daily). Temple of Mithras visible as a reconstructed display of original material in Queen Victoria Street. The Lower Thames Street bath house can be visited by prior arrangement with the Museum of London (020 7600 3699; www.museumoflondon.org.uk) (**50**).

Rochester, *Durobrivae,* Kent
A small section of city wall is visible beside the High Street at the eastern end by the Eagle Tavern. However the City Museum, at the west end (open daily), contains a collection of Roman material from the city and some of the extensive pottery-producing sites that grew up alongside the Medway and the south bank of the Thames near here.
(01634 848717; www.kent-museums.org.uk/muscat.html)

St Albans, see Verulamium

Silchester, *Calleva Atrebatum*, Hampshire (SU 640625)
Of all Roman Britain's towns, Silchester is now so isolated it seems impossible to believe this was once a road hub, and had an earlier existence as a tribal *oppidum*. The town defences are visible almost in their entirety but the gates are not well preserved (**47**). The cleared and consolidated amphitheatre is accessible outside the walls just north of the church in the eastern sector (**32 & 33**). A few finds are displayed in a little museum (open daily) about 0.5 mile along a track leading from the west gate. The main collections are in Reading Museum (closed Sunday mornings and Mondays).
(0118 939 9800; www.museumreading.org.uk)

Verulamium (St Albans), Hertfordshire
Verulamium Museum (closed Sunday mornings) with its revamped displays of finds from one of Roman Britain's premier towns (the second largest) is in the little village of St Michael's just west of modern St Albans. Across the dangerously busy A4147 that bisects the Roman town is the theatre, the only complete example visible in Britain (open daily) (**29 & colour plate 17**). Parts of the defences in the southern part of the town can still be seen and a mosaic is visible in its original location a short walk from the museum. (01727 751810; www.stalbansmuseums.org.uk)

Vindolanda (Chesterholm), Northumberland (NY 771664)
Vindolanda was a fort on the Stanegate road that ran east-west a few miles south of Hadrian's Wall. The *vicus* settlement is laid out just outside the fort's west gate. It is the only example of a military *vicus* visible in Britain (**colour**

plate 19). Various buildings, including a baths and *mansio*, can be seen and an extensive range of displays is on view in the museum (open daily). (01434 344277; www.vindolanda.com)

Wall, *Letocetum*, Staffordshire (SK 099067)
The only small town of Roman Britain where the *mansio* and baths can be seen. There is also a small site museum (open daily April-September). (English Heritage 01543 480768)

Water Newton, *Durobrivae*, Cambridgeshire (TL 122908)
Accessible from the A1 (southbound traffic only), in the lay-by after the second turning marked to Water Newton village. Defences visible as mounds, and the *agger* of Ermine Street from London on its way to Lincoln. Finds from the site can be seen at Peterborough Museum, but the Christian treasure is in the British Museum, London.

116 *Wroxeter, the 'Old Work'. The masonry formed part of the south wall of the basilican palaestra (beyond) and at this point visitors could pass through the doorway into the frigidarium. Although severely damaged, traces of three arches can be seen in the brickwork. These are the lower parts of the vaults that roof the frigidarium. The small holes in the walls were for securing scaffolding. Veneers and plaster would have covered these up*

Winchester, *Venta Belgarum*, Hampshire
Almost nothing of the town is visible, but the City Museum on the north-west side of the Cathedral Green has a fine, and well-lit, collection of finds from the town (**39** & **76**) and other sites scattered about including the Sparsholt villa (closed Sunday mornings, and Mondays in the winter). (01962 848269; www.winchester.gov.uk/arts_museums/museums/citymuseum.shtml)

Wroxeter, *Uriconium Cornoviorum*, Shropshire (SJ 568088)
The Roman city is a few miles east of Shrewsbury off the B45061. The 'Old Work' (**116**) and the baths complex, along with the *macellum* can be fully explored, and compared with reconstruction paintings placed at strategic locations. Nearby part of the forum colonnade is also visible (**56**). There is a site museum (open daily, except Monday and Tuesday in winter). Other finds are at Rowley's House Museum in Shrewsbury (closed Sundays except in the afternoon during the summer). (Wroxeter: 01743 761330. Shrewsbury: 01743 361196; http://shrewsburymuseums.com/museums/shrews_museum)

FURTHER READING

General

There are a number of modern books that cover the history of Roman Britain, for example Sheppard Frere's *Britannia* (1987), and Peter Salway's *Roman Britain* (1981). The latter has now been reissued in an abridged and illustrated form as *The Oxford Illustrated History of Roman Britain* (1993). Catherine Johns and the late Tim Potter of the British Museum co-wrote *Roman Britain* (British Museum Press, second edition 2002), a book that benefits from two lifetime experiences of dealing with Britain's premier Romano-British collections.

For an excellent survey of Roman Britain and how it functioned in terms of the landscape, the reader will find *An Atlas of Roman Britain* (1990) by Barri Jones and David Mattingly of great value. A more detailed general look at towns can be found in John Wacher's *Towns of Roman Britain* (second edition, 1995) and *The 'Small Towns' of Roman Britain* (1990), the latter written in association with Barry C. Burnham. The books are indispensable surveys and classify towns according to their type and date. Each town is fully discussed with plans and accounts of development and individual structures. The present author's *Buildings of Roman Britain* (second edition, Tempus 2001) contains many reconstruction drawings of buildings in Roman towns. The aesthetics of Romano-British life are covered by Martin Henig in his *Art in Roman Britain* (Batsford 1995). Ken and Petra Dark's *The Landscape of Roman Britain* (Sutton 1997) seeks to explain how Roman Britain was defined by the physical background. Hugh Davies deals with the engineering logistics of roads in his *Roman Roads in Britain* (Tempus 2002).

Three recent books feature articles by several authors, all tackling how the study of Roman Britain has changed in recent years. Simon James and Martin Millett have edited *Britons and Romans: advancing an archaeological agenda* (CBA Research Report 125, 2001). Peter Salway has edited *The Roman Era* (2002) for Oxford University Press's *Short Oxford History of the British Isles*. Both of these titles are affordable and accessible. Malcolm Todd has edited *A Companion to Roman Britain* (Blackwell 2003), but this is an extremely expensive book beyond most people's reach. All these books have a wide range of topics discussed in the light of modern thought and research by a variety of experts and scholars. Roman Britain's towns feature prominently in all three. The articles vary in their usefulness to the general reader or student, but overall they illustrate the different types of approach, from the highly theoretical to the pragmatic and imaginative.

Tempus has been responsible for providing today's archaeological readership with an exceptional range of choice. Those interested in how Roman Britain's towns functioned in the latter days of the province will find the author's *Golden Age of Roman Britain* (Tempus 1999) and Neil Faulkner's *The Decline and Fall of Roman Britain* (Tempus 2000) offer completely different approaches to this difficult period. The author's *Eagles over Britannia* (Tempus 2001) is a history of the Roman army in Britain and its exceptional contribution to the development of towns, and his *Companion to Roman Britain* (Tempus 1999) is a catalogue of the literary and epigraphic evidence for the history of Roman Britain.

The *Lactor* series of booklets provides an excellent summary of epigraphic sources in Volume 4 *Inscriptions of Roman Britain*, and historical sources in Volume 11, *Literary Sources for Roman Britain*. They can be obtained from LACT Publications Secretary, 5 Normington Close, Leigham Court Road, London SW16 2QS. Stanley Ireland's *Roman Britain: A Sourcebook* (Croom Helm 1986 and later reprints) provides all the literary sources in translation and a number of inscriptions, coins and other references.

RIB is a reference to the catalogue of inscriptions: *The Roman Inscriptions of Britain,* 1965, Collingwood, R.G., and Wright, R.P., Oxford, revised by R.S.O. Tomlin in 1995 for Sutton Publishing. Other references are to the annual journal *Britannia*, published by the Society for the Promotion of Roman Studies, London (see Further Reading).

Individual towns

Books concerned with the Roman history and archaeology of individual towns are frustratingly limited, with the result that coverage is really very patchy. Fortunately, though, there are some outstanding new books around which have made a considerable difference to the subject. One of the most comprehensive and recent surveys is Rosalind Niblett's *Verulamium: The Roman City of St Albans* (Tempus 2001), which brings the story of this exceptional Roman town right up-to-date. Roger White and Philip Barker's *Wroxeter: Life and Death of a Roman City* (Tempus 1998) makes the most of the authors' years of excavation at this vitally important town, and one which has helped transform our picture of urban life in the fourth and fifth centuries.

Others include George Boon's *Silchester: the Roman Town of Calleva* (David & Charles 1974), which remains the standard account of studies of this town before the modern series of excavations started, Peter Marsden's *Roman London* (Thames & Hudson 1980), and Gustav Milne's *The Port of Roman London* (Batsford 1985). A slightly more up-to-date and very useful survey of work done in the capital is Dominic Perring's *Roman London* (1991) in Seaby's Archaeology of London series. Barry Cunliffe's *Roman Bath Discovered* (RKP 1984, and now reissued by Tempus) covers the recent excavations in a very special case of urban development. Mike McCarthy's *Roman Carlisle and the Lands of the Solway* (Tempus 2002) and David J.P. Mason's *Roman Chester: City of the Eagles* (Tempus 2001) look at two major military bases but include discussion of the extensive civilian settlement at both places. Mick Jones has produced *Roman Lincoln* (Tempus 2002), an account of one town that in its time served as a legionary fortress and colony and which has some of the most remarkable surviving physical remains of any Roman town in Britain. Patrick Ottaway's *Roman York* (Batsford/English Heritage 1993) is due for reissue shortly under the Tempus label and provides probably the only general overview of Roman York ever published.

Apart from these, the other books that are directly concerned with individual towns are the archaeological reports prepared by excavators. Amongst the most recent to have appeared are M.G. Fulford's reports on new excavations at Silchester. The amphitheatre is covered in a monograph published by the Society for the Promotion of Roman Studies (Britannia Monograph No. 10, 1989), with work on the forum-basilica site in *Late Iron Age and Roman Silchester* following in 2000 (Britannia Monograph No. 15). The important excavations at Wroxeter were published by English Heritage in 1997 as *The Baths Basilica, Wroxeter: Excavations 1966-90* by Philip Barker, Roger White and others. 'Standard' excavation reports also include a number published by the Society of Antiquaries in London in its Research Report series. Many of these are strictly speaking becoming out-of-date in terms of discussion and conclusions, but the data they contain are still invaluable. The most important are M.R. Hull's *Roman Colchester* (1958) that includes an examination of the defences and the Temple of Claudius, and Sheppard Frere's three volumes of Verulamium *Excavations* (1972, 1983, 1984). The first volume covers the *Insula XIV* shops, the second includes sections on the basilica and houses while the third contains detailed catalogues of finds. Previous excavations by Sir Mortimer Wheeler were covered earlier in the same series in *Verulamium: a Belgic and two Roman cities*, published in 1936.

Information about current excavations often appears first in abbreviated form in the pages of *Current Archaeology*, published at 9 Nassington Road, London NW3 2TX and available bi-monthly on annual subscription (website at www.archaeology.co.uk; telephone 020 7435 7517). Working through back issues of this magazine is an extremely useful way of reading preliminary summaries of very recent excavations that may not reach final publication for a decade or more. The Society for the Promotion of Roman Studies at Senate House, Malet Street, London WC1E 7HU, includes a more comprehensive survey in the 'Roman Britain in 19-' section of its annual journal *Britannia*. Membership of the Society grants access to its comprehensive library.

Economics and industry

Kevin Greene's *The Archaeology of the Roman Economy* (Batsford 1986) is a very useful introduction to understanding something of how production and trade functioned in the Roman world. The excavations on the site of the New Fresh Wharf in London produced a wealth of evidence for the extent and sources of traded goods that entered Britain through the province's busiest port (Dyson, T.(ed.), *et al.*, *The Roman Quay at St Magnus House*, London, Special Paper No. 8 of the London and Middlesex Archaeological Society (1986)). For coinage see Richard Reece's *Coinage of Roman Britain* (Tempus 2002). A. Trevor Hodge's *Roman Aqueducts and Water Supply* (Duckworth 1991) covers the whole Empire, but provides a wealth of information about how this most fundamental urban necessity was managed.

Religion

Romano-British religion is a popular subject amongst academics and there has been much lively debate about how Roman and Celtic cults were synthesized by Romano-British culture. Martin Henig's *Religion in Roman Britain* (1984) covers most aspects while the present author's *Gods with Thunderbolts* (Tempus 2002) is a narrative history of religion in Roman Britain and includes a full list of all the deities recorded on inscriptions in Roman Britain.

Three of the most useful surveys of death and burial are: the Royal Commission on Historical Monuments for England's volumes on *Roman London* (1928), and *Eboracum, Roman York* (1962), and Alan McWhirr *et al.*, *Romano-British Cemeteries at Cirencester* (Cirencester Excavation Committee 1982). The first two contain extensive catalogues of burials, tombstones and grave goods while the third is a comprehensive survey of an inhumation cemetery with discussions about the make-up, ages and diseases of the buried population. See also Ann Woodward's *Shrines and Sacrifice* (Batsford 1992).

This is only a very brief survey of some of the literature available concerned with Roman towns and related aspects of Roman life. Many are 'popular' works that can be found in large bookshops, at major site museums or local libraries, and most contain extensive bibliographies that can guide the reader further. The more academic excavation reports are sometimes available at academic bookshops but are more usually only found in university libraries or occasionally at specialist secondhand bookshops.

GLOSSARY

Aedile
Magistrate with responsibility for managing civic and cantonal public services like buildings, water and drainage, food supply and public entertainment. The term originated in the Latin word for a sacred building, *aedes*.

ala
A body, literally a 'wing', of auxiliary cavalry (auxiliaries were provincials attached to the Roman army; their units served alongside the legions).

Amphora
The universal means of transporting perishables in the ancient world. There were many forms of this heavy pottery container, but almost all had handles and could be stacked against one another. The neck was usually plugged with wood and a painted inscription recorded the nature, quantity and owner of the contents.

As
Small denomination coin, struck in copper or bronze. There were four to a *sestertius* (see below).

Aureus
The standard Roman gold coin until 312 (see *solidus* below). Struck at 60 to one pound of gold.

Axonometric
Form of projection used to show buildings by drawing vertical lines directly from a plan. In this way the absolute dimensions are retained to scale.

Basilica
A kind of town hall. Rectangular in shape with a nave and, usually, a pair of aisles. The building type has remained in use for churches.

Canton
See *civitas*.

Cantonal capital
See *civitas* capital.

Censitor
The *censitor* divided up citizens according to voting tribes and other criteria such as age, class and wealth to produce a property value for tax assessment. The post was similar to that of *censor*, of whom two were elected annually in Rome, but who came to exercise authority over public morals.

Civitas
The body of citizens combined as a political entity, usually translated in English as 'canton'.

Civitas capital
The town from which a tribal *civitas* (canton) was ruled. It was not legally distinct from the canton.

Client kingdom
During the first century, the Roman government sometimes used tame native chieftains to act as puppet administrators of their regions. Provided with financial and military support, the client kingdom could help stabilise a region as well as act as a buffer zone. However, they were unstable and could easily dissolve into factions without warning. By the end of the first century AD in Britain they had been abandoned and their territory annexed to the province.

Collegium
Generic term for a 'guild' or organized group, usually of men who shared a craft, or perhaps worshipped a particular god. They had their own articles of association, elected officials, and finances to protect members' interests, pay for religious dedications, funerals and so on. They resembled modern Masonic organizations.

Colonia
A town founded for the use of retired military veterans and their families as a way of granting them land and assisting in the control of provinces. Its inhabitants were normally Roman citizens. Britain had at least four: Colchester, Gloucester, Lincoln and York. London also may have been elevated to colony status though this is far from certain.

Decuriones
Members of the town council, *ordo* (see below).

Denarius
The standard silver coin, around 20mm in diameter. Around the year 100 a legionary soldier was paid 300 *denarii* a year.

Duovir
Literally 'One of the two men'. Two magistrates were elected annually, modelled on the consulships at Rome. They were the senior magistrates in town and canton government. The idea of having two was to prevent one man becoming too powerful and unchecked.

Forum

An open piazza or market square in front of the basilica. The other three sides were usually made up of rows of shops and covered colonnades.

Isometric

Form of projection similar to axonometric but the plan has its angles altered to create an illusion of perspective. The dimensions are retained to scale.

Macellum

A kind of miniature forum, probably associated with a specific trade. The literal meaning is 'meat market' but in practice it meant 'provision market', and was an important place where news and gossip were exchanged, while commercial transactions went on.

Magistrates

The *decuriones* on the town council competed for annually elected magistracies. The two most senior were the *duoviri iuridicundo*. They were in charge of the council and justice in the canton. Aediles dealt with public services. In the *coloniae* the *quaestores* administered finances.

Mansio

An official inn or staging post. Usually a large courtyard building with stores and baths. The word means literally 'a time of staying in one place', which is much clumsier in English.

Martyrium

A chapel attached to the tomb of a Christian martyr that often developed into a major church or cathedral.

Mithraeum

Temple dedicated to the worship of Mithras. Although similar to the basilica the temple was windowless and often partly subterranean to emulate Mithras' cave.

Municipium

A *civitas* capital (usually) singled out for special treatment. Its citizens were elevated to 'Latin status', which meant more than just provincial but was not as prestigious as Roman citizenship. Verulamium is the only certain example in Britain. After 313 and the edict of universal citizenship this ceased to be of significance.

Oppidum

The Latin word for a town. It was used by ancient authors like Julius Caesar to describe large low-lying native settlements in Britain and northern Gaul. It is still used to describe such settlements which are generally defined as zones demarcated with lengths of ditches.

Ordo

The town council, made up of 100 men who fulfilled a property qualification and had successfully competed for annually elected magistracies.

Quaestor

Magistrate for dealing with public finances, literally 'the inquirer'. The word originated in the verb *quaerere*, 'to investigate' or 'inquire', i.e. 'inquire into public finances'.

Samian ware

A fine red-slip ware manufactured mainly in what is now central and southern France. There were many forms, plain and decorated, and they were shipped into Roman Britain in enormous quantities during the first and second centuries. Production had ceased by the mid-third century.

Sestertius

The largest denomination base-metal coin, struck in brass. There were 4 to a *denarius*, the standard silver coin. Around the year 100 a legionary soldier was paid 300 *denarii* a year.

Sevir Augustalis

Town-based priest of the imperial cult, usually a member of a board of six men, who were normally freedmen. The board was elected from a group of peers and former members were liable to 'influence' the election of successors. Their duties will have involved presiding at ceremonies that celebrated events in the imperial family's calendar.

Solidus

Standard gold coin of 312 and later. Struck at 72 to a pound of gold.

Terminus ante quem

Literally 'time before which', a term used by archaeologists when a dated feature lies over another, earlier, feature. Suppose the occupation debris of a gatehouse on a city wall contains a coin dated AD 212 then it is clear that the gatehouse, and probably the wall must have been built before 212.

Terminus post quem

The opposite of *terminus ante quem* and means 'time after which'. Suppose a building is undated, but lies over a filled-in ditch that contains a coin dated to AD 100. The house must have been built after AD 100, but *how long* is often difficult to determine.

Territorium

Land associated with a colony, divided up amongst the colonists.

Tetrastyle

Classical temple form where the pediment is supported by four columns.

Vicus

A small settlement or town. Normally used now to refer to the civilian townships that grew up around forts.

INDEX

Page numbers in **bold** refer to illustrations

Please note that towns are referred to by their modern names except Verulamium (St Albans) and Vindolanda (Chesterholm). The Roman settlements at both these places are distinct from modern settlements and are normally published and promoted under their ancient names.

General index